Vocabulary in use

High Intermediate

Second Edition

100 units of vocabulary practice in North American English

with answers

Michael McCarthy
Felicity O'Dell
with John D. Bunting

CAMBRIDGE
UNIVERSITY PRESS

University Printing House, Cambridge CB2 8BS, United Kingdom

One Liberty Plaza, 20th Floor, New York, NY 10006, USA

477 Williamstown Road, Port Melbourne, VIC 3207, Australia

4843/24, 2nd Floor, Ansari Road, Daryaganj, Delhi – 110002, India

79 Anson Road, #06–04/06, Singapore 079906

Cambridge University Press is part of the University of Cambridge.

It furthers the University's mission by disseminating knowledge in the pursuit of education, learning and research at the highest international levels of excellence.

www.cambridge.org

© Cambridge University Press 2001, 2010

This publication is in copyright. Subject to statutory exception
and to the provisions of relevant collective licensing agreements,
no reproduction of any part may take place without the written
permission of Cambridge University Press.

First published 2001
Second edition 2010

20 19 18 17 16 15 14 13 12 11

Printed in Great Britain by CPI Group (UK) Ltd, Croydon CR0 4YY

ISBN 978-0-521-12386-0 paperback High Intermediate Student's Book with answers
ISBN 978-0-521-12367-9 paperback Basic Student's Book with answers
ISBN 978-0-521-12375-4 paperback Intermediate Student's Book with answers

Cambridge University Press has no responsibility for the persistence or accuracy of URLs for external or third-party internet websites referred to in this publication, and does not guarantee that any content on such websites is, or will remain, accurate or appropriate. Information regarding prices, travel timetables, and other factual information given in this work is correct at the time of first printing but Cambridge University Press does not guarantee the accuracy of such information thereafter.

Contents

Acknowledgments   vi
Introduction   vii

Strategies for learning vocabulary

1. Learning vocabulary: general advice
2. Learning vocabulary: specific techniques
3. Organizing a vocabulary notebook
4. The names of English language words
5. Using your dictionary
6. Reviewing vocabulary
7. Guessing and explaining meaning

Word formation

8. Suffixes
9. Prefixes
10. Roots
11. Abstract nouns
12. Compound adjectives
13. Compound nouns: noun + noun
14. Compound nouns: verb + preposition
15. Words from other languages
16. Abbreviations and acronyms
17. New words in English

Words and pronunciation

18. Words commonly mispronounced
19. Onomatopoeic words
20. Homonyms

Connecting and linking words

21. Time
22. Condition
23. Cause, reason, purpose, and result
24. Concession and contrast
25. Addition
26. Text-referring words
27. Discourse markers in speech
28. Discourse markers in writing

Countable and uncountable nouns

29. Uncountable nouns
30. Nouns that are usually plural
31. Countable and uncountable nouns with different meanings
32. Collective nouns
33. Making uncountable nouns countable
34. Containers and contents

iii

Topics

35 Countries, nationalities, and languages
36 The weather
37 Describing people's appearance
38 Describing people's character
39 Relationships
40 At home
41 Everyday problems
42 Global problems
43 Education
44 Work
45 Sports
46 The arts
47 Music
48 Food
49 The environment
50 Towns
51 The natural world
52 Clothes
53 Health and medicine
54 Transportation
55 Vacations
56 Numbers and shapes
57 Science and technology
58 Computers and the Internet
59 The media and the press
60 Politics and public institutions
61 Crime
62 Money and finances

Feelings and Actions

63 Belief and opinion
64 Pleasant and unpleasant feelings
65 Likes, dislikes, and desires
66 Speaking
67 The six senses
68 What your body does

Basic Concepts

69 Number, quantity, degree, and intensity
70 Duration of time
71 Distances and dimensions
72 Obligation, need, possibility, and probability
73 Sound and light
74 Possession, giving, and lending
75 Movement and speed
76 Texture, brightness, density, and weight
77 Success, failure, and difficulty

Idiomatic expressions

- 78 Idioms and fixed expressions: general
- 79 Everyday expressions
- 80 Similes
- 81 Binomials
- 82 Idioms describing people
- 83 Idioms describing feelings and mood
- 84 Idioms connected with problematic situations
- 85 Idioms connected with praise and criticism
- 86 Idioms connected with using language
- 87 Miscellaneous idioms
- 88 Proverbs

Phrasal verbs and verb-based expressions

- 89 Expressions with *do* and *make*
- 90 Expressions with *bring* and *take*
- 91 Expressions with *get*
- 92 Expressions with *set* and *put*
- 93 Expressions with *come* and *go*
- 94 Miscellaneous expressions

Special Topics

- 95   Headline English
- 96   The language of signs and notices
- 97   Words and gender
- 98   Formal and informal words
- 99   Varieties of English
- 100 American English and British English

Pronunciation symbols	202
Index	203
Answer key	236

Acknowledgments

We wish to thank the following reviewers, whose comments were so helpful in improving this book: Julien Park, English Language Academy, South Korea; Nick Taggert, Instructor, Interactive College of Technology, Chamblee, Georgia; and Nina Ito, Academic Coordinator, American Language Institute, California State University, U.S.A.

We also wish to acknowledge the insightful suggestions provided by reviewers at Cambridge University Press: Emeric Lau, Singapore; Jinhee Park, South Korea; Satoko Shimoyama, Japan; and Alex Martinez, Mexico.

Many thanks are due to the *Corpus* consultant Randi Reppen, who made sure the text was faithful to contemporary American usage. But above all, we are indebted to our American adapter John D. Bunting. Without John's collaboration, this second edition would not be published.

We would also like to express our appreciation to the following editorial staff at Cambridge University Press: Caitlin Mara, Karen McAlister Shimoda, Katherine Wong, Kathleen O'Reilly, Keiko Sugiyama, and Richard Walker. Our special thanks go to Bernard Seal, who guided this book through the editorial process with his usual calm and professionalism.

Finally, we would like to thank all those who helped in the making of the first edition of *Vocabulary in Use High Intermediate*, especially Ellen Shaw, our original American adapter.

Michael McCarthy
Felicity O'Dell

January 2010

Layout and design: Transnet Pte Ltd.
                            based on a design by Tanky Media
Cover design: Studioleng

Illustrations by Jonathan C. Shih, LiDan Illustration & Design Studio, Richard Peter David, and Tanky Media.

The authors and publishers would like to thank Stephen Forster, and would also like to thank the following for permission to reproduce copyright material and photographs:

p.2, extract from *The English Language* by David Crystal (London: Penguin Books, 1988), reproduced by permission of Penguin Books; p.3, ©iStockphoto.com/mikheewnik; p.10, 11, definitions of "hairy" and "slip" adapted from *Cambridge Dictionary of American English*, Second Edition (2008), and reproduced by permission of Cambridge University Press; p.12, extract from *Language Learning Strategies: What Every Teacher Should Know*, by Rebecca L. Oxford (1990), reproduced by permission of Heinle; p.15, ©iStockphoto.com/DNY59; p.17, (*left to right*) ©iStockphoto.com/anlogin, ©iStockphoto.com/ritajaco, ©iStockphoto.com/peolsen, ©iStockphoto.com/Spiderstock, ©iStockphoto.com/sweetym; p.77, ©iStockphoto.com/bluestocking; p.100, extract from *The Great Towns of the West*, David Vokac (San Diego: West Press, 1985), reproduced by permission of West Press; ©iStockphoto.com/zzwarnock; p.103, 243, extracts from *The Cambridge Encyclopedia* by David Crystal (1991), reproduced by permission of Cambridge University Press; p.124, ©iStockphoto.com/igenkin; p.166, 167, ©iStockphoto.com/cteconsulting

Introduction

This new edition of *Vocabulary in Use High Intermediate* still retains the features that made the first edition so popular:

- The format of presentation on the left-hand page and practice on the right-hand page.
- It opens with a section on skills for vocabulary recording and memorizing.
- It approaches English vocabulary from a range of different angles – looking not just at topics, but also at word formation, at words and grammar, at functions like *Connecting and linking*, at concepts like *Time* or *Distance*, and at varieties of English.
- A student-friendly Answer key, including not only correct answers to right/wrong exercises, but also possible answers for more open-ended exercises.
- It contains language and usage notes that are ideal for self-study learners.
- It has a complete Index, which lists all the target words and phrases covered.

What is different about the new edition?

The first thing you will notice is that the new edition is in color. This makes the text and the artwork more attractive, and it also makes the book easier for you to use: the different headings and sections are now clearer, and the usage notes are shown against their own color background, so you can find them and read them more easily.

All the artwork is new: the full-color illustrations are clearer and more attractive, and they reflect recent changes in technology.

This new edition has made use of the *Cambridge International Corpus* of written and spoken English. This is important in several ways:

- The *Corpus* has been used to check that all language and content is contemporary, natural, and accurate.
- The frequency information in the *Corpus* has helped guide the selection of words and phrases in the book and ensure that the vocabulary is suitable for learners of English at a high intermediate level.
- Example sentences are the same or similar to those in the *Corpus*. In other words, the examples show you words and phrases being used in their most typical contexts.

The process of updating the materials has also allowed us to introduce some new units, as requested by teachers and students. This edition contains a unit on *Guessing and explaining meaning* (Unit 7) and a unit on *Music* (Unit 47). *New words in English* (Unit 17) and *Computers and the Internet* (Unit 58) have both been totally revised to match changes in the language since the first edition.

In this second edition, we have reorganized the units in a more logical way and have introduced clearer headings for some of the sections. We have also created a new section, *Words and pronunciation*. In addition, we have made changes to the presentation materials and the exercises which we hope will make the book easier for students to use.

The Index is now organized unit by unit, allowing learners to see at a glance the key words and phrases of any unit.

Using this book

Who is this book for?

Vocabulary in Use High Intermediate has been written to help learners at this level to improve their English. The material corresponds approximately to level B2 of the Council of Europe's CEFR (Common European Framework of Reference for Languages). It will help students to learn not only the meanings of words but also how they are used. *Vocabulary in Use High Intermediate* has been designed for students who are studying on their own, but it can also be used by a teacher in the classroom with a group of students.

How is the book organized?

The book has 100 two-page units. The left-hand page explains the new words and expressions chosen for that unit. Where appropriate, it gives information about the meanings of words as well as how to use them. The right-hand page gives you a chance to check your understanding through a series of exercises which practice the new vocabulary. Sometimes, the right-hand page will also teach you some more new words.

There is an Answer key at the back of the book. It will help you learn more about the words and expressions studied in the unit. Some questions have only one correct answer. Other questions have more than one correct answer. You will find comments on the answers giving reasons why one answer may be more appropriate than another. You will also find suggested answers for more open-ended questions. These suggested answers are intended to be used as possible examples and are not the only correct answer.

There is also an Index at the back of the book. This lists all the words and phrases introduced in the book.

How should I use the book?

The book is divided into a number of sections. Start by working through the first seven units. These units not only teach you some new vocabulary but they also help you with useful techniques for vocabulary learning in general. After completing those units, you may want to work straight through the book, or you might prefer to do the units in any order that suits you.

What else do I need in order to work with this book?

You need some kind of vocabulary notebook where you can write down the new words you are learning (see Unit 3 for advice on how to do this).

It is also important to have access to a good dictionary. This book selects the words that are most useful for you to learn at your level and it gives you the most essential information about those words, but you will sometimes need to refer to a dictionary as well for extra information about meaning and usage. Remember, you can always go to http://dictionary.cambridge.org/ to look up words and learn more about them.

Companion Web site: www.cambridge.org/vinu

On the *Vocabulary in Use* Companion Web site, you will find a range of free additional activities for vocabulary and listening practice.

We hope you enjoy learning with *Vocabulary in Use High Intermediate*.

Good luck!

Unit 1
Learning vocabulary: general advice

A What do you need to learn?

1. How many words are there in English?
   a) 10,000   b) 100,000   c) 250,000   d) 500,000

2. How many words does the average English speaker use in everyday speech?
   a) 2,500   b) 5,000   c) 7,500   d) 10,000

3. How many words make up 45% of everything written in English?
   a) 50   b) 250   c) 1,000   d) 2,500

4. What do you think are the twenty most common words in English?

Answers are on page 236. They show the following basic facts about English vocabulary.

- There are many words in English that you don't need at all.
- There are words that you need to be able to use yourself.
- There are other words you need simply to understand when you read or hear them.
- The most common words in English are the grammar words, which you already know.

Clearly you need to spend the most time learning words that you need to be able to use yourself. In the text below, underline the words you want to understand. Then, circle the words you want to understand *and* be able to use.

> English vocabulary has a remarkable range, flexibility, and adaptability. Thanks to the periods of contact with foreign languages and its readiness to coin new words out of old elements, English seems to have far more words in its core vocabulary than other languages. For example, alongside *kingly* (from Anglo-Saxon), we find *royal* (from French) and *regal* (from Latin). There are many such sets of words, which add greatly to our opportunities to express subtle shades of meaning at various levels of style.

B What does knowing a new word mean?

It is not enough just to know the meaning of a word. You also need to know the following:

- Which words it is usually associated with, such as
    adjectives and nouns (e.g., *classical music, common sense*)
    verbs and nouns (e.g., *to express an opinion, to take sides*)
    nouns in phrases (e.g., *in touch with, a sense of humor*)
    words with prepositions (e.g., *at a loss for words, thanks to you*)
- Its grammatical characteristics, for example,
    irregular verbs (e.g., *take, took, taken*)
    uncountable nouns (e.g., *luggage*)
    nouns that are only used in the plural (e.g., *clothes*)
- How it is pronounced (see Units 4 and 18)
- Its register – whether it is formal, informal, or neutral (see Units 95 and 96)

Unit 1

1. What phrases could you write to help you remember the following words?
   a) chilly   b) dissuade   c) up to my neck   d) independent   e) get married

2. What grammatical notes could you write next to the following words?
   a) scissors   b) weather   c) teach   d) advice   e) lose   f) pants

3. What pronunciation notes could you write next to the following words?
   a) subtle   b) catastrophe   c) photograph/photography   d) answer

4. What notes could you write about the register of the following words?
   a) guys   b) persons   c) people

C Can you learn just by reading or listening to English?

You can help yourself learn English vocabulary by reading and listening to English as much as possible. Rank each item below from 0 to 4 to describe how important the way of learning vocabulary is for you personally (with 4 being the most important). You can add more items to the list if you like.

reading newspapers or magazines	....	watching TV, movies, or DVDs	....
listening to podcasts or the radio	....	listening to CDs or MP3 files	....
reading books, comics, or blog sites	....	surfing the Internet	....
talking to English speakers	....	attending lectures	....

D What should you do when you come across new words?

- When you are reading something in English, don't stop to look up every new word or expression in a dictionary – this slows down your reading and your comprehension. Look up only those words that are really important for understanding the text. When you have finished reading, look back at what you have read and then perhaps look up some extra words and write down new expressions that interest you.
- When you listen in English, don't panic when you hear words or expressions that you don't know. Keep listening for the overall meaning.
- When you read or listen to English, it is sometimes possible to guess the meaning of a word you don't know before you look it up. Decide first which part of speech the word is, and then look for clues in its context or form.

Look at the following text. Before you read it, see if you know what the underlined words mean. After you read the text, try to guess the meaning of the underlined words from the context or from the way the word is formed. Then, if necessary, check a dictionary.

A <u>tortoise</u> is a <u>shelled</u> <u>reptile</u> <u>famed</u> for its slowness and <u>longevity</u>. The giant tortoise of the Galapagos may <u>attain</u> over 1.5 meters in length and have a <u>life span</u> of more than 150 years. Smaller tortoises from southern Europe and North Africa make popular pets. They need to be <u>tended</u> carefully in cool climates and must have a warm place in which they can <u>hibernate</u>.

Unit 2

Learning vocabulary: specific techniques

A Learning associated words together

- Learn words with associated meanings together.

    Complete this bubble network for the word *cat*. Add as many other bubbles as you like. Then, if possible, compare networks with your classmates. If you like, add any of their ideas to your own network.

    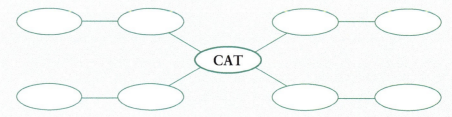

- Learn words that form collocations together. Sometimes similar words do not make equally strong collocations (such as *a big day* or *a big race*, but not *a large day* or *a large race*). The best way to build your collocation knowledge is to notice what other words usually appear with the words you want to learn. This takes a long time, so you should also use a good learner's dictionary to find common collocations.

    For these groups of words, decide which words might make the strongest collocations.

draw	*point* . . .	utter	*highly* . . .
make	a gun	horrible	complex
write	a finger	extreme	enjoyable
. . . *a line*	a book	. . . *nonsense*	successful

- Learn words based on the same root together.

    Can you add any other words or expressions to these two groups?
    1. price   priceless   overpriced
    2. handy   single-handed   give me a hand

B Using pictures

- Pictures might help you remember vocabulary visually.

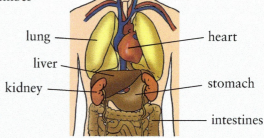

Can you draw any pictures that would help you remember the following vocabulary?

skeleton   skinny   receipt

C Using diagrams

- Word trees can help you make connections between related words.

  Look at the word tree for *vacation*. Now complete a tree for *school*.

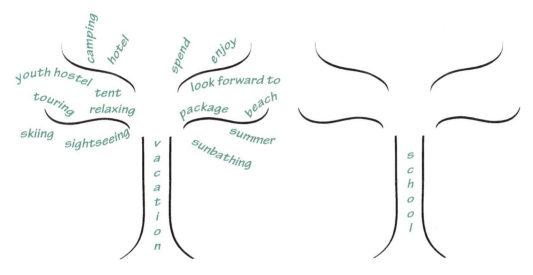

- Word forks are a good way of learning adjectives and verbs.

  Look at the complete word forks for adjectives that go with *idea* and verbs that go with *a movie*. What words can you use to complete the word forks for *view* and *a ball*?

original		shoot		magnificent		kick	
brilliant		edit		breathtaking		hit	
unusual	idea	direct	a movie	superb	view	bounce	a ball
great		star in					
excellent		review					

- Tables can also help clarify collocations.

  Look at this example of a table. Then complete the sentences below by using the correct form of the verbs **fly**, **drive**, or **ride**.

	a car	a motorcycle	a truck	a horse	a plane
to fly					✓
to drive	✓		✓		
to ride		✓		✓	

  1. Her mother .... a truck for 15 years, but now she's retired.
  2. Have you ever .... a plane?
  3. .... a motorcycle can be very dangerous.

Unit 3
Organizing a vocabulary notebook

> **tip** *While you are learning vocabulary, you should keep a vocabulary notebook, either on paper or electronically. There are many different ways to organize your notebook. This unit provides some ideas and examples.*

A Organizing words by meaning

Try dividing your notebook into general sections, with different sections for *words for feelings*, *words to describe places*, *words for movement*, *words for thinking*, etc. In each section you can build families of words related in meaning.

B Using various types of diagrams

- Words can be grouped under a heading, or a more general word can be drawn as a tree diagram. (See Unit 2.) In the example below, the dotted lines show that you can add more words to a diagram as you learn them.

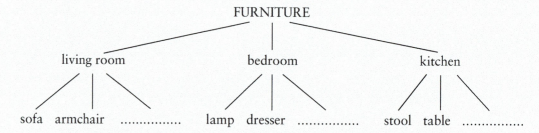

- A bubble network is also useful since you can make it grow in whatever direction you want it to grow.

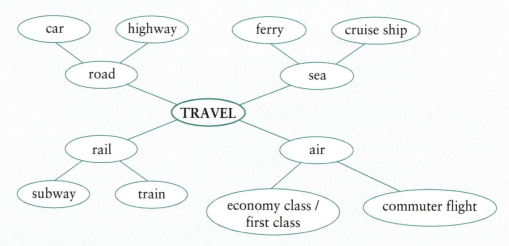

C Adding synonyms and antonyms

When you find a synonym or an antonym of a word you already have in your vocabulary notebook, enter it next to that word with a few notes.

> urban ≠ rural   stop = cease (more formal)

Unit 3

Exercises

3.1 Here is a list of words a Spanish learner of English made in her vocabulary notebook. How could she improve the list and organize it better?

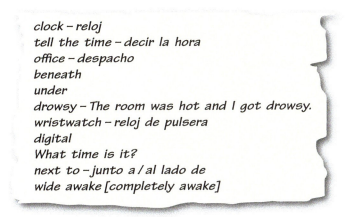

clock – reloj
tell the time – decir la hora
office – despacho
beneath
under
drowsy – The room was hot and I got drowsy.
wristwatch – reloj de pulsera
digital
What time is it?
next to – junto a / al lado de
wide awake [completely awake]

3.2 This word map is a variation on the bubble network. Write the word that you think belongs in the middle of the map.

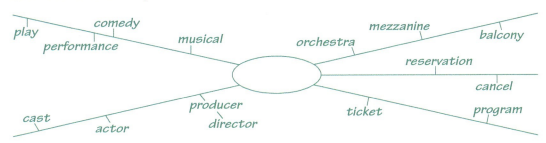

3.3 Complete this table by filling in synonyms and antonyms for the words in the center.

Synonyms	=		≠	Antonyms
dominant, controlling	=	powerful	≠	weak, ineffective
	=	ready	≠	
	=	transport	≠	
	=	destroy	≠	

3.4 Talk with other people who are learning English. Compare your ideas for learning vocabulary and list useful ideas in your notebook. For example, one learner tested himself regularly with his notebook, covering up the word and guessing it from his translation or from his other notes. Here is his system.

- If his translation and notes were clear, but he couldn't guess the word, he put a small red mark in the margin. Three red marks meant "needs extra effort."
- If his translation and notes couldn't help him guess the word, then he put a blue mark in the margin. This meant "need more information about this word."

Unit 4 The names of English language words

A The names of basic parts of speech in English

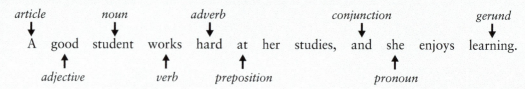

B Words relating to nouns

Look at this sentence: *An artist loves beauty*. *Artist* is **countable** – it has a plural form: *artists* – but *beauty* is **uncountable**. *Artist* is the **subject** of the verb – it describes who does the verb. *Beauty* is the **object** of the verb – it describes who or what is affected by the verb.

C Words relating to verbs

infinitive (*to go*)   **-ing form** (*going*)   **past participle** (*gone*)   **past tense** (*went*)

Go (*go, went, gone*) is an **irregular** verb, but *live* (*live, lived, lived*) is **regular**. *Go* is also **intransitive** because it does not need an object (e.g., *Has Luis gone?*). *Make* is **transitive** because it is followed by an object (e.g., *you make something*).

D Words relating to the construction of words

In the word *irregularity*, *ir-* is a **prefix**, *regular* is a **root**, and *-ity* is a **suffix**. *Thin* is the **opposite** or **antonym** of *fat*; and *slim* has the same meaning, or is a **synonym**, of *thin*. A **word family** is a set of words based on one root (e.g., *word, wordy, to reword*). A **phrase** does not include a **main verb** – *in a minute* is an example of a phrase. A **sentence** has a main verb; the first word of a sentence begins with a **capital letter** and ends with a **period** (or **question mark** or **exclamation point**).

E Words relating to pronunciation

A **syllable** is the minimum sound unit of a word, consisting of at least one vowel sound. There are three syllables (or beats) in the word *opposite* ('op•po•site), and the **stress** is on the first syllable.

F Words and their associations

There are different styles of speaking and writing appropriate to different situations. **Slang** is an extremely informal style. A **colloquial** style is suitable mainly for conversation (e.g., *a nice guy*). **Pejorative** words have a negative association (*pigheaded* is pejorative, whereas *determined*, although very close in meaning, is not).

G Words describing punctuation

. period   , comma   ; semicolon   ' apostrophe
- hyphen   – dash   ! exclamation point ? question mark
( ) parentheses   " " quotation marks   B capital letter   : colon

Unit 4

Exercises

4.1 Look at the paragraphs in D, E, and F on page 8. Find one example for each of these items.

1. a noun that is countable ....
2. a transitive verb ....
3. a regular verb ....
4. an adjective ....
5. a preposition ....
6. a noun that is uncountable ....
7. an intransitive verb ....
8. an irregular verb ....
9. an adverb ....
10. an article ....

4.2 Complete this table.

Verb	Infinitive	-ing form	Past participle
define	....	....	....
mean	....	....	....
write	....	....	....

4.3 Think about the word *informal*.

1. What is its root, its prefix, and its suffix?
2. What is its opposite or antonym?
3. Does it have any synonyms?
4. Name some words that are included in its word family.

4.4 Look at all the words in bold in E, F, and G on page 8. For each word with more than one syllable, underline the stressed syllable. (e.g., pe•*jor*•a•tive)

4.5 Match the following colloquial words below with their more formal equivalents in the box.

| man | converse | tolerate | relax | exhausted |

1. chat (verb)   2. guy   3. put up with   4. beat (adjective)   5. hang out (verb)

4.6 The following pairs of words are close in meaning, but one word in each case is pejorative. Circle the pejorative one. Use your dictionary if necessary.

1. scheme / plan
2. slim / skinny
3. eloquent / wordy
4. stingy / thrifty
5. cunning / shrewd
6. smug / confident

4.7 Cover page 8 and write the names of these punctuation marks.

( ) ....   ? ....   , ...
; ....   – ....   - ....
, ...   " " ....   ! ....

Unit 5 Using your dictionary

A Good dictionaries in general, and learner's dictionaries in particular, can tell you a lot more about a word than just its meaning, including the following:

- Part of speech (e.g., **n**: *noun*; **v**: *verb*; **adj**: *adjective*; **adv**: *adverb*), whether a noun is countable (**C**) or uncountable (**U**), and whether a verb is normally transitive (**T**) or intransitive (**IT**)
- Synonyms and the ways that they differ (e.g., **mislay** and **misplace**)
- Antonyms (e.g., **friend** ≠ **enemy/foe**)
- Collocations (e.g., **living** is often used in these collocations: **make a living; cost of living; standard of living**)
- Pronunciation, which requires learning some symbols that are different from the letters of the English alphabet

/θ/	th in **thick**	/ð/	th in **then**	/tʃ/	ch in **church**
/ʃ/	sh in **she**	/dʒ/	j in **jam**	/ʒ/	s in **pleasure**
/ŋ/	ng in **ring**	/æ/	a in **bad**	/ɑ/	o in **top**
/ɔː/	o in **form**	/ʊ/	u in **put**	/ə/	a in **about**
/ʌ/	u in **up**	/ɜr/	ir in **bird**		

- Word stress, which is usually shown by a mark (ˈ) before the stressed syllable (e.g., /ɪkˈspek·tən·si/ for **expectancy**, which is stressed on the second syllable)
- Syllable division (e.g., reg·u·lar·ly)
- Differences between varieties of English, such as American, Australian, and British English
- How a word is used and any special grammatical pattern that goes with it (e.g., **suggest** + that + clause: *I suggest that you call her*)
- Information about style and use in special situations (formal, informal, taboo, technical, dated, etc.)

B Don't forget that most words have more than one meaning. In this example, only the second meaning corresponds to the way **hairy** is used in this sentence:
It was a really hairy ride down the mountain road.

> **Hairy** /ˈher·i, ˈhær·i/ *adj* having a lot of hair, esp. on parts of the body other than the head ○ *hairy arms*

> **Hairy** /ˈher·i, ˈhær·i/ *adj informal* difficult, dangerous, or frightening ○ *The roads were really icy, and it was definitely a hairy situation even going slow.*

 tip If you own a dictionary, make a little mark in the margin each time you look up a word. If a word gets three or more marks, it is worth an extra effort to learn it.

Unit 5

Exercises

5.1 Some learner's dictionaries have *guide* words. These are the various definitions of a word, and they are usually boxed. Look at all the guide words for *slip* in these example entries. Then look at the sentences below the entries. For each sentence, write the correct guide word on the blank.

> **slip** SLIDE /slɪp/ *v* [I] -pp- to slide suddenly and without intending to • *He slipped on an icy sidewalk and broke his hip.* • *The blanket began to slip off my shoulders.*
> **slip** GET WORSE /slɪp/ *v* [I] -pp- to change to a worse state or condition • *We've slipped even further behind schedule.* • *After slipping into a coma, he never woke up.*
> **slip** PIECE OF PAPER /slɪp/ *n* [C] a small piece of paper • *You get a slip from the cash machine when you take out money.*
>
> **slip** MISTAKE /slɪp/ *n* [C] a mistake that someone makes when they are not being careful • *She has made some slips lately that show she's thinking about other things.*
> **slip** UNDERWEAR /slɪp/ *n* [C] women's underwear that is shaped like a skirt or a dress
> **slip** ESCAPE /slɪp/ *v* [I/T] -pp- to get away from or get free from something • [T] *The dog slipped its leash and ran off.* • [I always + adv/prep] *The ball slipped through my fingers.*

1. You can't wear that white dress with a black slip underneath. ....
2. He slipped on the ice and fell. ....
3. I meant to call you yesterday, but it slipped my mind. ....
4. Our profits are slowly slipping. ....
5. If you want to return something to a store, you need a sales slip. ....
6. I didn't mean to make that negative comment; it was just a slip. ....

5.2 Read the pronunciation symbols for the words below. Figure out what English words they are, how many syllables each word has, and which syllable has the most stress in each word. Then fill in the blanks with the correct words and underline their stressed syllables. Use the pronunciation key on page 202.

1. /ˌedʒ·əˈkeɪʃən/   3. /ˈlɪb·ərt̬·i/   5. /ˈpæsˌpɔːrt/
   ....

2. /rɪˈvɪʒ·ən/   4. /leŋθ/   6. /ˈbrʌð·ər/
   ....

5.3 In the dictionary entry for *hairy* in B on page 10, how many synonyms can you find?

> *follow-up* Go to the Internet site for Cambridge University Press dictionaries at http://www.dictionary.cambridge.org/ and look at the different kinds of dictionaries available for learners of English. Which one do you think would work best for you?

Unit 6   Reviewing vocabulary

A Here is an extract from a book about language-learning strategies on the importance of reviewing in an active way.

> Reviewing . . . is especially useful for remembering new material in the target language. It entails reviewing at different intervals, at first close together and then increasingly far apart. For instance, Misha is learning a set of vocabulary words in English. He practices them immediately, waits 15 minutes before practicing them again, and practices them an hour later, three hours later, the next day, two days later, four days later, the following week, two weeks later, and so on until the material becomes more or less automatic. In this way he keeps spiraling back to these particular vocabulary words, even though he might be encountering more material in class. Each time he practices these vocabulary words, Misha does it in a meaningful way, like putting them into a context or recombining them to make new sentences. Naturally, the amount of time needed to make new material automatic depends on the kind of material involved. (From *Language Learning Strategies: What Every Teacher Should Know*, by Rebecca L. Oxford)

B **Reviewing vocabulary with this book**

When you review a unit, first read through it completely. Next, look at anything you wrote in your vocabulary notebook connected with the unit. Then, and most importantly, try to do something different with the new words and expressions in that unit in order to help fix them in your memory. Here are some suggestions for reviewing vocabulary.

- Highlight any words or expressions that you had forgotten or were not sure about.
- Look at the unit and choose ten words and expressions that you particularly want or need to learn. Write them in your vocabulary notebook.
- Look up any words that you selected in an English-English dictionary. Do these words have any other uses or associations that might help you learn them? For example, looking up the word **heart** might lead you to the adjective **heartbroken** or the phrase **heart of the matter**. Write words that especially interest you in an appropriate phrase or sentence.
- The dictionary can also help you find some other words based on the same root. Looking up the noun **employment** will lead you to the verb **employ**, to the nouns **employer** and **employee**, and, perhaps, to the adjectives **employable**, **unemployed**, and **self-employed**.
- Note the pronunciation of the words and expressions you wish to learn. Try to write them down using the pronunciation symbols (they are shown on page 202). Include the syllable stress. Use a dictionary if necessary.
- In your notebook, consider writing the words and phrases from each unit in a slightly different way – for instance, put them into a network or a table. Then test yourself. Cover part of a word or phrase. Can you remember the complete word or phrase?

When you have done all the steps above that you feel are useful, close your book and notebook, and go over what you have been studying. How much can you remember?

Unit 6

C Making the new words active

One of the great advantages of reviewing vocabulary is that it should help you to make the step from having a word or phrase in your receptive vocabulary to having it in your active vocabulary. Here are some suggestions for making new words active.

- Write the words and expressions you are trying to learn in a sentence relating to your life and interests at the moment.
- Make an effort to use the new words and expressions in your next class or homework or in some other way.
- Keep a learning diary in which you note down things that particularly interest you about the words you have learned.
- Watch out for the words and expressions you are trying to learn in your general reading of English. If you come across any of them, write them down in their context in your diary or notebook.
- Write a paragraph or story linking the words and expressions you want to learn.

D What can you remember?

1. What do you remember from the first six units of this book about how to learn new vocabulary effectively? Answer without looking back at the units.
2. Now read through the units again.
3. How much do you remember about the units now?
4. Choose at least one word and expression from each unit and work through all the suggestions made in B and C above. It may not always be appropriate in your future study to do all the steps in B, but try them now for practice.

E Planning your work with this book

1. How often are you going to review what you have done? Every week? Every five units?
2. Which techniques are you going to use for reviewing?
3. Now write some notes to remind yourself of when you are going to review.
   For instance, you might like to write *review vocabulary* in your calendar for the next eight Fridays if you decided to review every week. Alternatively, you could write *REVIEW* in capital letters after every five units in the book.

Unit 7

Guessing and explaining meaning

A Inferring meaning from context

A number of clues may help you figure out the meaning of an unfamiliar word.

- **The context in which it is used**
  Visual clues: A picture in a book or film footage in a TV news broadcast may help you.

  Your own background knowledge about a situation: For example, if you already know that there has just been an earthquake in California, then you will find it easy to understand the word *earthquake* when you hear a news broadcast about it.

  The immediate context (other words around the unfamiliar word) that may make the meaning absolutely clear: *Suzanna picked one tall yellow gladiolus to put in her new crystal vase*. Even if you have never seen or heard the word *gladiolus*, it will probably be obvious to you from the context that it is a type of flower.

  Grammatical clues in the context: It is not difficult to understand that *superstitious* must be an adjective in the sentence *Marsha is very superstitious*, or that *gingerly* is an adverb in *Jackie tiptoed gingerly down the stairs*.

- **Similarity to other words you already know in English**
  A large number of words in English are made up of combinations of other words. You may never have seen the word *headscarf*, for example, but the meaning is easy to figure out from its two components. Units 12–14 will help you improve your skills in understanding how English uses everyday words to build up new concepts.

- **Structure**
  A prefix or suffix may give you a clue to the meaning of a word. Units 8–11 focus on different aspects of word formation in English and should help you exploit those clues in making sense of unfamiliar words.

- **Similarity to a word you know in your own (or some other) language**
  If your first language is of Latin or of Germanic origin, you will come across many words in English that resemble words in your own language. However, English has taken words from many other languages too (see Unit 15). So make use of any other languages you know. But remember that some words are "false friends" – they sound as if they mean the same, but in fact, they have a different meaning. (A good dictionary will give lists of false friends for a lot of European languages.)

B Explaining unknown words

The following expressions can be useful when you are trying to explain what a word or expression means.

It's (a bit) like (a chair) . . .
It's something you use for (painting pictures / cleaning the kitchen floor . . .)
It's a kind of / sort of / type of (bird / musical instrument / building . . .)
It must/could be . . .

Unit 7

Exercises

7.1 Look at the following text. Before you read it, see if you know what the underlined words mean. After you read the text, try to guess the meaning of the underlined words from the context or from the way the words are formed. Then, if necessary, check a dictionary.

> High blood pressure, also called <u>hypertension</u>, is a common problem and needs <u>ongoing monitoring</u>. Doctors identify high blood pressure when the <u>sphygmomanometer</u> reading is 140/90 mmHg or more. This <u>malady</u> can lead to kidney <u>failure</u>, heart attacks, and other <u>debilitating</u> health conditions. Making positive changes in diet and lifestyle can significantly lower blood pressure in many cases. In certain cases, <u>medication</u> can be used to <u>remedy</u> this condition.

7.2 Use the context to figure out the meanings of the underlined words. Explain the words by using the expressions in B on page 14.

1. Above the trees at the edge of the meadow, a <u>buzzard</u> hangs for a moment on the wind before soaring towards the hills.
   A buzzard must be a kind of big bird.
2. The long-beaked <u>echidnas</u> of New Guinea are at risk of extinction because their meat is valuable and their forest habitat is disappearing.
3. Using a large <u>chisel</u>, the police broke through the front door and surprised the robbers.
4. We ate a delicious chicken noodle soup from a big <u>tureen</u> and enjoyed several bowls each.
5. We walked to the top of the cliff and <u>clambered</u> over the bushes to get a better view of the sunset.
6. Some people get really <u>cranky</u> when they haven't had enough sleep.

7.3 Use your knowledge of basic English words to help you figure out the meanings of these underlined words and expressions. Rewrite them using simpler words or explanations.

1. It says on the can that this drink is <u>sugar-free</u>.
   It says on the can that this drink contains no sugar.
2. Many countries require <u>identification</u> cards for anyone who lives there.
3. I find Max to be a very <u>warm-hearted</u> person.
4. I've been <u>up to my eyes in work</u> all week.
5. We walked down a <u>tree-lined</u> street towards the station.
6. The little boys were fascinated by the <u>cement-mixer</u>.

7.4 Use your knowledge of prefixes and suffixes to suggest what these phrases mean.

1. uncontrollable anger
2. anti-government feelings
3. my ex-boss
4. pre-dinner drinks
5. bimonthly report
6. undelivered letters

Unit 8

Suffixes

A Common noun suffixes

- **-er** is usually used for the person who does an activity, e.g., **writer, worker, programmer, teacher**. You can use **-er** to turn many verbs into nouns.
- In a few cases, the **-er** suffix is written as **-or**, e.g., **doctor, supervisor, governor**.
- **-er/-or** are also used for things to describe their purpose, e.g., **pencil sharpener, computer, bottle opener, coffeemaker, projector**.
- **-er/-or** and **-ee** can contrast with each other, **-er/-or** meaning *person who does something* and **-ee** meaning *person who receives or experiences the action*, e.g., **employer/employee; sender/addressee; payer/payee** (e.g., of a check).
- **-tion/-sion/-ion** are used to form nouns from verbs, e.g., **complication, pollution, reduction, donation, promotion, admission**.
- **-ism** (an activity or ideology) is used for beliefs, and sometimes professions, e.g., **liberalism, Buddhism, journalism, environmentalism, racism**.
- **-ist** (a person) is used for beliefs, and sometimes professions, e.g., **Buddhist, journalist, artist, physicist, pianist**.
- **-ness** is used to form nouns from adjectives, e.g., **sadness, goodness, thoughtfulness**. Note what happens to adjectives that end in **-y**: **laziness, friendliness, happiness**.

B Adjective suffixes

-able/-ible combined with verbs often means *can be done*, e.g., **erasable** [can be erased] or **flexible** [can be bent]. Other examples are

   breakable   edible [can be eaten]   **profitable   reliable   rewritable   variable**

C Verbs

-ize forms verbs from adjectives or nouns, e.g., **alphabetize, digitize, industrialize, popularize**.

D Other suffixes that can help you recognize parts of speech

-**ment:** (nouns) excitement   enjoyment   replacement
-**ity:** (nouns) flexibility   productivity   scarcity
-**ive:** (adjectives) passive   productive   active
-**y:** (adjectives) windy   wealthy   angry
-**al:** (adjectives) brutal   legal   (nouns) refusal   arrival
-**ous:** (adjectives) delicious   outrageous   furious
-**ful:** (adjectives) forgetful   hopeful   useful
-**less:** (adjectives) useless   harmless   homeless
-**ify:** (verbs) beautify   purify   terrify
-**ly, ally:** (adverb) actively   wildly   curiously

Unit 8

Exercises

8.1 Use the suffixes *-er/-or*, *-ee*, and *-ist* to form the names of these people or objects.

1. A person who plays jazz on the piano. *a jazz pianist*
2. The thing that wipes rain off your car windshield.
3. A person who takes photographs professionally.
4. A person who is employed by someone else.
5. An appliance for washing dishes.
6. A person who creates art.
7. A person who works to save the environment.

8.2 Each picture is of an object ending in *-er* or *-or*. Name the objects

1.   2.   3.   4.   5.

8.3 List six jobs you would like to have in order of preference. How many different suffixes are there in your list? Which of the job names do not have a suffix (e.g., *pilot*, *movie star*)?

8.4 Do these words mean a person, a thing, or both?

1. a cleaner
2. a computer
3. a dishwasher
4. a dresser
5. a governor
6. a marker
7. an MP3 player
8. a singer

8.5 Fill in each blank with a form of the underlined word and a suffix from page 16. Make any necessary spelling changes.

1. Most of his crimes can be <u>forgiven</u>. Most of his crimes are ..*forgivable*............. .
2. This job looks like we can easily <u>do</u> it. This job is definitely ....
3. Her only fault is that she is <u>lazy</u>. Her only fault is ....
4. The company has <u>produced</u> a lot in recent years. The company has been very .... in recent years.
5. The audience was <u>outraged</u> by the play. The play was ....

8.6 Think of any industry or service in your country that should be *nationalized* (e.g., airlines) or any that should be *privatized*. Think of processes that have recently been either *modernized* or *computerized*.

8.7 Which word is the odd one out in each group and why?

1. actively   wildly   timely   quickly
2. appointment involvement   compliment   arrangement
3. tearful   spiteful   dreadful   handful
4. worship   relationship   friendship   partnership

17

Unit 9 Prefixes

A Prefixes usually change the meaning of a word, and are most often used to show a negative or opposite meaning. For example, comfortable/**un**comfortable, convenient/**in**convenient, and similar/**dis**similar are opposites. Other examples are **un**just, **in**edible, **dis**loyal. Unfortunately, there is no easy way of knowing which prefix is used to form a word's opposite.

Note that the prefix **in-** often changes depending on the first sound of the root word.

- **in-** becomes **im-** before a root beginning with *m* or *p*, e.g., **im**mature, **im**patient, **im**partial, **im**probable.
- **in-** becomes **ir-** before a word beginning with *r*, e.g., **ir**replaceable, **ir**reversible.
- **in-** becomes **il-** before a word beginning with *l*, e.g., **il**legal, **il**legible, **il**literate.
- The prefix **in-** (and its variations) does not always have a negative/opposite meaning – often it gives the idea of *inside* or *into*, e.g., **in**ternal, **im**port, **in**sert, **in**come.

B The prefixes **un-** and **dis-** can also form the opposites of words (often verbs), e.g., tie/**un**tie, appear/**dis**appear. These prefixes are used to reverse the action of the verb. Here are some more examples: **dis**agree, **dis**approve, **dis**connect, **dis**credit, **dis**like, **dis**prove, **dis**qualify, **un**bend, **un**do, **un**dress, **un**earth, **un**fold, **un**load, **un**lock, **un**veil, **un**wrap.

C Here are some examples of other prefixes in English. Some of these words are used with a hyphen. Check a dictionary if necessary.

Prefix	Meaning	Examples
anti	against	antisocial antitrust antiwar
auto	of or by oneself	autograph autopilot autobiography
bi	two, twice	bicycle bilateral bilingual
ex	former	ex-husband ex-smoker ex-boss
ex	out of	extract exhale excommunicate
micro	small	micromanage microwave microscopic
mis	badly, wrongly	misunderstand misbehave misinform mispronounce
mono	one, single	monotonous monologue monogamous
multi	many	multinational multitasking multimedia
over	too much	overdo overqualified oversleep overdose overwork
post	after	postwar postgraduate postdated
pre	before	preschool preconceived prerequisite precaution
pro	in favor of	proponent pro-choice pro-democracy
pseudo	false	pseudonym pseudo-intellectual
re	again or back	retype reread replace refill
semi	half	semicircular semicolon semifinal
sub	under	subway submarine subconscious
under	not enough	underestimate underused undercooked underpay

Unit 9

Exercises

9.1 Replace the underlined words with words that contradict the statements. Not all the words you need are on page 18.

1. She looks very <u>comfortable</u>. *uncomfortable*
2. I think she's very <u>mature</u>.
3. It's a <u>convenient</u> location.
4. That's a <u>reversible</u> medical procedure.
5. They have such <u>similar</u> attitudes.
6. He's very <u>efficient</u>.
7. She's always been <u>patient</u>.
8. The punishment seems harsh but <u>just</u>.
9. I'm sure she's <u>loyal</u> to the company.
10. That is a <u>logical</u> argument.

9.2 Fill in the blanks with negative adjectives that match these definitions.

1. .... = impossible to eat
2. .... = unable to read or write
3. .... = not having a job
4. .... = unable to be replaced
5. .... = against the law
6. .... = not enjoying social events

9.3 Fill in the blanks with a negative verb from B on page 18. Put the verbs in the correct form.

1. The runner was ....*disqualified*.... after a blood test.
2. I almost always find that I .... with her opinion.
3. I'm sure he's lying, but it's going to be hard to .... his story.
4. Even though she always smiled, it was clear that she .... him immensely.
5. It took the movers an hour to .... our things from the van.

9.4 Answer these questions, using words from C on page 18.

1. What kind of oven cooks things very quickly?
2. How would you describe someone who is too well prepared for a particular job?
3. What kind of company has branches in many countries?
4. What is a university student who is studying for an advanced degree?
5. What is a person who used to smoke but has now quit smoking?
6. What is a vessel that travels under the water?

9.5 Replace the underlined words with words from C on page 18.

1. People often <u>pronounce</u> my name <u>incorrectly</u>.   *People often mispronounce my name.*
2. Most people say they <u>have to work too hard</u> and <u>are paid too little</u>.
3. It's a good idea to use an alarm clock so you don't <u>sleep later than you should</u>.
4. She's still on good terms with <u>the man who used to be her husband</u>.
5. For very difficult books, it is a good idea to <u>read them a second time</u>.
6. I can tell by her response that she <u>did not understand me at all</u>.
7. I am always impressed with people who are <u>able to speak two languages</u>.

Unit 10 Roots

A Many words in English are formed from Latin roots and are often considered fairly formal in English. Here are some examples of the more common Latin roots, with some of the English verbs derived from them.

- **duc, duct** [lead]
  She was **educated** [went to school] abroad.
  He **conducted** [led] the orchestra brilliantly.
  Japan **produces** [makes] a lot of electronic equipment.

- **port** [carry, take]
  How are you going to **transport** [carry or ship] those boxes overseas?
  The U.S. both **imports** [brings into a country] and **exports** [takes out of a country] cars.
  The roof is **supported** [holds the weight] by the old beams.

- **pose, pone** [place, put]
  The meeting has been **postponed** [changed to a later date] until next week.
  The king was **deposed** [put off the throne] by his own son.
  I don't want to **impose** [force] my views on you.

- **press** [press, push]
  I was **impressed** [full of admiration and respect] by your presentation.
  This dreary weather **depresses** [makes one feel miserable] me.
  She always **expresses** [puts thoughts into words] herself articulately.

- **spect** [see, look]
  You should **respect** [look up to, think highly of] your parents.
  The police **suspected** [had a feeling] they were guilty but had no proof.
  Many American pioneers traveled west to **prospect** [search] for gold.

- **vert** [turn]
  I tried an electronic dictionary, but I soon **reverted** [turned back to] to my old paper dictionary.
  What is an easy way to **convert** [change] pounds into kilograms?
  The scandal **diverted** [turned away] attention from the political crisis.

B The words listed in A are verbs, but for all the roots listed, there is at least one noun and one adjective form as well. The following are examples of roots and their various forms.

Verb	Person noun	Abstract noun	Adjective
intro**duc**e	introducer	introduction	introductory
de**port**	deportee	deportation	deported
com**pose**	composer	composition	composite
op**press**	oppressor	oppression	oppressive
in**spect**	inspector	inspection	inspecting
ad**vert**ise	advertiser	advertisement	advertising

Unit 10

Exercises

10.1 Complete this table by using other forms of words in A on page 20. Use a dictionary if necessary.

Verb	Person noun	Abstract noun	Adjective
convert	convert		
produce			
conduct			
impress	X		
support			
impose	X		

10.2 Figure out the meanings of the underlined words in the sentences below. Use the Latin prefixes in the box to help you.

intro [within, inward]	o, ob [against]	re [again, back]
de [down, from]	ex [out of]	sub, sup [under]

1. She's a very introverted person, but her husband is very expressive.
2. It seems like he opposes everything that I believe in.
3. I don't think it's healthy to repress one's emotions too much.
4. Perhaps you can deduce what the word means from the way it is formed.
5. The documentary exposed corruption in high places.
6. She tried hard to suppress a laugh.

10.3 Match the verbs on the left with verb phrases on the right. Then put a check (✓) next to the column of words that is more informal.

1. respect   put off
2. postpone   turn away
3. oppose   look at
4. inspect   go against
5. revert   take/send out
6. export   look up to
7. divert   turn back to

10.4 Fill in the blanks with words from B on page 20.

1. He was .... for having a forged passport.
2. This magazine has nothing in it but .... for cosmetics.
3. May I .... you to my boss?
4. This heat is so .... - I can barely stand it!
5. Before you buy a new home, be sure to .... it thoroughly.
6. Tchaikovsky .... some incredible music.

> **follow-up** Find two other words based on each of the roots listed in A on page 20. Try to think of how you would use them, and write an appropriate phrase or sentence for each one in your notebook.

Unit 11

Abstract nouns

A An abstract noun represents an idea, experience, or quality, rather than an object that you can touch. **Happiness, intention,** and **shock** are abstract nouns, but **pen, bed,** and **clothes** are not.

B Suffixes are letters added to the ends of words to form new words. Certain suffixes are used frequently in abstract nouns. The most common are **-ment, -ion, -ness,** and **-ity.** The suffix **-ion** sometimes becomes **-tion, -sion, -ation,** or **-ition.**

achievement	action	aggressiveness	absurdity
adjustment	collection	attractiveness	anonymity
amazement	combination	bitterness	complexity
discouragement	illusion	carelessness	curiosity
improvement	imagination	consciousness	generosity
investment	production	friendliness	hostility
replacement	recognition	kindness	originality
resentment	reduction	tenderness	sensitivity

> **note** **-ment** and **-ion** are usually used to make verbs into abstract nouns. The suffixes **-ness** and **-ity** are often added to adjectives.

C Other suffixes that form abstract nouns are **-ship, -dom, -th,** and **-hood.**

apprenticeship	boredom	breadth	adulthood
companionship	freedom	depth	brotherhood
membership	kingdom	length	childhood
ownership	martyrdom	strength	motherhood
partnership	stardom	warmth	neighborhood
relationship	wisdom	width	(wo)manhood

> **note** The suffixes **-ship** and **-hood** are often added to nouns to form abstract nouns. The suffix **-th** is often added to adjectives, and the suffix **-dom** can combine with either nouns or adjectives.

D Many abstract nouns do not use any suffix at all.

anger	faith	luck	sense
belief	fear	principle	sight
calm	hope	rage	speed
chance	idea	reason	thought

(You can find more examples of suffixes in Units 8 and 10 and of abstract nouns in Units 63–65.)

Unit 11

Exercises

11.1 Find abstract nouns on page 22 that are related to these adjectives.

1. amazed
2. attractive
3. complex
4. discouraged
5. fearful
6. friendly
7. generous
8. hopeful
9. hostile
10. kind
11. prosperous
12. reasonable
13. resentful
14. sensitive
15. warm
16. wise

11.2 Which verbs are related to these abstract nouns?

Example: argument   *to argue*

1. achievement *achieve*
2. belief *believe*
3. boredom *bore*
4. collection *collect*
5. imagination *imgie*
6. improvement *improve*
7. investment *investi*
8. ownership *own*
9. production *product*
10. recognition *recogne*
11. replacement *replace*
12. thought *think*

11.3 Find synonyms on page 22 to match the suffixes in parentheses for these nouns.

1. animosity (-ness)
2. inquisitiveness (-ity)
3. fraternity (-hood)
4. possibility (no suffix)
5. awareness (-ness)
6. fame (-dom)
7. decrease (-tion)
8. community (-hood)
9. vision (no suffix)
10. angry disappointment
11. fury (no suffix)
12. creativity (-ity)

11.4 Find abstract nouns on page 22 to match these definitions.

1. not upset or excited
2. being very aggressive
3. a country ruled by a monarch
4. something that appears to be real or true, but isn't
5. when two people or groups join together

11.5 Write your own statements to describe what these abstract nouns mean to you.

1. freedom   *I believe freedom means being able to live the way you want to live.*
2. strength
3. faith
4. childhood
5. imagination

> **follow-up** Think of at least one more noun using each of the suffixes in B on page 22 (*-ment*, *-ion*, *-ness*, and *-ity*). Then think of at least one more noun using each of the suffixes in C on page 22 (*-ship*, *-dom*, *-th*, and *-hood*). Write the nouns in your notebook.

Unit 12: Compound adjectives

A A compound adjective is made up of two parts – sometimes written with a hyphen, e.g., **good-natured** – or as one word, e.g., **nearsighted**. Its meaning is usually clear from the words combined. The second part of the compound adjective often looks like a present or past participle (someone with red hair is described as red-hair**ed**). Note that some compound adjectives use a hyphen before a noun, e.g., a **well-known** singer, but not after a noun, e.g., *That singer is **well known**.*)

B Compound adjectives describing personal appearance

Martin was a **curly-haired, suntanned, blue-eyed, rosy-cheeked, thin-lipped, broad-shouldered, left-handed, slim-hipped, long-legged, flatfooted** young man, wearing **brand-new, tight-fitting** jeans, and **open-toed** sandals.

C Compound adjectives describing a person's character

Sonya was **absent-minded** [forgetful], **easygoing** [relaxed], **good-natured** [cheerful], **warmhearted** [kind], and **quick-witted** [intelligent] if perhaps a little **pigheaded** [stubborn], **two-faced** [hypocritical], **self-centered** [egotistical], **quick-tempered** [easily angered], and **stuck-up** [conceited] at times.

D Compound adjectives with a preposition in the second part

Note that these adjectives are listed here with a typical noun.

an **all-out** [total] effort
a **broken-down** [it won't work] car
a **rundown** [in poor condition] area
a **burned-out** [nothing left after a fire] building

built-in [can't be removed] furniture
a **built-up** [covered with buildings] area
worn-out [can't be worn anymore] shoes

E Other useful compound adjectives

air-conditioned	handmade	longstanding	sugar-free
interest-free	part-time	nearsighted	time-consuming
duty-free	last-minute	off-peak	top-secret
first-class	long-distance	so-called	world-famous

F You can sometimes vary compound adjectives by changing either the first or last part of the adjective. For example, **curly-haired, long-haired, red-haired,** and **straight-haired**; **self-absorbed, self-reliant, self-righteous,** and **self-taught**.

Unit 12

Exercises

12.1 Use the words in the box to create new compound adjectives below.

> broken   care   fire   fool   hard   hot   light   narrow   open   starry   tax   wide

1. .... -eyed
2. .... -proof
3. .... -minded
4. .... -free
5. .... -headed
6. .... -hearted

12.2 List as many compound adjectives beginning with *self* as you can. Mark them *P* or *N* for positive or negative characteristics, or write *neutral*.

12.3 Answer these questions with a compound adjective that is opposite in meaning. Choose words from E on page 24.

1. Is he working full time?   *No, part time.*
2. Isn't she a little farsighted?
3. Is this vase mass-produced?
4. Do you like food with sugar in it?
5. Do you like to fly economy class?

12.4 Create more compound adjectives. Fill in the blanks below with a preposition from the box.

> down   back   up   out   on   of

1. She's been working at the same low-paying job for so long that she's really fed .... with it.
2. The two cars were involved in a head- .... collision.
3. He has a very casual, laid- .... approach to life in general.
4. Unfortunately, recycling is practically unheard .... in my country.
5. After working for two years without a vacation, she was completely worn- ....
6. The apartment was wonderful, but it was in a run .... area.

12.5 Think of two nouns that would usually go with any ten compound adjectives listed in E on page 24. Write them in your notebook.

12.6 Put the compound adjectives on page 24 into categories that will help you learn them. You can put them into topic-related categories (e.g., *money/finance* for adjectives like *interest-free*) or word-related categories (e.g., *-ing* endings for adjectives like *longstanding*).

> *follow-up*   Use adjectives from this unit to describe yourself, your classmates, or members of your family. Write your descriptions in your notebook.

25

Unit 13
Compound nouns: noun + noun

A A compound noun is a fixed expression, made up of two or more words that function as a noun. Compound nouns are usually combinations of two nouns, e.g., **address book**, **human being**, **bedroom**. A number of compound nouns are related to phrasal verbs; these are dealt with in Unit 14.

B If you understand both parts of the compound noun, the meaning will usually be clear. Compound nouns are often written as two words, e.g., **health care**, **alarm system**, or as one word, e.g., **notebook**, **trademark**. Occasionally they may be written with a hyphen, e.g., **baby-sitter**.

C Usually the main stress is on the first part of the compound noun, but sometimes it is on the second part. The word with the main stress is underlined in the compound nouns below.

<u>foot</u>ball   <u>credit</u> card   <u>bus</u> driver   <u>reference</u> book

<u>alarm</u> clock   <u>bus</u> stop   <u>phone</u> book   <u>waste</u>basket
<u>assembly</u> line   <u>gas</u> station   <u>rain</u>coat   <u>wind</u>mill
<u>bank</u> account   <u>heart</u> attack   <u>status</u> symbol   <u>windshield</u> wiper
<u>blood</u> donor   <u>light</u> year   <u>touch</u> screen   <u>youth</u> hostel

D Compound nouns may be countable, uncountable, or used only in the singular or only in the plural. C (above) gives examples of countable compounds. Here are some common examples of the other types.

- uncountable compound nouns

  air-traffic control   business class   family planning   income tax
  birth control   computer technology   food poisoning   Internet banking
  blood pressure   data processing   hay fever [pollen allergy]   junk food

- compound nouns generally used only in the singular

  death penalty   labor force
  generation gap   mother tongue
  greenhouse effect   sound barrier
  brain drain [highly educated people leaving their country to work abroad]

- compound nouns usually used only in the plural

  grass roots   luxury goods   race relations
  human rights   public works   sunglasses

Unit 13

Exercises

13.1 Complete these bubble networks with any appropriate compound nouns from page 26. Add extra bubbles if necessary.

13.2 Sometimes more than one compound noun can be formed from one particular word. For example, *blood pressure* and *blood donor* are formed from *blood*, or *birth control* and *self-control* are formed from *control*. Complete these compound nouns, using nouns other than the ones on page 26.

1. junk ....
2. computer ....
3. bus ....
4. heart ....
5. .... station
6. .... processing
7. .... tax
8. food ....
9. .... account

13.3 Find compound nouns on page 26 that these quotes describe.

1. "Using these in windy places could be a great source of energy." *windmills*
2. "I had it checked at the doctor's office this morning and it was a little high."
3. "It's partly caused by such things as pollution and air conditioning."
4. "Coca-Cola is the best known in the world."
5. "Some people use an expensive car or a big house to show how successful they are."
6. "Some people think it's justified for brutal crimes like murder. Do you agree?"
7. "To keep my home and family safe, I installed one."
8. "All that processed food, with not one green vegetable in sight!"
9. "Sometimes I use it to pay bills directly from my computer. It's more convenient and less expensive than going to a bank."

13.4 Make up some quotes like the ones in 13.3 for the compound nouns you created in 13.2.

13.5 Look at all the compound nouns from this unit. Circle the ones that you would like to use in your own speaking or writing.

> *follow-up* Find an article in a magazine or newspaper that interests you and look for compound nouns. Determine if the nouns are countable or uncountable. Then make a list of the compound nouns in your notebook.

Unit 14 Compound nouns: verb + preposition

A Some compound nouns are based on phrasal verbs, e.g., **takeover**, which comes from **to take over**. Nouns based on phrasal verbs are often informal and are common in newspaper reporting. To form the plural, add -s to the end, e.g., **pinups**.

The army forced an end to the **standoff** [stalemate or standstill] with rebel troops.
There will be a **crackdown** [action against] on wasteful government spending.
There has been a **breakout** [escape] from the local prison.
The government-ordered **breakup** [change into smaller pieces] of the telecommunications industry created a dramatic shift in the market.
Last month saw a big **shakeup** [change] in personnel.

B Compound nouns with economic associations

The **takeover** [purchase by another company] of a leading hotel chain has just been announced.
We're trying to find some new **outlets** [places to sell things] for our products.
Cutbacks [reductions] will be essential until the company becomes profitable again.
The company has begun a series of **layoffs**. [ending employment]
There's been a **downturn** [decline] in the stock market recently.

C Compound nouns associated with technology and other aspects of contemporary life

What the computer produces depends on the quality of the **input**. [information that is entered in]
We had unusually high staff **turnover** [change] last year.
A high school **dropout** [person who withdraws from school early] has few career choices.
Let me get you a **printout** [paper on which computer information is printed] of the latest figures.
A **breakthrough** [important discovery] has been made in AIDS research.
You should make a **backup** [duplicate or substitute] of your work.

D Compound nouns used in more general circumstances

Many of the problems were caused by a **breakdown** [failure] in communication.
The **outlook** [prospect] for titanium is strong.
There are **drawbacks** [negative aspects] as well as advantages to every situation.
The **outcome** [conclusion] of the situation was not satisfactory.
Some TV stations welcome **feedback** [comments] from viewers.
New enterprises often suffer **setbacks** [circumstances that delay progress] in the early stages.

> *tip* When you learn a compound word that you want to use in your speaking and writing, find out if you can make a phrasal verb that has the same meaning (make a backup / you should back up your files).

Unit 14

Exercises

14.1 Here are some more compound nouns based on phrasal verbs. Guess the meaning of each underlined compound noun from its context.

1. "Cabin crew, please prepare for <u>takeoff</u>."
2. Residents are alarmed over the increased number of <u>break-ins</u> in this area.
3. The news media are claiming the president ordered a <u>cover-up</u> about the fundraising scandal.
4. She went to the <u>tryouts</u> for the tennis team.
5. There was a <u>holdup</u> at the bank. The robbers got away with $1 million.
6. The robbers made their <u>getaway</u> in a stolen car.

14.2 Find compound nouns on page 28 that would most likely follow these adjectives.

1. nervous ....
2. computer ....
3. final ....
4. retail ....
5. positive ....
6. drastic ....

14.3 Fill in the blanks with appropriate compound nouns from page 28.

1. It is common in the telecommunications industry for larger companies to make .... bids for smaller companies.
2. In response to heavy criticism, the president announced a major .... in the cabinet yesterday.
3. Human rights groups are concerned about the government's violent .... on opposition groups.
4. She provided some very valuable .... to the discussion.
5. The new vaccine is a real .... that could save tens of thousands of lives.
6. Despite all the bad news, the overall .... remains good.

14.4 Create more compound nouns based on phrasal verbs. Each sentence below has the preposition but not the verb. Fill in the blanks with verbs from the box.

| clean | hand | hold | push | stand | turn | work |

1. Negotiators met in an attempt to resolve the 12-hour .... off with the kidnappers.
2. The lecturer distributed .... outs before she started speaking.
3. Jack has a daily .... out at the gym, starting with twenty .... -ups.
4. I'm giving my office a major .... up this week.
5. Did you read about the .... up at our bank?
6. There was a surprisingly large .... out for the concert.

14.5 Explain the differences between these pairs of words. Use a dictionary if necessary.

1. outlook/lookout
2. outbreak/breakout
3. setup/upset
4. outlay/layout

Unit 15 Words from other languages

A English has borrowed words from many other languages. It has taken many expressions from the ancient languages Latin and Greek, and these expressions often have academic or literary associations. Other European languages such as French, Spanish, Italian, and German have contributed lots of words related to cooking, the arts, politics, and more. Words borrowed from other languages usually relate to things that English speakers experienced for the first time in other countries.

B English has borrowed from a wide range of languages. For example, from Japanese, **tycoon, karate, origami, judo, futon,** and **bonsai**; from Chinese, **tofu, tea, kumquat,** and **kung fu**; from Arabic, **mattress, alcove, carafe, algebra,** and **harem**; from Turkish, **yogurt, jackal, kiosk, tulip,** and **caftan**; from Farsi, **caravan, shawl, taffeta,** and **bazaar**; from Inuit, **kayak** and **igloo**; and from Hindi, **bungalow, pajamas,** and **shampoo**.

C This map of Europe shows the places of origin of some English words and expressions borrowed from other European languages. Use a dictionary to check the meanings if necessary.

Norway
fjord
lemming
ski
slalom

Sweden
ombudsman
smorgasbord

Finland
sauna

Russia
cosmonaut
mammoth
steppe
tsar
tundra

Netherlands
cruise
easel
landscape
yacht

Germany
blitz
dachshund
delicatessen
frankfurter
hamburger
kindergarten
poodle
seminar
snorkel
waltz
wanderlust

Spain
bonanza
embargo
guerrilla
guitar
junta
lasso
macho
mosquito
patio
siesta
vanilla

France
avant-garde
boutique
chauffeur
coup
cuisine
cul-de-sac
elite
résumé
sauté

Italy
alarm
balcony
ballerina
bandit
bankrupt
casino
confetti
fiasco
ghetto
piano
soprano
spaghetti
vendetta

Greece
academy
alphabet
catastrophe
cemetery
democracy
drama
holocaust
lexicon
mystery
pseudonym
psychology
synonym
theory

Portugal
cobra
marmalade
molasses

Unit 15

Exercises

15.1 Circle the words listed on page 30 that are also used in your native language.

15.2 If your native language is represented on page 30, add other words you can think of to the lists. If your native language is not represented, make a list of any words that English has borrowed from your language. Do the words have the same meaning in English as in your language? Are they pronounced in the same way?

15.3 Look at the words in B and C on page 30, and complete these bubble networks.

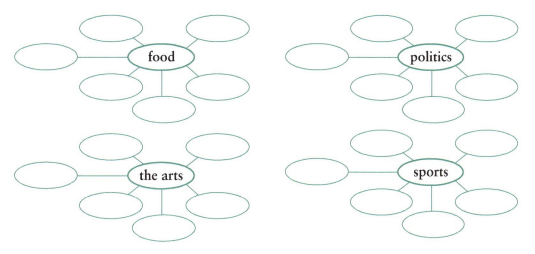

15.4 Make two or three other networks to help you learn the words on page 30.

15.5 Find the word on the right that is most likely to follow the word on the left. Use a dictionary if necessary.

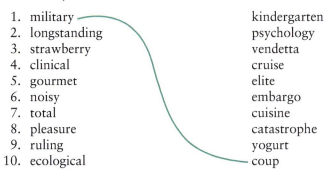

1. military
2. longstanding
3. strawberry
4. clinical
5. gourmet
6. noisy
7. total
8. pleasure
9. ruling
10. ecological

kindergarten
psychology
vendetta
cruise
elite
embargo
cuisine
catastrophe
yogurt
coup

15.6 Write the languages that these words are borrowed from. Try to guess if you aren't sure.

1. opera: *Italian*
2. garage:
3. guru:
4. tomato:
5. intelligentsia:
6. coffee:
7. haiku:
8. anonymous:

15.7 List examples of words or expressions that your native language has borrowed from English. Have they kept exactly the same meaning as they have in English? Are they pronounced in the same way?

31

Unit 16: Abbreviations and acronyms

A Abbreviations read as individual letters, usually representing the initials, or first letters, of each word

(an) ID [identification]
R&D [research & development]
the UN [the United Nations]
(an) ATM [automated teller machine]
the U.S.A. [the United States of America]
the IRS [the Internal Revenue Service (U.S. government tax agency)]

B *Acronyms* - abbreviations read as words

OPEC [Organization of Petroleum Exporting Countries]
PIN [Personal Identity Number (e.g., for a credit card)]

Some acronyms have become so normal as words that people no longer think of them as abbreviations, and they are no longer written in all capital letters.

radar [radio detecting and ranging]
laser [light wave amplification by simulated emission of radiation]
yuppie [young urban professional]

C Abbreviations used for written forms only

Dr. [Doctor]   **Mr.** [Mister]   **Rd.** [Road]   **St.** [Saint or Street]
Mrs. /ˈmɪs·əz/   **Ms.** /mɪz/

D Abbreviations used in the organization of language

etc. [and so on (Latin: *et cetera*)]   **i.e.** [that is to say (Latin: *id est*)]
e.g. [for example (Latin: *exempli gratia*)]

E Words normally used in a clipped form, especially in informal situations

lab [laboratory]   **phone** [telephone]   **typo** [typographical error]
dorm [dormitory]   **memo** [memorandum]   **fax** [facsimile]

F Abbreviations used with e-mail messages, letters, faxes, or envelopes

P.S. [postscript (extra message after the letter has ended)]
P.O. Box [post office box]
enc. [enclosed (e.g., an application form)]
RSVP [please reply (French: *répondez s'il vous plaît*)]
ASAP [as soon as possible (e.g., call me ASAP)]
cc [carbon copy (someone other than the addressee receives a copy)]
re: [regarding]
FYI [for your information]

G Abbreviations related to time and location

a.m./p.m. (time)
Days of the week (**Mon, Tue**, etc.)
Months (**Jan, Feb, Mar**, etc.)
Direction: **N** (north), **S** (south), **NE** (northeast), etc.

Unit 16

Exercises

16.1 Underline the words in these addresses that you think are normally abbreviated.

1.
Mister Henry Chen
Post Office Box 2020
Saint Louis, Missouri
United States of America

2.
Doctor Maria Rivera
430 Yonge Street
Apartment 5
Toronto, Ontario
Canada

3.
Lowe Plastics, Incorporated
7 Bridge Road
Freeminster
United Kingdom

16.2 Match the abbreviations on the left with their meanings on the right.

1. B.A. — extension
2. the FBI — condominium
3. Prof. — Federal Bureau of Investigation
4. MYOB — self-contained underwater breathing apparatus
5. TOEFL — frequently asked questions
6. TBA — Bachelor of Arts
7. ext. — mind your own business
8. FAQ — Professor
9. condo — Test of English as a Foreign Language
10. scuba — to be announced

16.3 Change the abbreviations to full words to translate this e-mail message from a boss to the workers in an office.

```
From: Mr. Braneless              To: All staff
Sent: Mon, Mar 24, 2010          cc: Ms. Hothead, Supply Dept.
Subject: lab equipment

All new lab equipment should be registered with the Supply
Dept., Rm. 354 (ext. 2683). New items must be registered before
5 p.m. on the last day of the month of purchase, i.e., within
the current budgeting month. FYI: All nos. must be recorded.
```

16.4 Find words on page 32 to match these descriptions.

1. a room for sleeping: *dorm*
2. you need to do something right away:
3. a mistake on a written page:
4. title for a married woman:
5. the number you use to access private information:
6. a group of countries that produce oil:
7. a sharp beam of light:
8. this group develops new ideas for a company:

33

Unit 17 New words in English

No language stands still. New words and expressions are always being created. Below are some new words and expressions and new uses of old words. Note that all of these words had been in use for at least a few years before the publication of this book.

A Science and technology

cyberspace [the realm where electronic data is stored or transmitted by computers]
DNA fingerprinting [the use of genetic material (DNA) to identify an individual]
MP3 [a type of computer file that holds high quality sound and music]
sound bite [a brief excerpt from a speech or statement, used in broadcast news]
spam [junk mail sent via e-mail]
surfing the Net [exploring the World Wide Web]
technophobe [a person who is afraid of using technology]
webcast [a presentation, sometimes interactive, shown via the Internet]

B Health and medicine

attention deficit disorder (ADD) [an illness characterized by inattention and hyperactivity]
eating disorder [a serious disturbance in eating habits, often from emotional causes]
information overload [becoming overwhelmed by the amount of information available online and through other media]
managed care [a plan providing comprehensive health services at reduced costs]
repetitive strain injury (RSI) [soreness, numbness, and pain (usually) in the hand, wrist, or arm caused by repeated movement (e.g., keyboarding)]

C Business

e-commerce [business based on the Internet]
downsizing [reducing the size of a company, usually by laying people off]
outsourcing [hiring outside workers to do work away from the company site]
telecommuting [working from home, communicating with the office by computer]

D Social trends and entertainment

audio book [an audio recording of a book read aloud, sometimes condensed]
blended family [when two single parents marry, and join their families together]
cybercafé [a café where people can eat, drink coffee, and use the Internet]
family leave [time that an employee takes off in order to care for family members]
road rage [extreme anger resulting in reckless driving and attacks on other drivers
snowboarding [gliding on snow by standing upright on a large single ski]
spin doctor [someone who manipulates public opinion to benefit a public figure]
texting [sending written messages via cell phone]

Unit 17

Exercises

17.1 The words and expressions on the left are fairly new. Match them with their definitions on the right.

1. wannabe (*informal*) — television programs that document non-actors in contrived situations
2. greening — ordinary mail sent through the postal service
3. plus-size — a television commercial that lasts 15 to 30 minutes
4. reality TV — the process of using fewer natural resources and becoming more environmentally aware
5. snail mail — someone who wants to be like someone else, especially someone famous
6. infomercial — clothes for overweight or large people

17.2 Fill in the blanks with words from page 34.

1. He lost his job of 20 years when the company began ....
2. They say that in the next few years more and more people will start .... It should certainly ease traffic during rush hours.
3. Every morning, there is so much .... in my e-mail inbox that it takes 10 minutes to delete it.
4. My grandfather is a .... He doesn't even own a computer.
5. The president has a dozen .... around him to make his foolish actions appear wise.
6. If you want to check your e-mail, we can go to a .... and get a coffee at the same time.
7. Nick is taking a month off work for .... He's taking care of his father, who is very ill.
8. They're a .... He has two children from a previous marriage, and she has one child from her first marriage.

17.3 If you see a new word, you can sometimes figure out the meaning from the context. Using the context, explain what these underlined words might mean.

1. This area attracts quite a few <u>ecotourists</u>, who come to watch the wildlife.
2. So many people got sick after we moved to the new building that we checked to see if it had <u>sick building syndrome</u>.
3. When you're communicating on the Internet, it's considered bad <u>netiquette</u> to use all capital letters because it looks as if you're SHOUTING.
4. You don't have to pay anything for this computer program. It's <u>freeware</u>.
5. She has <u>cyberphobia</u>. She refuses to go on the Internet.

Unit 18 Words commonly mispronounced

Some English words cause pronunciation difficulties for learners of English. The phonetic transcription is provided for some of these words below. If you are not sure of the pronunciation of any of the other words, check the Index on page 203 and the list of pronunciation symbols on page 202.

A To master English pronunciation, it is helpful to learn the phonetic symbols for English vowel sounds. It is not so important to learn the consonant symbols because it is usually not difficult to know how consonants are pronounced. However, the vowel letters can be pronounced in many different ways. (*Note*: Some dictionaries may use a slightly different phonetic system.)

a	about /ə/	wander /ɑ/	last /æ/	late /eɪ/
i	alive /aɪ/	give /ɪ/		
u	put /ʊ/	cut /ʌ/	stupid /u:/	
ie	fiend /i:/	friend /e/	science /aɪ·ə/	
ei	rein /eɪ/	receive /i:/	reinforce /i·ə/	
e	met /e/	meter /i:/		
o	hot /ɑ/	go /oʊ/	lost /ɔ:/	to /u:/
ea	head /e/	team /i:/	react /i'æ/	
ou	out /aʊ/	soup /u:/	would /ʊ/	
oo	cool /u:/	cook /ʊ/	cooperate /o'ɑ/	

B These letters in bold are silent.

p	**p**sychic /'saɪ·kɪk/	**p**sychiatry	**p**neumonia	receipt	**p**seudonym	**p**sychology
b	com**b** /koʊm/	dum**b**	clim**b**	dou**b**t	su**b**tle	de**b**t
l	cou**l**d /kʊd/	shou**l**d	wou**l**d	ha**l**f	ta**l**k	sa**l**mon
h	**h**onor /'ɑn·ər/	**h**onorable	**h**onest	**h**our	**h**ourly	**h**eir
t	cas**t**le /'kæs·əl/	lis**t**en	whis**t**le	fas**t**en	sof**t**en	Chris**t**mas
k	**k**nowledge /'nɑl·ɪdʒ/	**k**nife	**k**not	**k**nob	**k**nock	**k**nee
w	**w**rite /raɪt/	**w**rong	**w**rist	**w**rap	**w**reck	**w**hole

C In two-syllable words in English, the stress is often on the first syllable if it is a noun and on the second syllable if it is a verb, e.g., *We gave her a present* (noun); *She's going to present the award* (verb).

compound	contract	desert	increase	reject
conduct	convict	detail	insult	subject
conflict	decrease	export	object	suspect
contest	defect	import	record	upset

D Here are other words often mispronounced or given the wrong stress.

apostrophe /ə'pɑs·trə·fi/	photographic /,foʊt̬·ə'græf·ɪk/
industry /'ɪn,də·stri/	photographically /,foʊt̬·ə'græf·ɪ·kli/
interesting /'ɪn·trə·stɪŋ/	photography /fə'tɑg·rə·fi/
library /'laɪ,brer·i/	recipe /'res·ə·pi/
muscle /'mʌs·əl/	sword /sɔrd/
photograph /'foʊt̬·ə,græf/	vegetable /'vedʒ·(ə)·tə·bəl/

Unit 18

Exercises

18.1 Choose words from A on page 36 that rhyme with each of these words.

1. passed ....
2. liter ....
3. lend ....
4. eight ....
5. pain ....
6. said ....

18.2 Which word is the odd one out in each group and why? (Check the vowel sounds.)

1. come   some   dome
2. head   plead   tread
3. land   wand   sand
4. took   boot   foot
5. could   doubt   would
6. though   rough   tough

18.3 Circle all the silent letters in each of these nonsense sentences.

1. Your knowledge of psychology should help soften the blow.
2. It was an honest mistake when the psychiatrist wrote down the wrong name.
3. It should take you half an hour to follow the whole recipe for salmon.
4. I doubt that we could wrap all these presents before Christmas.

18.4 Circle the stressed syllable in each of these underlined words.

1. Although the police suspected several people, Joe was the main suspect.
2. I object to having that ugly object in our home. It is not art!
3. There are conflicting views as to the cause of the conflict.
4. I know you think it's an insult, but I'm sure he didn't mean to insult you.
5. The cost of living has increased while there has been no increase in wages.
6. A work permit will permit you to keep the job for a period of six months.
7. If I make enough progress, I can progress to the next level.
8. Despite the bad conduct of the audience, he continued conducting the band.

18.5 Write these words using the normal English alphabet and spelling.

1. /koʊˈɑp·əˌreɪt/   3. /ˈvedʒ·tə·bəl/   5. /ˈsʌt·əl/   7. /nʊˈmoʊn·jə/
   ....

2. /ˈkɑmˌpaʊnd/   4. /ˈkɑnˌflɪkt/   6. /ˈɑn·ər·ə·bəl/   8. /riː·ənˈfɔːrs/
   ....

18.6 Underline the stressed syllable in each of these words. Use a dictionary if necessary.

1. photograph   photography   photographer   photographic
2. politics   political   politician
3. economy   economical   economics
4. psychology   psychologist   psychological
5. psychiatry   psychiatric   psychiatrist
6. mathematics   mathematician   mathematical

Unit 19 Onomatopoeic words

A Onomatopoeic words are words that seem to sound like their meaning. The most obvious examples are verbs relating to the noises that animals make, e.g., cows **moo** and cats **meow**.

B Certain combinations of letters have particular sound associations in English.

- **cl-** at the beginning of a word can suggest something sharp and/or metallic, e.g., **click** [a short, sharp sound]; **clang** [a loud ringing noise]; **clank** [a dull metallic noise, not as loud as a **clang**]; **clash** [a loud, broken, confused noise as when metal objects strike together]; **clink** [the sound of small bits of metal or glass knocking together].

- **gr-** at the beginning of a word can suggest something unpleasant or miserable, e.g., **groan** [to make a deep sound forced out by pain or despair]; **grumble** [to complain in a bad-tempered way]; **grumpy** [bad tempered or moody]; **grunt** [to make a low, rough sound like pigs do]; **growl** [to make a deep, threatening sound].

- **sp-** at the beginning of a word can have an association with water or other liquids or powders, e.g., **splash** [to cause a liquid to scatter in the air in drops]; **spit** [to send liquid out from the mouth]; **sputter** [to say something using short breaths, often when confused or upset]; **spray** [to send liquid through the air in a mist either by wind or some instrument]; **sprinkle** [to scatter small drops]; **spurt** [to come out in a sudden burst].

- **wh-** at the beginning of a word often suggests the movement of air, e.g., **whistle** [to make a high-pitched noise by forcing air or steam through a small opening]; **whisper** [to speak softly]; **whirr** [a sound like a bird's wings moving rapidly]; **whiz** [the sound of something rushing through the air]; **wheeze** [to breathe noisily, especially with a whistling sound in the chest]; **whip** [to move a long piece of rope or leather quickly through the air].

- **-ash** at the end of a word can suggest something fast and violent, e.g., **smash** [to break something violently into small pieces]; **dash** [to move or be moved quickly or violently]; **crash** [to suddenly strike something violently and noisily]; **mash** [to make something soft or pulpy by beating or crushing it]; **gash** [a long, deep cut or wound], **bash** [to strike something hard enough to break or injure it].

- **-ckle, -ggle,** or **-zzle** at the end of a word can suggest something light and repeated, e.g., **trickle** [to flow slowly in a thin stream or in drops]; **crackle** [to make a series of short, sharp sounds]; **tinkle** [to make a series of light ringing sounds]; **giggle** [to laugh lightly]; **wriggle** [to move with quick, short twists of the body]; **sizzle** [to make a hissing sound like something cooking in fat]; **drizzle** [a light, fine rain].

sizzle

trickle

clash

growl

Unit 19

Exercises

19.1 Which of the consonant combinations listed in B on page 38 exist in your native language?

19.2 Fill in the blanks with words from B on page 38. You may need to change the word form to fit the sentence.

1. The dog began to .... at the strange person at the door.
2. He's such a .... old man – does he ever smile?
3. Do you like your potatoes baked, fried, or .... ?
4. They .... glasses and drank to each other's health.
5. There was a terrible car .... on the freeway today.
6. Everyone .... with disappointment at the news.
7. That .... on your forehead really needs medical attention.
8. It's not raining hard yet; it's just ....

19.3 Almost all the words in B on page 38 can be both nouns and regular verbs. However, answer these questions to find some common exceptions.

1. Which of the following verbs is irregular: *whip*, *grunt*, *spurt*, *spit*, or *wriggle*?
2. Which word is only an adjective: *gash*, *grumpy*, *wheeze*, or *whir*?
3. Which word is both a verb and a noun, but the noun has a different meaning: *trickle*, *growl*, *splutter*, *spit*, *splash*, or *crash*?

19.4 Match the noun phrases on the left with the appropriate verbs on the right.

1. an angry animal   smashes
2. a dish falling on the floor   clangs
3. a bored child   growls
4. someone with asthma   wriggles
5. a church bell   wheezes

19.5 Guess the meaning of each underlined word from the context and the sound of the word.

1. If your throat hurts, try <u>gargling</u> with salt water.
2. Please speak up. Don't <u>mumble</u> when you talk.
3. The floor in this old house is always <u>creaking</u>.
4. He really <u>whacked</u> the ball!

19.6 Choose the appropriate words from page 38 to match these pictures.

1.
2.
3.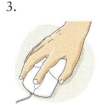
4.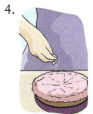
5.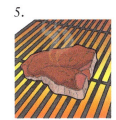

> **follow-up** Look in your dictionary for other examples of words beginning with *cl-*, *gr-*, *sp-*, or *wh-* that have the associations described on page 38.

Unit 20 Homonyms

A **Homonyms** can be subdivided into **homographs** and **homophones**.

| Homographs are written in the same way but have different meanings and may be pronounced differently. Compare **bow** in *He took a* **bow** /baʊ/ *at the end of the concert and He was wearing a* **bow** /boʊ/ *tie*. | Homophones are words with different meanings that are pronounced the same way but spelled differently. Compare **sale** and **sail** /seɪl/ as in *We bought this TV on* **sale** *and I love to* **sail** *my boat*. |

B Examples of English homographs

- They lived in a large old **house**. /haʊs/
  The buildings **house** /haʊz/ a library and two concert halls as well as a theater.
- The **lead** /liːd/ singer in the group is great.
  Lead /led/ pipes are dangerous.
- I **live** /lɪv/ in California.
  Your favorite rock group is performing **live** /laɪv/ on TV tonight.
- It will only take a **minute** /ˈmɪn·ət/ to pick this up.
  There were **minute** /maɪˈn(j)uːt/ traces of mercury in the water.
- I **read** /riːd/ in bed every night.
  I **read** /red/ *War and Peace* last year.
- We will **resume** /rɪˈzuːm/ programming after this commercial break.
  It's a good idea to send a cover letter and a **résumé** /ˈrez·ʊ·meɪ/ to each prospective employer.
- A single **tear** /tɪr/ rolled down her cheek.
  Be careful not to **tear** /ter/ the document.
- This book is called *Vocabulary in Use*. /juːs/
  You need to know how to **use** /juːz/ words, as well as to know their meanings.
- The **wind** /wɪnd/ blew the tree down.
  If you treat people badly, you'll **wind** /waɪnd/ up alone.
- The party **wound** /waʊnd/ down after the band left.
  He suffered a terrible **wound** /wuːnd/ in the fight.

C Examples of English homophones

air/heir	its/it's	raise/rays	some/sum
aloud/allowed	mail/male	read/reed	steak/stake
break/brake	meat/meet	red/read	tea/tee
dough/doe	mown/moan	right/write	there/their/they're
fare/fair	our/hour	scene/seen	through/threw
faze/phase	pair/pear/pare	sea/see	toe/tow
flu/flew	pale/pail	sent/scent	waist/waste
grate/great	pane/pain	sew/so	wait/weight
groan/grown	peal/peel	sight/site	weak/week
hoarse/horse	pray/prey	sole/soul	wood/would

Unit 20

Exercises

20.1 Circle the word in parentheses that rhymes with, or sounds similar to, the underlined word.

1. The woman I <u>live</u> (five / **give**) with knows a good club with <u>live</u> (**five** / give) music.
2. It's no <u>use</u> (snooze / juice)! I can't <u>use</u> (snooze / juice) this device.
3. The violinist in the <u>bow</u> (now / go) tie took a <u>bow</u> (now / go).
4. He's the <u>lead</u> (head / deed) singer in the heavy metal group <u>Lead</u> (head / deed) Bullets.
5. Does he still suffer from his war <u>wound</u> (found / mooned)?
6. I <u>wound</u> (round / tuned) the rope around the tree.
7. I didn't mean to <u>tear</u> (near / wear) up the contract, but I was so angry.
8. Now that the party is starting to <u>wind</u> (find / thinned) down, let's go home.

20.2 Complete each sentence by circling the word in parentheses that uses the correct spelling for that sentence.

1. I should get some exercise or I'll never lose (**weight** / wait).
2. Watching TV game shows is such a (waist / waste) of time.
3. There is a hole in the (sole / soul) of my shoe.
4. He broke a (pane / pain) of glass in the kitchen window.
5. You are not (aloud / allowed) to talk during the test.
6. She's going (through / threw) a rather difficult (faze / phase).
7. Don't throw away that orange (peal / peel). I need it for a recipe.
8. Most people (right / write) with their (right / write) hand.
9. That cold knocked me out for a whole (weak / week).

20.3 Many jokes in English are based on homophones and homographs. Match the first part of each of these children's jokes on the left with the second part on the right. Then explain why you think the joke is funny.

1. What did the big chimney say to the little chimney?   a nervous wreck
2. Why did the man take his pencil to bed?   because it's full of dates
3. What's pale and trembles at the bottom of the sea?   a newspaper
4. Why is history the sweetest lesson?   He wanted to draw the curtains.
5. What's black and white and red all over?   "You're too young to smoke."

20.4 Choose the appropriate word pairs from C on page 40 to match these pictures.

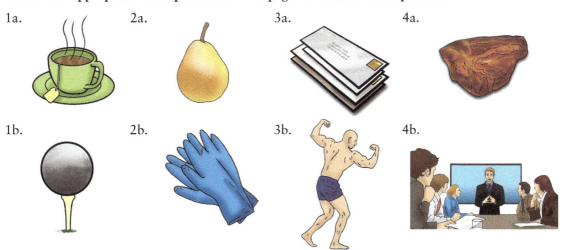

Unit 21 Time

A One thing before another

Before (most common form) I went to work, I fed the cat.
Before / Prior to going (formal/written style) **to** work, I ran a mile.
I spent a week in Mexico City. **Before that** (more formal: **Previously/Earlier,** I . . .), I went to Cancun and Guadalajara.
I was in the office at 2:30. **Before then** (more formal: **Earlier,** I . . .), I was out.
The city's name is New York. **Formerly,** it was called New Amsterdam. (**At an earlier time,** it was called . . . ; less formally: It **used to** be called New Amsterdam.)

B Things happening at the same time

While I waited, I read the newspaper. (The waiting and reading happened together; more formal: **While waiting,** I read . . .)
As I was driving to work, I saw an accident. (**As** describes the background information, contrasting with the more important information in the main clause.)
I saw her **just as** she was turning the corner. (The two actions happened simultaneously; at precisely the same moment.)
During the war, I lived in Canada. (This does not specify how long the person lived in Canada.)
Throughout [from beginning to end] the war, food was rationed.
Whenever [every time] I see a sentimental movie, I start crying.

C One thing after another

After (more formal: **After locking up,** . . .) I locked up, I went to bed.
First, we went to the movies. **After that,** we went out for coffee.
He had a stroke and was rushed to the hospital. He died soon **afterward.** (**After that** and **afterward** are interchangeable here.)
Following (fairly formal) my visit to Beijing, I bought lots of books about China.

D Connecting to the future

When I'm rich, I'll buy a yacht. (*Note:* not When I will be rich . . .)
As soon as [immediately after] we finish packing, we can leave.
Once (after, but a less specific time) we finish packing, we can go get some coffee.
The moment / The minute I saw his face, I knew I'd met him before.
I met her at my sister's party last year. **At that time,** she was with her old boyfriend.

E Connecting two periods or events

Dinner will take about an hour. **Meanwhile / In the meantime** [between now and dinner], relax and have a drink.
The new computers are arriving soon. **Till then** (more formal: **Until then**), we'll just use the old ones.
By the time I retire, I will have worked here for 26 years.
I last saw him in 2004. **Since then,** I haven't seen him.

Unit 21

Exercises

21.1 Look at these pages from the personal diary of Sandra, a businesswoman who travels a lot. Then complete each sentence below, using time connectors from page 42.

1. .... going to Boston, Sandra was in Toronto.
2. Her next trip after Boston is on the 30th. ...., she can spend some time at home.
3. She was in Toronto for over a week. .... she got home, there was a big pile of mail waiting for her.
4. .... she was at Nick's place on the 15th, she met Maria.
5. She went to a concert in Toronto on Monday. ...., she went to Eaton Centre.
6. .... she said goodbye to Nick, she left.
7. .... she had answered all her letters, she watched TV for a while.
8. .... she hung up the phone, it rang again. This time it was James.

21.2 Make sentences that describe what happened to you last week. Use time connectors from page 42.

21.3 Think of things that are true for you in these situations and complete the sentences. Add more sentences if you can.

1. While I'm asleep, *I usually dream a lot.*
2. When I finish studying English, I'll ....
3. After I eat too much, I ....
4. The minute I wake up, I ....
5. Throughout my childhood, I ....
6. I'm working on vocabulary right now. Earlier, I was ....
7. I bought this laptop recently. Since then, I ....
8. I hope to take a vacation soon. In the meantime, I ....
9. Whenever I have an argument with someone, I always feel ....
10. After I bought my new cell phone, I ....

Unit 22
Condition

A Conditions with *if* and other words and phrases

1. **If** you don't have a ticket, you can't get into the theater.

3. You can use this book **provided (that)** you return it by 5:00.

2. **In case of** fire, dial 911.

4. You can stay **as long as** you don't mind sleeping on the sofa.

- You can use **unless** instead of **if** + a negative statement, e.g., *You can't get into the theater unless you have a ticket*.
- **on condition that** is a more formal way of saying **provided (that)**
- Don't confuse **in case of** with **in case**, e.g., *Take your umbrella in case it rains*. (It isn't raining, but there's a chance of rain today.)

B Possibility with *supposing / suppose* and *what if*

Supposing/Suppose and **What if** express possible situations in the future (usually in spoken language). For example:

Supposing/Suppose a new clean energy source is found – how will it change our lives?
What if he doesn't turn up – what will we do then?

C Conditions with *-ever*

- The **-ever** suffix means *it doesn't matter which*.

  However you do it, it will cost a lot of money.
  You'll get to the train station **whichever** bus you take.
  Whoever wins the election will have a difficult job.
  That box is so big, it will be in the way **wherever** you leave it.

- The four sentences above can also be expressed using **no matter**.

  No matter *how* you do it, it will cost a lot of money.
  You'll get to the train station **no matter** *which* bus you take.

D Nouns that express condition

Certain **conditions** must be **met** before the peace talks can begin.
Proficiency in English is a **prerequisite** [absolutely necessary (formal)] for admission to an American university.
What are the **requirements** [official conditions] for obtaining a driver's license?
I would not move to a big city **under any circumstances**. I hate big cities!

Unit 22

Exercises

22.1 Fill in the blanks with appropriate words or phrases from A or B on page 44.

1. You can come to the party .... you don't bring that awful friend of yours.
2. .... an emergency in the factory, sound the alarm and notify the supervisor at once.
3. .... you're not here by 6:00, I'll leave without you.
4. Applicants may take the driving test again .... they have not already taken a test within the past 14 days.
5. .... I lent you my car, would that help?

22.2 Each picture shows a condition that must be met to do a certain thing. Write two different sentences for each picture, using words and phrases from page 44.

Example: *You can have a passenger on a motorcycle provided the passenger wears a helmet.*
or *Unless you wear a helmet, you can't ride on a motorcycle.*

22.3 Change these sentences with *-ever* to *no matter*, and vice versa.

1. Wherever she goes, she always takes that dog of hers.
2. I don't want to speak to anyone, no matter who it is.
3. No matter what I do, I always seem to do the wrong thing.
4. No matter how I do it, that recipe never seems to work.
5. Whichever color I choose, I always end up liking another color better.

22.4 Answer these questions, using vocabulary from this unit.

1. What are the prerequisites for the job you have now or would like to have?
2. Under what circumstances would you move from where you're living now?
3. What are the normal admission requirements for universities in your country?
4. On what condition would you lend a friend a large amount of money?

45

Unit 23: Cause, reason, purpose, and result

A Cause and reason

- You probably know how to use words like **because** and **since** to refer to the **cause** of or **reason** for something. Here are some other ways to express **cause** and **reason**.

    Owing to / Because of the icy conditions, the two trucks collided.
    The collision was **due to** the icy conditions.
    The collision was **caused by** ice on the road.
    The cause of the collision was ice on the road.
    Due to the fact that there was ice on the road, the two trucks collided.

- Here are some other **cause** words and typical contexts.

    The budget cuts in education **sparked/ignited** a new round of bitter protests.
        (These are often used for very strong, perhaps violent, reactions to events)
    The president's statement **gave rise to / provoked / generated** a lot of criticism.
        (These are not as strong as **spark** or **ignite**.)
    The peace talks have **brought about / led to** a cease-fire. (These are often used for political/social change.)
    Unemployment in the region **stems from** [the direct origins of events and states] the steady decline in manufacturing jobs.
    The court case **arose from** allegations made in a newspaper. (The allegations started the process that led to the court case.)

B Reasons for and purposes of doing things

Her **reason for** leaving her job was that she was offered a better position at another company. *or* **The reason** she left her job was that . . .
The purpose of his visit was to establish goodwill.
I wonder what his **motives** were **in** [purpose (more formal)] sending that e-mail.
I wonder what **prompted** [reason/cause (more formal)] him to send that e-mail.
She wrote to the newspaper **with the aim of** [purpose (more formal)] exposing the scandal.
She refused to answer **on the grounds that** [reason (more formal)] her lawyer wasn't present.

C Results

He didn't study. **As a result / Therefore / As a consequence / Consequently**, he failed his exams.
The result/consequence of all these changes is that no one is happy.
    (**Consequence/consequently** sounds more formal than **result**.)
His remarks **resulted in** (verb + **in**) an explosion of anger.
The meeting had an **outcome** [result of a process or events, or of meetings, discussions, etc.] that no one could have predicted.
The **upshot of** (less formal than **outcome**) all these problems was that we had to start again.

Unit 23

Exercises

23.1 Make sentences using *cause* and *reason* words from A on page 46.

Example: decision to raise tuition → protests on campus
*The decision to raise tuition **sparked** protests on campus.*
Or *Protests on campus were **ignited** by the decision to raise tuition.*

1. the new tax law → changes in the tax system
2. faulty wiring → an electrical fire
3. a violent storm → widespread flooding
4. food shortages → riots in several cities
5. declining profits → layoffs and salary cuts
6. more Internet advertising → increased sales

23.2 Combine two sentences into one, using the *reason* and *purpose* words in parentheses. Look at B on page 46 if necessary.

1. There was a controversial decision. She wrote to the local newspaper to protest. (prompt)
   The controversial decision prompted her to write to the local newspaper to protest.
2. I didn't call you. I'd lost your phone number. (reason)
3. I will not sign. This contract is illegal. (grounds)
4. Lawmakers passed a new bill. It was in order to balance the budget. (aim)
5. She sent everyone flowers. I wonder why. (motives)
6. The salary was high. She applied for the job. (prompt)

23.3 Describe *causes* and *results* of the events in these pictures, using different words or phrases from page 46.

1. The road was blocked.

3. The customers got angry.

2. Everyone got a refund.

4. We had to walk home.

23.4 Fill in the blanks with words from page 46.

1. My reasons .... not joining the club are personal.
2. The purpose .... this key is to restart the computer.
3. All this confusion arose .... one small mistake we made.
4. The new policy was introduced .... the aim .... lowering inflation.
5. The ideas in that book have .... rise .... a lot of criticism.

Unit 24

Concession and contrast

Concession means stating an idea or fact that **contrasts** with another idea or fact but is usually more important. For example:

> **Although** they were poor, they were rich in spirit.
> She is a little bit foolish. **Nevertheless/Nonetheless**, she's very kind.

A Verbs of concession

I **agree** that it was a bad idea, but it seemed sensible at the time.
I **admit** I was wrong, but I still think there was reason to doubt her.
I **concede/acknowledge** (formal) that you are right about the goal, but not the method.

B Adverbs and other phrases showing contrast

I expected Mr. Widebody to be heavy. **The reverse was true.**

A: Was the movie any good?
B: **Quite the opposite.** It was simply awful.

Even though / Although / Though I warned you about the dangers, you didn't listen.
You shouldn't seem so surprised. **After all**, I did warn you.
It's all very well saying you want a dog, but who'll take care of it?
He is boring and rude; but **despite all that**, he is your uncle and we should invite him.
In spite of the bad weather, we had a great vacation.
Our old house was sunny and bright. **In contrast**, our new place is dark and gloomy.
Admittedly, she put in a lot of effort, but sadly it was all wasted.
It's not raining now. **On the other hand**, it may rain later, so take the umbrella.
You think John is shy? **On the contrary**, he's the most outgoing person I know.

> **note** **On the other hand** shows that two contrasting facts are both true. **On the contrary** or **to the contrary** means that one statement is true and the other is not true.

C Collocating phrases for contrast

When it comes to politics, Jun and Anna are **poles apart**.
There's a **world of difference** between being a friend and a lover.
There's a **great divide** between liberals and conservatives, in general.
There's a **huge discrepancy** between his ideals and his actions.

Unit 24

Exercises

24.1 Rewrite these sentences using verbs from A on page 48. There is usually more than one possibility for each sentence.

1. I know that you weren't entirely to blame, but you have to take *some* responsibility.
2. He didn't deny that we had tried our best, but he still wasn't content.
3. The company will say you experienced a delay, but it does not accept liability.
4. OK, I was wrong and you were right; he is a nice guy.

24.2 Fill in the blanks with phrases from B and C on page 48.

1. I'm not worried; .... , I feel quite calm.
2. It's expensive, but .... we do need it.
3. There's a .... between what she says and what she does.
4. No need to rush. .... , the play doesn't start till six.
5. She's bossy and rude, but .... she is a friend.
6. There's a .... between being a student and being a teacher.
7. .... saying you'll pay me back soon; *when* is what *I* want to know!
8. .... , I could have tried harder, but I don't think I deserve all this criticism.

24.3 Try to complete this word puzzle from memory. If you can't, look at C on page 48.

Across
1. After .... , I did warn you to be careful.
2. There is a .... of difference between Mexican and Puerto Rican culture.
4. My old teacher was loud and funny; .... contrast, the new one just sits there and reads.
5. There is a .... discrepancy between what I want and what I can afford.

Down
1. Why are they getting married? They're poles .... about almost everything!
3. There's a great .... between Democrats and Republicans on the issue of health care.
5. I'd love to walk home after the movie; on the other .... it might not be safe at that hour.

Unit 25 Addition

You probably already know some ways to add one idea to another in English, using words like **and**, **also**, and **too**. Here are some other, more formal words and phrases.

A Addition words for linking sentences / clauses

Sentence / Clause 1	And	Sentence / Clause 2
For this job you need a degree.	**In addition,**	you need some experience.
Digital cameras are becoming easier to use.	**Furthermore, Moreover, What's more,***	they're becoming cheaper.
It'll take ages to get there, and it'll cost a fortune.	**Besides, Anyway,****	I don't really want to go.
Children should respect their parents.	**Likewise, Similarly,**	they should respect their teachers.
We'll definitely have to go to court.	**On top of (all) that,*****	we'll have to pay the lawyers' fees.

*   **Furthermore** and **moreover** are normally interchangeable. **What's more** is less formal; **What is more** is more formal.
**   **Besides** and **Anyway** are more emphatic.
*** **On top of (all) that** is even more emphatic; usually informal.

> **note** To keep fit you need a good diet **plus** regular exercise. **Plus** is normally used to connect noun phrases, but it can connect clauses in informal speech.

B Addition words at the end of sentences / clauses

They sell chairs, tables, beds, **and so on / etc.** (et cetera)
It'll go to the committee, then to the board, then to another committee, **and so forth**. [suggests a long continuation of actions]
He was a good athlete and an excellent musician **as well / to boot**. [emphasizes the combination of items (**to boot** is used for informal, spoken English)]

C Addition words that begin or come in the middle of sentences / clauses

Pursuant to / Further to my letter of May 1st, I am writing to . . . (a very formal opening for a letter referring back to earlier communication)
In addition to his B.A. in history, he has a Ph.D. in sociology.
He's on the school board, **as well as** being a volunteer firefighter.
Besides / Apart from having a full-time job, she also has a part-time job.
Jeremy Evans was there, **along with** a few other people I didn't know.

> **note** This last group is followed by nouns, noun phrases, or **-ing**. Don't say: *As well as she speaks French, she also speaks Japanese.* Say: *As well as speaking French, she . . .*

Unit 25

Exercises

25.1 Fill in the blanks in this formal job application letter with words and phrases that express addition. Try to fill in the blanks without looking at page 50.

> Dear Mr. Stoneheart:
>
> _____ (1) my letter of April 10th, I would like to give you more information concerning my qualifications and experience. _____ (2) holding a degree in hotel management, I also have an advanced certificate in catering. My hotel management studies covered the usual areas: finance, customer service, publicity, space allocation, _____ (3). I also wish to point out that _____ (4) having these qualifications, I have now been working in the hotel industry for five years. _____ (5), my previous experience was also connected with tourism and hospitality.
>
> I hope you will give my application due consideration.
>
> Sincerely,
>
> Ling Yuen

25.2 Rewrite these sentences using the words or phrases in parentheses.

1. Physical labor can exhaust the body very quickly. Excessive study can rapidly reduce mental powers too. (similarly)
2. My cousin turned up, and some classmates of his came with him. (along with)
3. He owns a big chemical factory, and he runs an enormous oil business. (as well as)
4. She was my teacher, and she was a good friend. (to boot)
5. I'm the scientific adviser and act as consultant to the director. (in addition to)

25.3 Correct the mistakes in the use of addition words and phrases in these sentences.

1. I work part time as well as I am a student, so I have a busy life.
2. Besides to have a good job, my ambition is to meet someone nice to share my life with.
3. Apart from I have many other responsibilities, I am now in charge of staff training.
4. In addition has a degree, she also has an advanced certificate.
5. My father won't agree. My mother's sure to find likewise something to object to.
6. He said he'd first have to consider the organization, then the system, then the finance, and so on so forth.

25.4 Make sentences about the following topics, using different words and phrases to add information.

1. What were/are your favorite school subjects? (Write about at least two subjects.)
2. What kind of movies do you enjoy? (Write about at least two types of movies, e.g., comedies, action, thrillers.)
3. How are you and your best friend similar? (Write about at least two ways.)

Unit 26 Text-referring words

A

Text-referring words take their meaning from the surrounding text. For example, the following sentence does not mean much when read in isolation.

We decided to look at the problem again and try to find a solution.

What problem? We need to refer to some other sentence or to the context to find out. The words **problem** and **solution** help organize the argument of the text, but they do not tell us the topic of the text. They refer to something somewhere else.

Here are some examples. The words in bold refer to the underlined words.

<u>Pollution is increasing</u>. The **problem** is getting worse each day.
<u>Should taxes be raised or lowered?</u> This was the biggest **issue** [topic causing argument and controversy] in the election.
<u>Whether the war could have been avoided</u> is a **question** that continues to interest historians.
Let's discuss <u>movies</u>. That's always an interesting **topic** [subject to argue about or discuss, e.g., in a debate or in an essay].
<u>Punishment</u> is only one **aspect** [part of the topic] of crime.

B Problem-solution words

- Text-referring words are often used with **problem-solution** types of text, where a problem is presented and ways of solving it are discussed. Try to learn these words as a family.

> The **situation** in our cities with regard to traffic is going from bad to worse. Congestion is a daily feature of urban life. The **problem** is now beginning to **affect** our national economy. Unless a new **approach** is found to control traffic, we will never find a **solution** to the **dilemma**.

- Text-referring words are useful to refer to complex ideas quickly. Note the use of the words in bold in these excerpts from a political debate.

> MS. RIGHT: You know, the **problem** with your **plan** for health care is that you want the government to pay for everything, without any personal responsibility.
> MR. LEFT: The **reason** why government should play a larger **role** is that the cost of private care is too high for anyone except the rich.
> MS. RIGHT: Oh, please! That **claim** about excluding the middle class is ridiculous. And the private sector is making **efforts** to include everyone. The **process** takes time, obviously...
> MR. LEFT: I understand that **view**, but the **question** is: are they doing enough?

Here are some other words associated with problem-solution texts.

information: fact, opinion, belief
situation: state of affairs, position, circumstance
problem: difficulty, crisis, matter, dilemma, controversy

response: reaction (to), attitude (toward)
solution: answer (to), resolution (to), key (to), way out (of), proposal (to)
evaluation (of the solution): assessment, judgment, appraisal

Unit 26

Exercises

26.1 Match the sentences on the left with the words on the right.

1. The earth is in orbit around the sun.
2. World poverty and overpopulation are the most serious.
3. You should treat others as you wish to be treated.
4. I've run out of cash.
5. It has proved to be most efficient.
6. They should get married, in my opinion.

problem
evaluation
fact
belief
view
issue

26.2 Fill in the blanks with an appropriate word that refers to the underlined words.

1. So you were talking about <u>animal rights</u>? That's quite a big .... nowadays.
2. We are <u>running out of funds</u>. How do you propose we deal with the .... ?
3. <u>Is there life on other planets?</u> This is a .... nobody has yet been able to answer.
4. (*teacher to the class*) You can write your essay on "<u>My best vacation ever.</u>" If you don't like that .... , I'll give you another one.
5. She thinks <u>we should all fly around in little helicopters.</u> This is a unique .... to the traffic problem in cities, but I doubt that it would ever be feasible.

26.3 Match these newspaper headlines with extracts from their texts below.

NEW APPROACH TO CANCER TREATMENT

PROPOSAL TO RAISE CABLE RATES DRAWS FIRE

NO RESOLUTION FOR UNEMPLOYMENT NUMBERS

SCIENTIST REJECTS CLAIMS OVER FAST FOOD

SOLUTION TO AGE-OLD MYSTERY IN KENYA

SITUATION IN SUDAN WORSENING DAILY

1. She said if the world community failed to respond, thousands of children could die.

3. The Secretary of Labor denied that this was true, pointing out evidence that . . .

5. The response of many customers and competitors is that the move is unfair.

2. Tests were being carried out to see if the new drug really did . . .

4. There was no proof at all that such additives were harmful, and in . . .

6. The bones proved beyond doubt that human beings had inhabited the region during . . .

Unit 27 Discourse markers in speech

A Discourse markers are words and phrases that organize, comment on, or in some way frame what we are saying or writing. One common discourse marker from spoken language is **well**.

A: So you live in Seoul?   B: **Well**, near Seoul.

Well here shows that the speaker is changing the direction of the conversation in some way (not giving the expected yes answer). In other words, **well** is a comment on what is being said.

B Here are some common markers that organize the different stages of a conversation.

Now, what shall we do next?
So, would you like to join us for dinner?
Good/OK, I'll call you on Thursday.
Well then, what was it you wanted to talk about?
Now then (said by someone in control of the conversation, e.g., a teacher), I want you to look at this picture.
Fine/Great, let's leave it at that, then, OK?

C In these mini-dialogs, the markers in bold modify or comment on what is being said.

A: It's cold isn't it?
B: Yeah.
A: **Of course** [an afterthought, used like *however*], it is November, so it's not surprising.

A: What's her number?
B: **Let's see / Let me see** [a hesitation – gaining time], I have it here somewhere . . .

A: It's quite a problem . . .
B: **Listen/Look** [introducing a suggestion / point], why don't you let me handle it?
A: Would you? Thanks a lot.

A: And he said he was go . . .
B: **Well**, that's typical!
A: **Hang on / Hold on** [preventing an interruption]! Let me tell you what he said!

Here are some other similar markers.

I can't do that. **You see** [explaining something], I'm not the boss here.
He was, **you know, sort of** [a hesitation] . . . just standing there.
So that's what we have to do. **Anyway** [signaling that the speaker thinks the topic or the conversation can now close], I'll call you tomorrow.
It rained all day yesterday. **Still** [contrasting two ideas with one another], we can't complain, it was fine all last week.
We shouldn't be too hard on him. **After all** [the final result of a discussion or argument is . . .], he's only a child.

In informal spoken language, people often use the letters of the alphabet (usually no more than *a*, *b*, and *c*) to list points they want to make.

I'm not going to London this summer because **a** it's too expensive, and **b** it's too far.

Unit 27

Exercises

27.1 Underline all the discourse markers in this monologue. Not all of them are on page 54.

> "Well, where should I start? It was last summer and we were just sitting in the garden, sort of doing nothing much. Anyway, I looked up and . . . see, we have this kind of long wall at the end of the garden, and it's . . . like . . . a highway for cats, for instance, that big fat black one you saw, well, that one considers it has a right of way over our vegetable patch, so . . . where was I? Yes, I was looking at that wall, you know, daydreaming as usual, and all of a sudden there was this new cat I'd never seen before, or rather, it wasn't an ordinary cat at all . . . I mean, you'll never believe what it was . . ."

27.2 Rewrite these sentences with the discourse markers in the box.

after all	still	a, b	of course	anyway

1. Yes, there is a lot of work to do. I must rush now. I'll call you tomorrow.
2. A: It is so hot in Mexico City just now!
   B: It is summer.
3. Money is not the most important thing in life. I really do believe that.
4. I never got a chance to tell him. I'm seeing him next week. I'll tell him then.
5. There're two reasons I think he's wrong. He has the facts wrong, and his conclusion doesn't make sense.

27.3 Here are some mini-dialogs without any discourse markers. Add markers from page 54 and from 27.1, where you think the speakers might use them.

1. A: Are you a football fan?
   B: I like it; I wouldn't say I was a fan.

2. A: I'll take care of these.
   B: That's everything.
   A: See you next week.
   B: That was a very useful meeting.

3. A: It was last Monday. I was coming home from work. I saw this ragged old man approaching me. I stopped him . . .
   B: Jim Dibble!
   A: Let me tell you what happened first.

4. A: Which number is yours?
   B: (*pause*) . . . it's this one here, yes, this one.

5. A: He's looking exhausted.
   B: Yes, he is.
   A: He has an awful lot of responsibility, so it's hardly surprising.

6. A: What do you mean, "cold?"
   B: She's not friendly, very distant. Last week I gave her a big smile and she . . . scowled at me.
   A: What do you expect? I've seen the way you smile at people – it makes them feel uncomfortable.

---

follow-up If you can, make a recording of a natural conversation between English speakers (get their permission, but don't tell them why you want to record them until after you have finished). Then listen to the recording and make a list of the markers the speakers use.

55

Unit 28　Discourse markers in writing

A　Organizing a formal written text from start to finish

First / Firstly / First of all, we must consider . . .
Next, it is important to remember that . . .
Second / Secondly and **Third / Thirdly** are also used with **First / Firstly** for lists.
Finally / Lastly (not *at last*), we should recall that . . .
Leaving aside the question of pollution [the writer will not deal with that question here], there are also other reasons . . .
In summary, to sum up [listing / summing up the main points], we may state that . . .
In sum [listing / summing up the main points: much more formal], the economic issues are at the center of this debate.
In conclusion / to conclude [finishing the text], I would like to point out that . . .

B　Markers for explaining, exemplifying, rephrasing, etc.

Some English words are hard to pronounce, **for example / for instance**, *eighth*.
He claims the resources are limitless. **In fact / Actually** [something needs correction or modification], we will run out within 40 years at current rates of consumption.
Congress has different committees. **Briefly** [the explanation will be short and not comprehensive], these consist of two main types.
Apparently [it may be true but it's not certain], it wasn't very popular with people.
To learn new words properly a lot of revision is needed; **in other words / that is to say** (**that is to say** is more formal), you have to study the same words many times.
These roads are crowded, **particularly/especially** [more than usual] during rush hour.
Politicians are being investigated; **in particular / specifically** [narrowing down a topic], they are focusing on the prime minister and her staff.

C　Signposts around the text

The following [used to introduce a list] points will be covered in this essay: . . .
It was stated **above/earlier** [earlier in the text] that the history of the U.S. is . . .
See **page 238** [go to page 238] for more information.
Many writers have claimed this (see **below**) [examples will be given later in the text].
For **further** details / discussion [more discussion / details], see Chapter 4.
May I **refer you to** (formal; *May I ask you to look at / read*) page 3 of my last letter to you?
In reference to / With reference to / Regarding (formal; often used at the beginning of a letter to link it with an earlier text) your fax of May 28, 2010, . . .

Unit 28

Exercises

28.1 Fill in the blanks with discourse markers from page 56. The first letter of each phrase or word is given.

> *Points for discussion – crime and punishment:*
>
> F....................... (1), it is important to understand why people commit crimes; i....................... (2), what are the motives that make people do things they would never normally do? F....................... (3), a young man steals clothes from a shop; is it because he is unemployed? a drug addict? mentally disturbed? N....................... (4), it is essential to consider whether punishment makes any difference, or is it just a kind of revenge? L....................... (5), how can we help victims of crime? I....................... (6), how can we get to the roots of the problem, rather than just attacking the symptoms?

28.2 Match the markers on the left with the appropriate functions on the right.

1. Leaving aside: moving to a more specific point
2. In fact: read something earlier in the text
3. In particular: this will not be discussed
4. In conclusion: this document is about another one
5. In reference to: to finish off
6. See above: to correct or modify something

28.3 Which marker(s) . . .

1. is based on the word *actual*?
2. is based on the verb to *follow*?
3. is a form of the word *far*?
4. means to restate something?
5. contains the word/syllable *sum*? (*Note:* There are three of them.)

28.4 Write a letter in response to an article you read about a local hospital closing down. Combine the discourse markers in the box with the sentences below the box to state why you believe the hospital should not close.

| with reference to the following | firstly, second(ly), third(ly), etc. that is to say | leaving aside to sum up | finally briefly |

The nearest other hospital is 50 miles away.
It is being closed for political reasons, not genuine economic ones.
Two hundred people work at the hospital; they will lose their jobs.
The hospital makes an important contribution to the local economy.
It is the only hospital in the region with a special cancer unit.

57

Unit 29 Uncountable nouns

Countable nouns can be used with **a/an** and made plural (e.g., **a building**, **two buildings**). Uncountable nouns are not normally used with **a/an** or the plural (e.g., **information**, *not* "an information" or "some informations"). You can learn uncountable nouns in groups associated with the same subject or area. Here are some groups.

A Travel

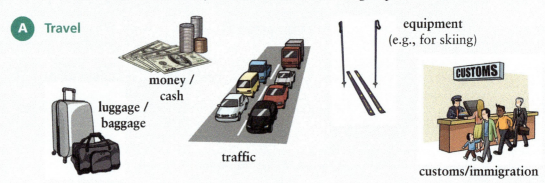

Travel is also an uncountable noun, e.g., *Travel broadens the mind*.

B Household items

soap   toothpaste   detergent   furniture   paper

C Food

The word **food** is uncountable. Try adding more uncountable words to this list.

sugar   rice   meat   butter   flour   soup

D Abstract uncountable nouns

She gave me some **advice** on how to reformat my hard drive.
Teachers need a great deal of **knowledge** about English grammar.
He's made a lot of **progress** in a very short time.
She has done some **research** on marine life.
They've done a lot of **work** on improving their search engine.

E Materials and resources

Clothing materials:	cotton	leather	polyester	wool	silk
Building materials:	cement	concrete	glass	plastic	wood
For energy:	coal	electricity	gas/gasoline	oil	wind/solar power

F Common mistakes

Don't say:	What a terrible weather!	I have so many homeworks.	I have a news for you.
Instead, say:	What terrible **weather**!	I have so much **homework**	I have (some) **news** for you.

Unit 29

Exercises

29.1 Decide whether these sentences need *a/an* or no article. Not all of the nouns are on on page 58. Use a dictionary that tells you whether the nouns are countable or uncountable.

1. He gave us ……………………… advice on what to take with us.
2. I'm sorry. I can't go. I have ……………………… homework to do.
3. She's doing ……………………… study of teenage slang for her university project.
4. You'll need ……………………… rice if you want to make a Chinese meal.
5. You're studying overseas? That's ……………………… wonderful news!
6. I need ……………………… cash to pay for parking. Can I borrow 10 dollars?

29.2 List these words in two columns side by side, one for uncountable nouns and one for countable nouns. Then join the words with similar meanings.

cotton	fact	suitcase	information	job	idea	soap	fuel
shirt	trip	work	baggage	advice	travel	engine	toothbrush

29.3 Imagine you are going away for a week's vacation and you pack a suitcase with a number of things. Make a list of what you would pack, and check off the items on your list that are uncountable nouns in English.

29.4 Correct the mistakes in the use of countable and uncountable nouns in these sentences.

1. We had such a terrible weather last night! The storm knocked out the electricities for hours.
2. I love antique furnitures, but I would need an advice from a specialist before I bought any. My knowledges in that area are very poor.
3. His researches are definitely making great progresses these days. He has done a lot of original works recently.
4. If your luggages are too heavy, it will cost a lot of monies to bring them.

29.5 Practice asking for these household items, using *Can I have . . . ?* Decide whether you should say *a* or *some* for each item.

broom	detergent	shampoo	flour	knife	soap

29.6 Personal qualities and skills use a lot of uncountable words. Choose the qualities from the list that the people with these jobs should have. Say whether they need *some*, *a lot*, or *a little bit* of the quality. Use a dictionary if necessary.

Jobs	actor	athlete	doctor	firefighter	teacher	writer
Qualities	charm commitment compassion	courage creativity determination	discipline empathy energy	experience goodwill intelligence	loyalty patience reliability	stamina talent training

Unit 30 — Nouns that are usually plural

A Tools, instruments, pieces of equipment

B Things we wear

C Other plural nouns

When will the **goods** [articles/items] be delivered?
He was seen leaving the **premises** around midnight.
The **fireworks** are amazing!
The military **authorities** established their **headquarters** in the town hall.
The **acoustics** in the new concert hall are excellent.
The **contents** of the house were sold after the owner's death.
Looks are less important than personality in a spouse.
Be careful! Those **stairs** are dangerous.
The industrial area is located on the **outskirts** of town.
This rainy weather gives me the **blues**. [feeling of sadness]
The **proceeds** of the concert are going to be donated to charity.
A prisoner has escaped and his **whereabouts** are unknown.

D Words with plural form but used mostly with singular verbs

Names of some games: **billiards   cards   checkers   darts   dominoes**
Names of some subjects/activities: **aerobics   arts   athletics   classics   economics   gymnastics   physics   sports**

> *note* Some words look plural but are not, e.g., series, means, news, spaghetti: a **series** of programs on TV; a cheap **means** of transportation

Unit 30

Exercises

30.1 Name the items listed in A on page 60 that can be used to . . .
1. pick up something hot.
2. protect your eyes from bright sunlight.
3. cut paper.
4. remove a splinter from your skin.
5. look at distant objects.
6. pull a nail out of a piece of wood.

30.2 Circle the articles on the clothesline that are plural nouns.

30.3 Fill in the blanks with appropriate plural nouns from page 60.
1. (*to a child*) Get your .... on! It's time to go to bed.
2. The .... of the rock concert are going to charity.
3. The escaped prisoner's .... are still unknown.
4. The .... have prohibited the import of all foreign ....
5. She always gets the .... in cold winter months.

30.4 In each group, circle the noun that must always be used in the plural. Then correct its spelling.

1. sleeve   pant   slipper
2. aerobic   squash   tennis
3. knife   tong   razor
4. suit   costume   clothe

30.5 In this story, change the singular nouns to plural where appropriate. Then change any incorrect verbs to singular or plural.

> After teaching gymnastic for years, I decided that I wanted to be a rock star and I moved to Los Angeles. I got a room, but it was on the outskirt of the city. The owner didn't live on the premise, so I could make as much noise as I liked. The acoustic in the bathroom was fantastic, so I practiced playing heavy metal music and rhythm & blue there. I went to the headquarter of the musicians' union, where a guy in pink short and large sunglass told me he liked my music but hated my taste in clothe.

30.6 Make a list of subjects you studied or would like to study, and a list of activities you like to do in your free time. How many of the words are plural? Use a dictionary if necessary.

Unit 31 — Countable and uncountable nouns with different meanings

A When we use a countable noun, we are thinking of specific **things** that can be counted, e.g., *two glasses*. When we use it as an uncountable noun, we are thinking of **stuff** or **material** or the **idea of a thing in general**, e.g., *Glass is breakable*.

Stuff / Material	*Things*
glass	a glass / glasses
cloth	a cloth
fish	a fish
thread	a thread

Here are some other nouns used in both ways. Make sure you know the difference between the uncountable and the countable meanings.

  hair – a hair   paper – a paper   land – a land
  people – a people   home – a home   trade – a trade

Waiter! There's **a hair** in my soup!
Did you buy **a paper** [a newspaper] this morning?
I love meeting **people** [individuals] from different **lands**. [countries]
Her grandmother lives in a **home**. [an institution]
Trade between the two countries has never been stronger.

B The names of food items often have a different meaning depending on whether they are used as countable or uncountable nouns (see *fish* above).

coffee/tea → a **coffee** and two **teas**

turkey → a turkey

Would you like some **chocolate**? → Would you like **a chocolate**?

salt and **pepper** → a pepper

Unit 31

Exercises

31.1 Complete this table with places or things where you might find these items in a home. Answer for both meanings (countable and uncountable).

Item	Countable	Uncountable
1. iron	in a laundry room or kitchen	in a frying pan (metal)
2. cloth		
3. pepper		
4. paper		
5. fish		
6. glass		

31.2 Practice asking for these items, using *Can I have/borrow . . . ?* Decide whether you should say *a* or *some* for each item.

1. chocolate

3. coffee

5. wine

2. pepper

4. turkey

31.3 Respond to these statements and questions by using the word in parentheses. Use *a/an* if the meaning is countable.

1. Oh no! I spilled milk on the floor! (cloth)
   Don't worry. Here's a cloth; just wipe it up.
2. How did you get a flat tire? (glass)
3. This soup tastes a little bland. What can we put on it? (pepper)
4. Why did you send back your soup? (hair)
5. There's something hanging on your shirt. (thread)

31.4 Explain the difference between the meaning of (a) and (b) in each pair. Use a dictionary if necessary.

1. a) Painting is a great way to relax.
   b) Are these paintings by Picasso?
2. a) Did you hear a noise coming from the basement?
   b) Will you kids stop making so much noise?
3. a) Can I have some light?
   b) Can I have a light?

Unit 32 Collective nouns

Collective nouns are used to describe **a group** of the same things.

A People

a **group** of people (small number)   a **crowd** of people (large number)   a **gang** of thieves (negative)

B Words associated with certain animals

A **flock** of sheep or birds, e.g., geese/pigeons; a **herd** of cattle, elephants; a **school** of fish; a **swarm** of insects (or any particular insect, most typically flying ones, e.g., a **swarm** of bees/gnats); a **pack** of . . . can be used for dogs, hyenas, wolves, etc., as well as for (playing) cards.

C People involved in the same job / activity

These phrases are used as singular nouns.

A **team** of doctors / experts / reporters / scientists / rescue workers / detectives arrived at the scene of the disaster.
The **crew** [workers on a ship] was saved when the ship sank.
The **company** [group of theater actors] is rehearsing a new production.
The **cast** [actors in a play or movie production] was composed entirely of amateurs.
The **public** [the people as a whole] has a right to know the truth.

> **note** The phrase **the people** takes a plural verb, e.g., *The people are tired of taxes*. The word **staff** can take either a singular or plural verb.

D Things in general

a **pile/heap** of papers (or clothes, dishes, etc.)   a **bunch** of flowers (or bananas, grapes, etc.)   a **stack** of chairs (or tables, boxes, etc.)   a **bundle** of firewood (clothing, papers)

a **set** of tools (or pots and pans, dishes, etc.)   a **clump** of trees (or bushes, grass, plants, etc.)   a **row** of chairs (or tables, houses: when they are in a line)   a **pair/couple** of birds (two of anything similar or the same)

Unit 32

Exercises

32.1 Fill in the blanks with appropriate collective nouns from page 64.

1. There was a .... of insects in my backyard this summer.
2. We saw a .... of brightly colored fish just below the surface of the water.
3. There is a .... of young people standing on the corner; they don't look too friendly.
4. I keep a .... of tools in the garage.
5. A .... of biologists is studying marine life in this area.

32.2 Circle the word that is the odd one out in each group

1. **Flock** is often used for: sheep   birds   pigs
2. **Cast** is often used for people in: a play   a book   a movie
3. **Crew** is often used for: a ship   a plane   a hospital
4. **Pack** is often used for: cats   dogs   wolves

32.3 Match the collective words on the left with the most appropriate nouns on the right.

1. a clump of   socks
2. a herd of   clothes
3. a row of   bushes
4. a swarm of   elephants
5. a pile of   bees
6. a pair of   chairs

32.4 Replace the underlined words with collective nouns. Change the verb to singular or plural where necessary and use the correct articles (a/an/the).

1. There are <u>some tables on top of one another</u> in the next room.
2. There are <u>a large number of people</u> waiting outside.
3. The <u>people who work there</u> are well paid.
4. He gave me <u>six identical sherry glasses</u>.
5. She gave me <u>five or six beautiful roses</u>.
6. We brought <u>many pieces of firewood</u> to burn in the bonfire.

32.5 Some collective nouns are associated with words describing language. Underline any you can see in this news text.

> THE JOURNALISTS raised a whole host of questions about the actions of the police during the demonstration. There had been a barrage of complaints about police violence. The Chief of Police replied that he would not listen to a string of wild allegations without any evidence. Eventually he gave reporters a series of short answers that left everyone dissatisfied.

Unit 33 — Making uncountable nouns countable

A You can make many uncountable nouns singular and countable by adding **a piece of** or **a (little) bit of**. Similarly, you can make such nouns plural with **pieces of** or (less frequently) **bits of**.

She bought an attractive **piece of** furniture at an antique shop.
Let me give you a **little bit of** advice?
Chopin wrote some wonderful **pieces of** music.
They created it from **bits of** metal and plastic.

B A number of other words go with specific uncountable nouns.

- Weather

    We've had a long **spell of** hot weather this summer.
    Did you hear that **rumble/clap** of thunder?
    Yes, I did. It came almost immediately after the **flash of** lightning.
    A sudden **gust of** wind turned my umbrella inside out.
    Did you feel a **drop of** rain just now?

    (See also Unit 36 for more weather words.)

- Groceries

two **pieces/slices*** of toast   a **carton of** milk   a **loaf of** bread   two **bars of** soap

a **bar of** chocolate   a **package of** cookies   a **tube of** toothpaste   **pound/kilo of** meat/cheese

***Slice** can also be used with *cake*, *bread*, *meat*, and *cheese*.

- Nature

    Look at the grasshopper on that **blade of** grass!
    What happened? Look at that **cloud of** smoke hanging over the city!
    Let's go out and get a **breath of** fresh air.

- Other

    I had an incredible **stroke of** luck this morning.
    The donkey is the basic **means of** transportation on the island.
    At the beach, the most important **item/article of** clothing is a hat.

C The phrase **a state of** can serve to make uncountable nouns singular. Those nouns are usually abstract and include *panic*, *shock*, *siege*, *emergency*, *uncertainty*, *poverty*, *disrepair*, *confusion*, *health*, *mind*, and *flux*, e.g., **a state of** shock.

Unit 33

Exercises

33.1 Match the words on the left with the most appropriate nouns on the right.

1. a stroke of   clothing
2. a rumble of   rain
3. a cloud of   thunder
4. an article of   transportation
5. a flash of   grass
6. a blade of   luck
7. a drop of   lightning
8. a means of   smoke

33.2 Change the uncountable nouns to countable nouns by using either *a piece of / a bit of* or one of the more specific words listed in B on page 66.

1. Could you get me some bread, please? *Could you get me a loaf/slice of bread, please?*
2. My mother gave me some advice that I have always remembered.
3. Suddenly the wind blew him off his feet.
4. Would you like some more toast?
5. Let's go to the park – I need some fresh air.
6. I can give you some important information about that.
7. I need to get some furniture for my apartment.

33.3 Complete this word puzzle, using words from C on page 66.

1. She wouldn't be in such a poor state of .... if she had stopped smoking.
2. The government announced a state of .... after the earthquake.
3. The economic collapse has left everyone in a state of .... about the future.
4. There was a general state of .... after the brutal attack.
5. Although this is supposed to be an affluent society, many people are living in a state of ....

33.4 Make your own puzzle like the one above, using words from page 66. If possible, ask someone to try doing your puzzle.

33.5 Make sentences in your notebook using *a state of* . . . and these words.

1. siege   2. flux   3. confusion   4. chaos   5. mind

67

Unit 34   Containers and contents

A Common containers

B Information about each of these types of containers

Container	Usually made of...	Typical contents
bag	cloth, paper, plastic	groceries, flour, rice
barrel	wood and metal	wine, beer, rainwater
basket	cane, wicker, bamboo	groceries, clothes, wastepaper
bottle	glass, plastic	milk, wine, other liquids
bowl	china, glass, wood	fruit, soup, sugar
box	cardboard, wood	matches, tools, cereal, chocolates
bucket	metal, plastic	sand, water
can	aluminum, tin	soda, beer, soup, vegetables
carton	cardboard, plastic	milk, eggs, cigarettes
case	leather, plastic, cardboard, wood	eyeglasses, jewelry, canned goods, beer
crate	wood, plastic	bottles
glass	glass, plastic	milk, water, other liquids
jar	glass, pottery	jam, honey, olives, instant coffee
jug	glass, pottery	milk, cream, water
mug	pottery	coffee, tea, cocoa
pack	cardboard, plastic	envelopes, gum, cards
package	paper, plastic	cookies, rolls
pot	metal, pottery	food, plant
sack	cloth, plastic	potatoes, onions, rice
six-pack	six cans or bottles	soda, beer
tube	soft metal, plastic	toothpaste, paint, ointment

Unit 34

Exercises

34.1 Fill in the blanks in this shopping list without looking at page 68.

2 .... of milk
4 .... of soda
a .... of tuna fish
a .... of chocolate chip cookies
a large .... of matches
a .... of honey
2 .... of mineral water
a .... of rice

34.2 Containers quiz

1. Which container would most likely be holding flowers from a garden?
2. Which three containers are you most likely to find in a basement?
3. Which five containers would you be likely to find in a liquor store?
4. Name at least five containers that you might see on the breakfast table.
5. Which two containers are often used for carrying groceries?
6. Which five containers might have juice in them?

34.3 Write the names of these containers and their contents.

1. 3. 5. 7. 9.

2. 4. 6. 8. 10.

34.4 Think of two words that are often used with these containers.

1. *shopping, garbage* bag
2. .... box
3. .... jug
4. .... can
5. .... crate
6. .... bowl
7. .... glass
8. .... pot

> **follow-up**   Look in a kitchen cupboard or in a supermarket. Name as many of the items you see in English (e.g., *a box of chocolates*). (Also see Units 33 and 48.)

Unit 35 Countries, nationalities, and languages

A Using *the*

Most names of countries are used without *the*, but some countries and other names have *the* before them, e.g., **the United States / the U.S.**, **the United Kingdom / the U.K.**, **the Philippines**, **the Netherlands**. For some countries, *the* is optional – **(the) Sudan**, **(the) Ukraine**.

B Adjectives referring to countries and languages

With *-ish*:	Spanish	British	Polish	Danish	Turkish	Irish
With *-(i)an*:	Canadian	Brazilian	American	Korean	Venezuelan	Mexican
With *-ese*:	Japanese	Congolese	Vietnamese	Portuguese	Lebanese	Chinese
With *-i*:	Israeli	Iraqi	Kuwaiti	Pakistani	Bangladeshi	Saudi
With *-ic*:	Icelandic	Arabic				

Some adjectives should be learned separately, e.g., **French**, **Swiss**, **Thai**, **Greek**, **Dutch**. **American** is sometimes used to refer to people or things from the U.S. or from all of North and South America.

C Nationalities

Some nationalities have nouns for referring to people, e.g., **a Spaniard**, **a Filipino**, **a Turk**, **a Swede**, **a Dane**, **a Briton**, **an Arab**. For most nationalities we can use the adjective as a noun, e.g., **a Canadian**, **a German**, **an Italian**, **a Greek**, **a South African**. Some need *woman / man / person* added to them (you can't say "a Dutch"), so if in doubt, add those words, e.g., **an English man (Englishman)**, **a Dutch man (Dutchman)**, **a Swiss woman**, **an Irish person**.

D World regions

E Peoples, races, and languages

People belong to **ethnic groups** and **regional groups** such as **African Americans**, **Asians**, and **Latin Americans**. They speak **dialects** [regional varieties of a language] as well as languages. Everyone has a **native language**, or **first language**; many have **second** and **third languages**. Some people speak more than one language **fluently** and are **bilingual** or **multilingual**.

Unit 35

Exercises

35.1 Some adjectives can form regional groups, e.g., Latin American countries are almost all described by *-(i)an* adjectives.

1. Complete this list of Latin American adjectives. Use a world map if necessary.
   Brazilian, Chilean, . . .
2. Complete this list of some Eastern European countries and parts of the former Soviet Union.
   Hungarian, Armenian, . . .
3. Find other regional groupings on page 70.
   (For example, many *-ish* adjectives are European.)

35.2 These nationality adjectives have a change in stress from the name of the country. Underline the stressed syllable in each word as in the example. Then try to pronounce each word.

1. Egypt → Egyptian
2. Italy → Italian
3. Canada → Canadian
4. Vietnam → Vietnamese
5. Jordan → Jordanian
6. China → Chinese

35.3 Correct the mistakes in these newspaper headlines.

1. A Spanish named as new UN leader
2. Britains have highest tax rate in EU
3. Canada Elections today
4. Police arrest Danish on smuggling charge
5. Iraqian delegation meets Pakistanian President
6. FOUR GOLD MEDALS FOR PORTUGALIAN TEAM!

35.4 World quiz.

1. What are the five most widely spoken languages?
2. What are the five countries with the largest populations?
3. Which countries are in Scandinavia?
4. Approximately how many languages are there in the world?
5. Where do people speak Inuit?
6. What are some of the main ethnic groups in Malaysia?

35.5 Describe your own nationality, country, region, ethnic group, language(s), etc., in English.

71

Unit 36 The weather

A Cold weather

> In Scandinavia, the **chilly**[1] days of autumn soon change to the cold days of winter. The first **frosts**[2] arrive and the roads become **icy**. Rain becomes **sleet**[3] and then snow, at first turning to **slush**[4] in the streets, with severe **blizzards**[5] and **snowdrifts**[6] in the far north. **Freezing**[7] weather often continues in the far north until May or even June, when the ground starts to **thaw**[8] and the ice **melts**[9] again.

[1]cold, but not extremely so; [2]thin, white coat of ice on everything; [3]frozen or partly frozen rain and snow mixed; [4]dirty half-melted snow; [5]heavy snow blown by high winds; [6]deep banks of snow against walls, etc.; [7]extremely cold, with temperatures at or below freezing; [8]changing from hard, frozen state to more liquid; [9]ice changing to water as it heats up

B Warm / hot weather

boiling [excessively hot], a **heat wave** [a period of unusually hot weather], **humid** [moist, damp air], **mild** [moderate; not severe or extreme (e.g., *a mild winter*)], **muggy** [unpleasantly warm and extremely humid; makes you sweat], **scorching** [burning heat], **stifling** [hot, uncomfortable; you can hardly breathe], **sweltering** [oppressive heat]

C Wet weather

This wet weather scale gets stronger from left to right.

damp → drizzle → pour/downpour → torrential rain → flood

It was absolutely **pouring**. / There was a real **downpour**.
In the tropics there is often **torrential rain**, and the roads get **flooded**.
This rain won't last long; it's only a **shower**. [short duration]
The **storm** [high winds and heavy rain] damaged several houses.
We got soaked in the **thunderstorm**. [thunder and heavy rain]
Hailstones [small balls of ice from the sky] battered the roof of our car.
The sky's **overcast** [very cloudy with no sunshine]; I think it's going to rain.
We had a **drought** [a long period with no rain] last summer. It didn't rain for six weeks.
It was so **foggy/misty** [moisture in the air] that I could barely see ahead of me.
It's so **hazy** [fog caused by water, smoke, or dust during extreme heat] that I can't see the buildings across the park.
There is a **smog** [a mixture of fog and smoke in the air] alert all week: Children and the elderly need to stay indoors.

D Wind

There was a gentle **breeze** on the beach, just enough to cool us.
It's a **blustery** day; the **gusts** of wind will just blow your umbrella away.
There's been a **gale** warning; it would be crazy to go sailing.
People boarded up their windows when they heard a **hurricane** was on the way.
The **tornado** destroyed over fifty homes in less than 10 minutes.

Unit 36

Exercises

36.1 Fill in the blanks with words from A on page 72.

> My first experience of real winter weather was when I went to northern Canada. I was used to the kind of snow that falls back home, which quickly turns into brown .... (1) with all the people walking in it. In fact, most of the time I was growing up, it didn't really snow at all – it was mostly .... (2). Otherwise, our winters meant a little bit of white .... (3) in my garden and occasionally having to drive very carefully on icy roads early in the morning. I had never experienced the .... (4) and .... (5) that can paralyze a whole city in less than an hour and close roads completely. However, when the earth finally .... (6) and all the snow .... (7) away in spring, everything comes to life again and looks more beautiful than ever.

36.2 Match each word below with a word from the box.

> stones   sky   drift   storm   warning   rain   wave   pour

1. thunder
2. torrential
3. down
4. heat
5. hail
6. snow
7. hurricane
8. overcast

36.3 What kinds of weather do you think caused the following events? Write a sentence that could go *before* each of these events, using words from page 72.

1. *It was terribly muggy*. The sweat was streaming down our backs.
2. .... We had to sit in the shade if we went outdoors.
3. .... I can hardly breathe; I wish it would rain to cool us down.
4. .... Even the mail carrier had to use a boat to get around.
5. .... They had to close the airport; it was 3 feet deep.
6. .... The earth became rock-hard and many plants died that summer.
7. .... It blew the newspaper completely out of my hands.
8. .... A row of big trees was uprooted like matchsticks.

36.4 Name the types of weather that are good and bad for these activities.

Activity	Good weather	Bad weather
1. planting flowers in a garden	mild; after rain	a drought; frost; snow
2. having an evening barbecue		
3. going out in a small sailboat		
4. sightseeing in a big city		
5. camping out in a tent		

> **follow-up** Watch a weather report on an English-language television channel or Web site (e.g., BBC, CNN, the Weather Channel). Listen for words from this unit, and try to learn other weather words.

Unit 37 Describing people's appearance

A Hair, face, and complexion

She has **straight black** hair and a **thin** face.

She has **long wavy** hair and a **round** face with a **double chin**.

She has **curly** hair (an **Afro**), and she is **dark-skinned** (or **black**).

He has a **crew cut** and **bushy eyebrows**.

He has a **receding hairline** and a few **wrinkles**.

He is **bald** and has **freckles**.

He has a **beard** and a **mustache**.

She has curly blond hair and a **fair complexion**.

He had **black** hair when he was younger, but now it's gone **gray**, almost **white**.
How would you describe your hair color? **Blond, brunette, dark/dark-haired, black,** or **red-haired / a redhead**?

> note Fair and dark can be used for hair or complexion.

B Height and build

a **plump** or **heavyset** man

a **slim** woman (positive)

an **obese** person (negative, very fat)

a **chubby** baby

Fat may sound impolite. Instead we might say **a bit overweight** or **heavy**. If someone is broad and solid, we say they are **stocky**. A person with good muscles can be **well built, athletic,** or **muscular**. Someone who is very thin may be described as **skinny** or **scrawny** (negative, impolite).

C General appearance and age

She's a very **stylish** and **elegant** woman, always **well dressed**; her husband is just the opposite, very **scruffy** and **messy/sloppy looking**.
He's very **good looking**, but his friend is rather **unattractive**.
Do you think **beautiful** women are always attracted to **handsome** men, and vice versa, or does personality matter more?
She's **middle-aged**. He's **in his early/mid-/late fifties**. She's **fortyish**. They're **thirty-something**.
He's **a teenager / in his teens**. She's **middle-aged**. They're **old/elderly**.
He's an **older** gentleman. They are **senior citizens / seniors**.

Unit 37

Exercises

37.1 Complete the responses with *opposite* descriptions, using words from page 74.

1. A: I thought you said he was the short, stocky one.
   B: No, just the opposite. *He's the tall, thin one.*
2. A: Was he the dark-skinned, wavy-haired man?
   B: No, just the opposite. Actually, he's ....
3. A: I've heard that she's always well dressed.
   B: What? Who told you that? Every time I see her, she's ....
4. A: Is Gina that plump, blond-haired woman over there?
   B: No, you're looking at the wrong one. Gina's ....
5. A: I don't know why, but I expected the tour guide to be middle-aged, or maybe elderly.
   B: No, apparently she's ....

37.2 Write one sentence to describe each of these people, giving information about their hair and face, height and build, age group, and general appearance. Then describe a famous person. Give some extra clues, e.g., *She's/He's a movie star / politician.* Ask someone to guess who you are describing.

1. yourself
2. your best friend
3. a neighbor
4. your ideal of a handsome man / a beautiful woman

37.3 Fill in the blanks in these WANTED posters.

WANTED FOR FORGERY
Will Prowse
height: 6 ft.
.... hair
.... complexion
with a .... face

WANTED FOR ARMED ROBBERY
Sandra King
height 5 ft., 3 in.
.... hair
.... build
with a .... face

MISSING
Louisa Yin
Age 10, Chinese
.... ;
....
.... hair.

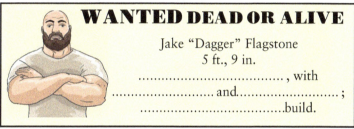

WANTED DEAD OR ALIVE
Jake "Dagger" Flagstone
5 ft., 9 in.
.... , with
.... and .... ;
.... build.

> **follow-up** Find descriptions of people in newspapers, magazines, and Web sites. Build your vocabulary for describing how people look by adding new words to your vocabulary notebook.

Unit 38 Describing people's character

A Intellectual ability

Ability: **intelligent bright smart able gifted clever shrewd talented brainy** (colloquial)
Lacking ability: **stupid foolish simple silly brainless dumb clueless** (the last three are colloquial)
Clever, in a negative way, using intelligence to trick or deceive: **cunning crafty sly**

B Attitudes toward life

Looking on the bright side or dark side: **optimistic, hopeful** or **pessimistic, cynical**
Outward-looking or inward-looking: **extroverted, outgoing** or **introverted, shy**
Calm or not calm: **relaxed, easygoing** or **tense, anxious**
Practical: **sensible, down-to-earth**
Feeling things intensely: **sensitive, thin-skinned**

C Attitudes toward other people

Enjoying others' company: **sociable gregarious congenial**
Disagreeing with others: **quarrelsome argumentative**
Taking pleasure in others' pain: **cruel sadistic**
Relaxed in attitude toward self and others: **even-tempered affable**
Not polite to others: **impolite rude ill-mannered**
Telling the truth / keeping promises: **honest trustworthy reliable sincere**
Unhappy if others have what one does not: **jealous envious**

D One person's meat is another one's poison

The words in the left column mean roughly the same as the words in the right column except that the words in the left column have positive rather than negative connotations.

Positive	Negative
ambitious	pushy (colloquial)
assertive	aggressive bossy (colloquial)
broad-minded	unprincipled permissive
determined	obstinate stubborn pigheaded
frank/direct/open	blunt abrupt brusque curt
generous	extravagant excessive
innocent	naive
inquiring	prying nosy
self-assured/confident	self-important arrogant smug cocky
thrifty/economical	stingy tight-fisted miserly cheap (colloquial)
unconventional/original	peculiar weird eccentric odd

(See also Unit 82.)

Unit 38

Exercises

38.1 Match the words on the left with their opposites on the right.

1. bright
2. extroverted
3. rude
4. cruel
5. generous
6. unsociable

introverted
tight-fisted
polite
gregarious
kindhearted
stupid

38.2 Choose a word from the box that completes each statement below.

| argumentative | extravagant | pessimistic | sensitive |
| assertive | inquiring | reliable | sociable |

1. If you arrange to meet someone at 7 p.m., and you arrive at 7 p.m., you are ...*reliable*...
2. If you prefer to be in the company of other people, you are ....
3. Look at the picture. If you think the glass is half empty, you are ....
4. If it is easy for you to tell your co-workers that they have treated you badly, you are ....
5. If you always look out the window when you hear a car pull up, you are ....
6. If you buy lots of things that you don't really need, you are ....
7. If you frequently disagree with what other people say, you are ....
8. If you lie awake at night because someone has said something unkind to you, you are ....

38.3 Make statements like those in 38.2 and complete the statements with these words.

1. thrifty   *If you save your money, you are thrifty.*
2. blunt
3. sensible
4. naive
5. even-tempered
6. unconventional

38.4 Rewrite these sentences to give the opposite tone, using words from D on page 76.

1. Diane's very thrifty. *Diane is very cheap. (negative)*
2. Nancy's usually frank.
3. Jim's really determined.
4. Paul can be bossy.
5. Dick is awfully pushy.
6. I find Annie so arrogant.
7. Molly is somewhat nosy.
8. Jack is kind of unconventional.

38.5 Choose at least five adjectives from page 76 that you think describe either your own or a friend's character. How do you or your friend demonstrate these characteristics?

Example: *Sociable – I am sociable because I love being with other people.*

Unit 39

Relationships

A Types of relationships

Here is a scale showing closeness and distance in relationships in different contexts.

	CLOSER ⟵	⟶ MORE DISTANT
friendship:	best friend good/old/dear friend	friend acquaintance
work:	close colleague	colleague/co-worker
love/romance:	lover boyfriend/girlfriend	ex-*
marriage:	wife / husband / spouse / partner	ex-*

*****ex-** can be used with or without another word: *That's my* **ex-boyfriend** or *She's my* **ex** (informal).

Mate is used as a suffix to describe a person you share something with, e.g., **classmate, roommate, teammate.**

Co-worker is used in most work contexts; **colleague** is used among professional people. English has no universally accepted word for "person I live with but am not married to," but **companion, partner,** and **significant other** are fairly common.

B Liking and not liking someone

Core verb	Positive	Negative
like	love adore worship idolize	dislike hate can't stand loathe
respect	look up to admire honor	look down on despise detest put down
attract	be attracted to turn someone on	disgust turn someone off
Note: **Put down, turn on,** and **turn off** are informal.		

She doesn't just like Bob; she **idolizes** him! I **can't stand** him.
I used to **look down on** my teachers; now I've begun to **admire** them.

C Phrases and idioms for personal and professional relationships

We **get along** [have a good relationship] well. / I **get along** (well) with her.
Paul and Liz don't **see eye to eye**. [often argue/disagree]
I've had **a falling out** [argument] with my parents again.
Tony and Sue have **broken up** / **split up**. [ended their marriage or relationship]
We have a **love-hate relationship**. [very emotional, with many changes in feeling]
She has a **crush on** [strong but temporary attraction] a famous movie star.
Let's try and **make up**. [be friends again after an argument]
She's **my junior** / I'm **her senior** / I'm **senior to her**. [refers to position / length of service at work] so she does what she's told

(See Unit 65 for more words relating to likes and dislikes.)

Unit 39

Exercises

39.1 Rewrite these sentences using words with the suffix *-mate*.

1. This is Jack. He and I share a room in the dormitory.
2. We were in the same class at Lincoln High School, weren't we?
3. She and I played on the softball team together.

39.2 Write sentences about any relationships you can find between the people mentioned in columns A and B, using words from page 78.

Example: *John Crosby and Bill Nash are colleagues.*

A	B
John Crosby: Works at a language school for businesspeople in Atlanta. Worked at the Sun School, Ottawa, 2002–2004.	**Nora Costa:** Was on the U.S. Olympic swimming team in 2004. Was in the same class at school as Ana Marquez.
Josh Yates: Politician. Met Bill Nash a couple of times.	**Bill Nash:** Works every day with John Crosby.
Lan Nguyen: Divorced from Bill Nash. Swam for the U.S. in the 2004 Olympics.	**Fred Park:** Politician. Knew Lan Nguyen years ago, but not very well.
Ana Marquez: Has been married to Fred Park for the past five years.	**Laura Fine:** Taught at Sun School in Ottawa, 1991–1996. Lives with Josh Yates in a serious relationship.

39.3 What do you think the relationships between the people below would be like? Use the language on page 78 to discuss the relationships.

Example: *A teenage pop music fan might not see eye to eye with his/her parents.*

1. teenage pop music fan
   (a) parents   (b) pop star   (c) strict teacher   (d) best friend
2. administrative assistant
   (a) another administrative assistant   (b) boss   (c) very attractive co-worker
3. 45-year-old bachelor
   (a) teenagers   (b) ex-girlfriend

39.4 Correct the mistakes in the use of phrases and idioms in these sentences.

1. Dave and Phil don't get along eye to eye.
2. I had a falling down with my boyfriend last night. It wasn't my fault.
3. We had an argument but now we've made well.
4. His girlfriend go along well with his mother.
5. Dana had a big fight with her fiancé and broke out with him.

Unit 40 At home

A Places in the home

master bedroom [the largest, most important bedroom]
den [an informal room for resting, watching TV, or studying]
attic [the room just below the roof, often used for storage]
basement [the room below ground level used for storage, relaxing, or living]
laundry room [a room with a clothes washer and dryer; in some apartment buildings, a large room with coin-operated washers and dryers for tenants' use]
hall/hallway [an open area as you come into a house (also called a **foyer** or **front hall**) or a long corridor between rooms]
landing [the floor at the top of a staircase]
walk-in closet [a clothes closet large enough to walk into, attached to a bedroom]
porch [a covered area outside an entrance door, used for sitting if large enough]
patio [an uncovered area adjoining a house or an apartment and used for sitting]
driveway [a (short) road leading from the street to a house, building, or garage]
garage [a closed space for parking a car (a more open space is a **carport**)]

B Small objects in the home

cutting board   grater   spatula   microwave   ironing board   dental floss

corkscrew   can opener   remote control   electrical outlet and plug   mop and bucket   stepladder

C Types of houses / places where people live

single-family house [a home for one family]
apartment [a unit of one or more rooms in an apartment building or complex that people rent to live in]
studio apartment / studio [a single room for living, eating, and sleeping]
apartment building [a building with individual apartments but a common entrance]
apartment complex [a large group of apartment buildings sharing common areas and managed by one company]
townhouse [a house, usually at least two stories high and attached to similar units]
mobile home / trailer [a manufactured home designed to be transported to a site]
condominium/condo [an apartment, owned by an individual instead of rented, in a building or on land that is owned in common by several people]

Unit 40

Exercises

40.1 Complete the labels for each part of the house, using words from page 80.

1. under the roof:
2. top of the stairs:
3. as you walk in:
4. the biggest bedroom:
5. cars are kept here:
6. leads from the street to the house:
7. a place to wash and dry clothes:
8. where people study, do paperwork, talk:

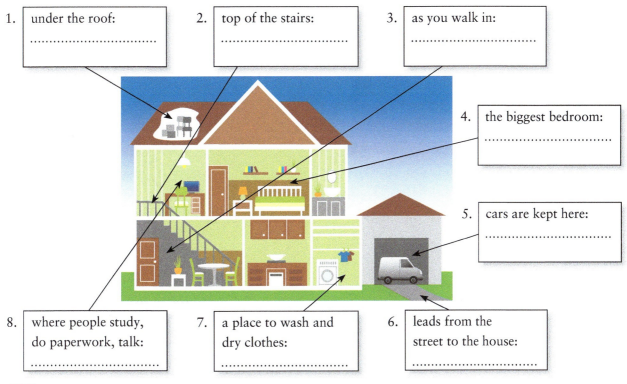

40.2 Fill in the blanks with words from page 80.

1. I have a darkroom in the .... where I develop film. It's perfect because there are no windows down there.
2. We keep our skis up in the .... during the summer.
3. Let's have a cold drink outside on the .... and watch the sunset.
4. The light switch is in the .... as you walk in the front door.
5. I can't go to work with my clothes all wrinkled like this; where is the .... ?
6. Is there an .... where I can recharge my cell phone?
7. We bought a .... It's just like an apartment, except we're the owners!
8. I've moved into a .... It's much easier with only one room to clean!

40.3 Write where you would usually find these items around a typical house.

1. a corkscrew *in the kitchen*
2. dental floss
3. a stepladder
4. a remote control
5. a computer
6. an ironing board
7. an electrical outlet and plug
8. a microwave

40.4 Answer these questions about yourself. If possible compare answers with another person.

1. Do you live in a house, an apartment, a townhouse, or some other type of home?
2. Have you ever been inside a mobile home? What was it like?
3. Are apartment buildings common in every part of your country? What about apartment complexes?
4. Would you rather rent a home or own one if you had a choice? Why?

Unit 41 Everyday problems

A Things that go wrong in houses and apartments

The lights are not **working**. There must be a **power failure / power outage**.

Oh no! The bathroom's **flooded**! Get a mop, quick!

The doorknob **came off**.

The batteries are **dead** / have **run out**. I'll have to get some more / recharge them.

The washing machine **broke down**. We'll have to do the laundry by hand.

Hey, this chair's **broken**! I wonder how that happened.

Can't you hear water **dripping** somewhere? I think a pipe is **leaking**.

All this furniture is **worn out**. We need to replace it, and it will be expensive!

B Everyday minor injuries

Maria **fell down** and **cut** her knee.

I **bumped/banged** my head against the door and got a **bruise**.

She **twisted/sprained** her ankle coming down the stairs.

C Other everyday problems

I **misplaced/lost** [put something somewhere and can't find it] Bob's letter. Have you seen it anywhere?
I knocked over the glass and it **smashed** on the floor.
Somebody **dented** my car door and just drove away!
My bike **got a flat tire** when I rode it on the dirt path.
She **spilled** coffee on the carpet. I hope it doesn't **stain**. [leave a permanent mark]
I **locked myself out**. Can I use your cell phone to call my wife?
The car **won't start**. I hope the battery isn't dead.
The clock's **slow/fast/stopped**. What time do you have?

Unit 41

Exercises

41.1 Write a statement that you think explains why these people said/did what they did.

1. We had to send for a plumber.
   A pipe was leaking. / Our basement was flooded.
2. I had to call a mechanic.
3. Our neighbors let us use their washing machine for a few days.
4. Don't try to walk on it! I'll take you to the doctor right away.
5. Come here and I'll put a Band-Aid on it.
6. How many batteries does it take? I'll get some for you.
7. I don't know where you put them. Try the bedside table.

41.2 Which word or phrase is the odd one out in each group and why?

1. break down   smash   break
2. fall down   bump   stain
3. leak   come off   spill
4. sprain   bruise   flood

41.3 What would you do if . . .

1. you misplaced your credit card?
2. you noticed water dripping from the ceiling?
3. one of your coat buttons came off?
4. your TV set broke down?
5. you bruised your elbow?
6. your watch was slow?

41.4 Match the pictures below with the things in the box that can go wrong with them. Not all of the words in the box are on page 82.

| bang | crack | rip | dent | wear out | drip |

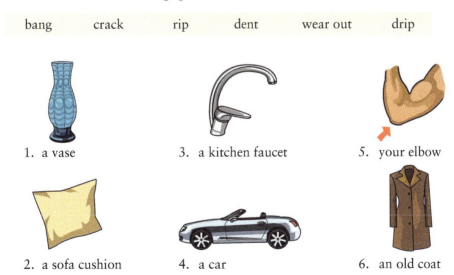

1. a vase
2. a sofa cushion
3. a kitchen faucet
4. a car
5. your elbow
6. an old coat

41.5 Complete these sentences with words and phrases from page 82.

1. We had to use flashlights *because there was a power outage.*
2. The wind blew the door shut, and I realized I'd ....
3. When I tried to climb that big rock, I ....
4. This flashlight doesn't work; maybe ....
5. I jumped in the car and backed up too quickly, so I ....

Unit 42 Global problems

A Disasters / tragedies

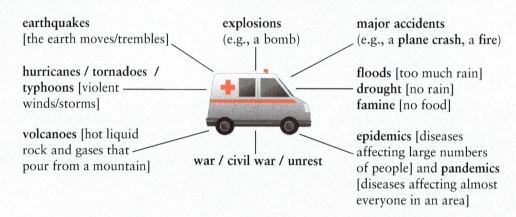

earthquakes [the earth moves/trembles]

explosions (e.g., a bomb)

major accidents (e.g., a **plane crash**, a **fire**)

hurricanes / tornadoes / typhoons [violent winds/storms]

floods [too much rain]
drought [no rain]
famine [no food]

volcanoes [hot liquid rock and gases that pour from a mountain]

war / civil war / unrest

epidemics [diseases affecting large numbers of people] and **pandemics** [diseases affecting almost everyone in an area]

Verbs connected with disaster/tragedy words

A volcano has **erupted** in Indonesia. Hundreds are feared dead.
The flu epidemic **spread** rapidly throughout the country.
Millions are **starving** as a result of the famine.
A big earthquake **shook** the city at noon today.
The area is **suffering** its worst drought in many years.
Civil war has **broken out** in the north of the country.
A tornado **swept** through the islands yesterday, **destroying** hundreds of homes.

> **note** **injure** is used with people, and **damage** is used with things, e.g., Many people were **injured** and dozens of buildings were **damaged** in the hurricane.

B Words for people involved in disasters / tragedies

It was a terrible accident, with only three **survivors**. [people who live through a disaster]
The real **victims** [people who suffer from a disaster] of the civil war are the children.
Thousands of **refugees** have crossed the border looking for food and shelter.
The explosion/typhoon/flood resulted in 300 **casualties**. [dead and injured people]

C Headlines about diseases and epidemics

Rabies out of control in many parts of Asia

New malaria drug tested

Cholera and typhoid shots not needed, claims Tourism Minister

disease that can be caused by a bite from a dog, raccoon, etc.

disease caught from certain mosquitoes, causing fever

diseases caused by infected food and water

84

Unit 42

Exercises

42.1 Write the type of disasters from A on page 84 that these situations are about. Then explain what each disaster means.

1. The lava flow destroyed three villages. *volcano; lava is hot liquid rock that comes from a volcano.*
2. The earth is cracked and vegetation has withered.
3. The tremor struck at 3:35 p.m. local time.
4. People boarded up stores and houses and stayed indoors.
5. Shelling and mortar fire could be heard all over the town.

42.2 Complete this table, using a dictionary if necessary. Where there are dashes, you do not need to write anything.

Verb	Noun: thing or idea	Noun: person/people	Adjective
destroy		-------	
erupt		-------	-------
	explosion	-------	
injure		the injured	
starve		-------	
	survival		-------

42.3 Read these headlines and say whether the situation is getting *worse* or *better*, or whether a disaster has *happened* or has been *avoided*.

42.4 Fill in the blanks with words from page 84. Try to answer from memory.

1. Another fifty people died today, all .... of the famine.
2. The government has agreed to allow 3,000 .... trying to escape the civil war to enter the country.
3. It was a tragic highway accident, with twelve ....
4. A: Were there any .... from the ship that sank?
   B: I'm afraid not. No one was rescued.

42.5 Disease quiz.

1. What disease can be caused by a mosquito bite?
2. What disease can you get by drinking infected water?
3. What disease can you get from an animal bite?

Unit 43 Education

A Stages of education before higher education in the United States

Level (different names)	Grades	Approximate age range
preschool, nursery school, Pre-K		2–5 years old
elementary school, primary school	kindergarten, 1–5 or 6	5–11 years old
junior high school, middle school	6–8 or 7–9	11–14 years old
high school, secondary school	9–12 or 10–12	14–18 years old

School attendance is **compulsory** [required] between the ages of 6 and 16 in most states in the U.S. **Public schools** are free, tax-supported schools, controlled by state and local governments and usually cover the span of **K–12** [kindergarten through 12th grade]. Students have the option of attending **private schools** or **parochial** [religious] **schools** (neither is free). Some people choose **homeschooling**, where parents teach their children at home.

A student **starts** school / college, **goes to** school / college, **drops out** of school / college, **graduates from** school / college.

B Higher education in the United States

Universities and **colleges** normally have an **undergraduate** division that gives out **bachelor's degrees**, e.g., Bachelor of Arts (B.A.) or Bachelor of Science (B.S.), and a **graduate** (or **postgraduate**) division that confers advanced degrees such as **Master of Arts (M.A.)** and **Doctor of Philosophy (Ph.D.)**. A student's main area of study is called a **major**.

Undergraduate study normally lasts four years, and postgraduate study can last from one year to seven or more years. **Community/junior colleges** [two years] and **state colleges / universities** [two or four years] are tax-supported and usually charge low **tuition** [payment]. A two-year degree is an **associate's degree**. Private universities and colleges are more expensive, though some **scholarships** or **grants** [financial aid] are offered. Certain **professional schools**, such as **medical**, **dental**, or **law schools**, are attended after one has earned a bachelor's degree. The **faculty** can include **professors**, **lecturers**, and **instructors**.

C Tests and exams

take a test

pass/ace (informal) a test

fail/flunk (informal) a test

If you want to get a **high score** or a **good grade** on a test, **review** the material beforehand, but don't wait until the night before a test to **cram** [prepare in a short period] for it.

Unit 43

Exercises

43.1 Fill in the blanks in this account of an American woman's education.

> Tammy Smith started her education at age three, when her mother enrolled her in .... (1). She "graduated" to .... (2) at age five. After Tammy completed .... (3) and .... (4) school, her family decided to send her to a .... (5) high school, rather than a public school. She got good .... (6) on her college admissions tests and entered a four-year university, where her .... (7) was economics. Upon receiving her .... (8) degree, she went on to .... (9) school, where she is now working toward a Ph.D. She hopes to become a .... (10) in a university someday.

43.2 Choose another country's education system and answer these questions for that system. Use friends, teachers, classmates, and the Internet to get information.

1. When do children start school?
2. How long are children required to stay in school (until what age)?
3. Is public education more common than private education? What options exist (such as homeschooling or parochial schools)?
4. Are there junior colleges and state colleges/universities? What is the cost compared with private colleges and universities? Are there any entrance requirements?
5. Can students get scholarships or grants to cover tuition costs?

43.3 Make a table for the stages of compulsory education in your country or region, like the table in A on page 86. How does it compare with the system in the U.S. or with systems in other countries that you know?

43.4 Complete each sentence with the most appropriate word in parentheses.

1. I have to study all night; I'm .... a test tomorrow. (flunking/passing/taking)
2. Congratulations! I hear you .... your exams! (aced / failed / studied for)
3. After finishing high school, she went directly to .... (law school / college / charter school)
4. .... schools in the U.S. are free. (parochial/private/public)

43.5 Write questions that match these answers.

1. No, I had to finance my own studies.
2. In most states, it's 16, but most kids stay on until 18.
3. Well, I was up all night cramming for an exam.
4. No, just the opposite; I flunked it!
5. No, both our kids started school in kindergarten. They didn't go to school before that.

Unit 44

Work

A Job titles that are common to a wide range of different workplaces

boss (informal)   supervisor   manager
executive   director   chief executive officer (CEO)
accountant   secretary   skilled worker
unskilled worker   entry-level employee   blue-collar worker
white-collar worker   union representative   administrative assistant

B *Fields* of employment and a few of the *occupations* in them

Health care	*Journalism*	*Construction /*
doctor (physician)	reporter	*home improvement*
registered/practical nurse	camera operator	construction worker
physical therapist	correspondent	carpenter
lab technician	editor	plumber
dietitian	photographer	electrician
Computers / Technology	*Arts / Entertainment*	*Engineering*
computer engineer	actor/actress	aerospace engineer
systems analyst	writer/playwright	chemical engineer
database manager	painter/artist	civil engineer
computer programmer	director	industrial engineer

C Collocations of words connected with *work*

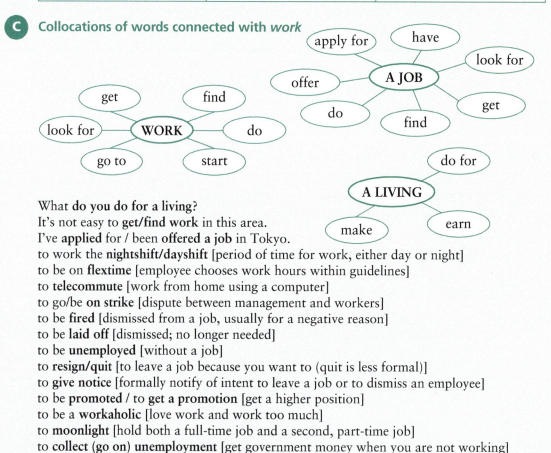

What **do you do for a living?**
It's not easy to **get/find work** in this area.
I've **applied for** / been **offered a job** in Tokyo.
to work the **nightshift/dayshift** [period of time for work, either day or night]
to be on **flextime** [employee chooses work hours within guidelines]
to **telecommute** [work from home using a computer]
to go/be **on strike** [dispute between management and workers]
to be **fired** [dismissed from a job, usually for a negative reason]
to be **laid off** [dismissed; no longer needed]
to be **unemployed** [without a job]
to **resign/quit** [to leave a job because you want to (quit is less formal)]
to **give notice** [formally notify of intent to leave a job or to dismiss an employee]
to be **promoted** / to **get a promotion** [get a higher position]
to be a **workaholic** [love work and work too much]
to **moonlight** [hold both a full-time job and a second, part-time job]
to **collect (go on) unemployment** [get government money when you are not working]

Unit 44

Exercises

44.1 Find job titles in A on page 88 that would best describe these people.

1. A person with a high position in a company and who makes important decisions
2. A person who represents the workers' interests in disputes with management.
3. A worker whose job requires no special training
4. A person who works in an office, bank, etc., as opposed to a factory
5. A person who keeps an eye on the day-to-day work of other workers
6. A person who keeps and checks financial records

44.2 Look at B on page 88 and think about which fields you would list these occupations in. Then think of at least one more occupation for each field.

1. bricklayer   *(field) Construction - (occupation) painter*
2. dental hygienist
3. electrical engineer
4. ballet dancer
5. TV news anchorperson
6. software developer

44.3 Using the expressions in C on page 88, make statements about what has happened or is happening.

1. Most employees work nine to five, but he comes in at ten and leaves at six.
   He's on flextime.
2. I lost my job. They had to make cutbacks.
3. I work from midnight until 8 a.m.
4. They've made her personnel manager as of next month!
5. I was late so often, I lost my job.
6. The working environment was so hostile that he left.
7. Your trouble is that you are obsessed with work!

44.4 Fill in the blanks with collocations from C on page 88.

> I'd love to .... (1) a job in journalism, but it's not easy without qualifications. Since I have to make a .... (2) somehow, I'll have to get .... (3) wherever I can find it. I've .... (4) for a full-time job doing data entry, but it doesn't pay very well. Even if the job is .... (5) to me, the salary may not be enough to pay the bills. I might just have to find a second job and .... (6).

44.5 Think of five people you know who work for a living. Name their jobs and the fields they are in, in English. Use a dictionary if necessary.

Unit 45 Sports

A Some interesting sports

scuba diving windsurfing horseback riding bowling

pool/billiards fencing auto racing cross-country skiing

B Sports equipment you hold in your hand

golf – **club**   squash/tennis/badminton – **racquet**   archery – **bow**
table tennis (Ping-Pong) – **paddle**   baseball – **bat**   fishing – **rod/line**
hockey – **stick**   pool/billiards – **cue**   canoeing – **paddle**   rowing – **oar**

C Some track and field events

discus javelin high jump long jump pole vault

She's a good **sprinter**. [fast over short distances]
He's a great **long-distance** (e.g., 5000 meters, marathon) runner.
Jogging around the park every Saturday is enough exercise for me.

D Verbs and their collocations in the context of sports

Our team **won/lost by** three **goals/points/runs**.
She **broke the** Olympic **record** last year. / She **set a** new Olympic **record**.
He **holds the record** for the 100-meter breaststroke.
Toronto **beat** New York 4–2 yesterday, and Los Angeles **lost to** Boston 6–0.
I'm planning to **take up** tennis.

E People who play particular sports

-er can be used for many sports, e.g., **swimmer, surfer, skater, golfer**.
Player is often necessary, e.g., tennis **player**, baseball player, pool player.
Some names must be learned separately, e.g., **cyclist, mountaineer, jockey, gymnast, archer**.

Unit 45

Exercises

45.1 Find the sports in A on page 90 that these people are probably talking about.

1. "The ball has a natural curve so it doesn't go down the lane in a straight line. You need to compensate for that when you are aiming."
2. "It's all a matter of balance, really."
3. "I like the noise, the speed, and the danger – there's nothing more exciting to watch."
4. "You need a good eye and a lot of concentration."
5. "At first you get sore and can hardly sit down, but that wears off."

45.2 Name a piece of equipment used in each sport below. Some are not on page 90. Use a dictionary if necessary.

1. golf: *club; ball*
2. Ping-Pong / table tennis:
3. billiards:
4. baseball:
5. basketball:
6. bowling:
7. horse racing:
8. squash:
9. soccer:
10. tennis:
11. swimming:
12. surfing:

45.3 What do you call a person who. . .

1. does the long jump?
2. rides horses in races?
3. drives cars in races?
4. throws the discus/javelin?
5. does gymnastics?
6. plays hockey?
7. runs long distance?
8. does the pole vault?

45.4 Fill in the blanks with appropriate verbs from D on page 90 to form collocations.

1. Were many records .... at the Olympics?
2. We've .... so often that we're at the bottom of the league!
3. Congratulations! How many points did you .... by?
4. Who .... the world record for the 1500-meter race?
5. You should .... jogging. You'd feel more energetic!

45.5 Name the sports that these places are associated with. Use a dictionary if necessary.

1. court: *tennis, squash, etc.*
2. course:
3. ring:
4. field:
5. rink:
6. alley:
7. slope:
8. track:

> **follow-up** Look at the sports page of a newspaper or a sports Web site (e.g., www.espn.com). Find sports not listed on page 90, and notice the language used to describe the sport. Use a dictionary if necessary.

Unit 46 The arts

A General branches of the arts

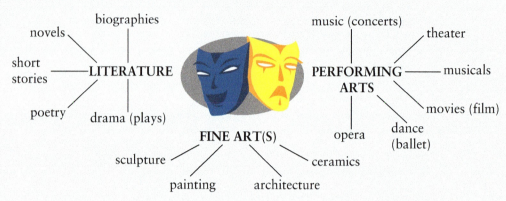

- **The arts** (plural) covers everything in the creative fields above. **Art** (singular / uncountable) usually means **fine art**, but it can also refer to technique and creativity.

  Have you read the **arts section** [covers all kinds of arts] in the paper today?
  She's a great **art lover**. [loves painting and sculpture]
  Shakespeare was skilled **in the art of** [creative ability] poetry.

- **Dance** refers to the art of dancing, especially **modern dance** or more traditional **ballet**.
  A novel is a long story; shorter works of fiction are usually called **short stories**.

- When we talk about a performing art in general, we can omit the definite article, e.g.,
  I love (the) opera / ballet / theater / movies. For a particular performance we say:
  Would you like to go to the opera / ballet / theater / movies tonight?

B Describing a performance

> We went to see a new **production**[1] of *Hamlet* last night. The **sets**[2] were incredibly realistic and the **costumes**[3] were wonderful. It was a good **cast**[4] and I thought the **direction**[5] was excellent. Anthony O'Donnell **gave** a **marvelous performance**[6]. It **got rave reviews**[7] in the papers today.

[1] the presentation of a work, especially a play or movie; [2] scenery, buildings, furniture on the stage or in a studio; [3] clothes the actors wear in the performance; [4] all the actors in the production;
[5] the way the director organizes the performance; [6] and [7] are typical collocations; [7] means "got very enthusiastic positive comments"

If there are very negative reviews or audiences stay away, then the play has **bombed**.

C Words connected with events in the arts

There's an **exhibit/exhibition** of paintings by Manet at the National Gallery.
They're going to **publish** a new **edition** of the **works** of Cervantes next year.
The Opera Society is doing a **performance** of *Don Giovanni*.
Scorsese's *The Departed* is **playing at** the Paradise Theater next week.

Unit 46

Exercises

46.1 Find the branch of the arts in A on page 92 that these people are talking about.

1. "It was a strong cast, but the play itself was weak." *theater*
2. "It's called *Peace*. It stands in the main square."
3. "It was so dull that I fell asleep during the second act."
4. "It was just pure movement, with very exciting rhythms."
5. "It doesn't have to rhyme to be good."
6. "Oils to me don't have the delicacy of watercolors."
7. "Her design for the new city hall won an award."
8. "I like to read them and imagine what they'd be like on stage."
9. "The first chapter was boring, but it got better later."
10. "The acting was marvelous, and I enjoyed seeing it on the big screen."

46.2 Correct the underlined word in each of these sentences. Use a dictionary if necessary.

1. The scene in this theater projects right out into the audience.
   not "scene" but "stage" [the place where the actors perform]
2. What's the name of the editorial of that book you recommended? Was it Cambridge University Press?
3. "Do I dare to eat a peach?" is my favorite stanza of poetry in English.
4. He's a very famous sculpture; he did that statue in the park, you know, the one with the soldiers.
5. Most of the novels in this collection are only five or six pages long. They're great for reading on short trips.
6. The cast wore beautiful sets in the new production of the play.

46.3 Write questions that match these answers.

1. It's an oil on canvas. *What kind of painting is it?*
2. Yes, it got rave reviews.
3. No, I'm not really a concertgoer, but thanks anyway.
4. Oh, some beautiful old buildings and some ugly new ones.
5. The cast was fine, but the direction was weak.
6. A new French film; would you like to see it?
7. It's OK, but I usually prefer modern dance.

46.4 Choose two or three of these categories of the arts. Make a list of your top five favorite items from each category you chose; for example, your five favorite novels or paintings.

ballets	music	plays
biographies	novels	poems
buildings	operas	sculptures
movies	paintings	short stories

Unit 47 Music

A Buying music

Many people now buy music online by **downloading MP3** files. Some people, however, prefer **CDs**.

album [a group of **songs/tracks** by an **artist** or group]
downloads [songs moved onto a **playlist** on
    a computer or **MP3 player**]
hit singles [best selling songs issued individually]

B Types of music

Music can be described in terms of the instrument(s) playing it: **piano** music, **guitar** music, **big band** music, **instrumental** music [music with instruments only and no **vocals** (voices, singing)], **electronic** music [played by a synthesizer], **orchestral** music.

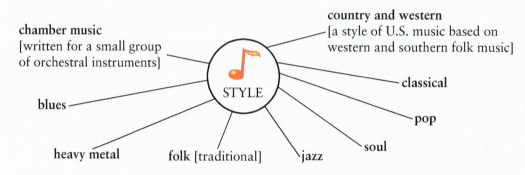

It's difficult to concentrate on my studies when there's **dance music** playing.
The **soundtrack** [music for a film] of that film is fantastic. I think it won an Oscar.
Music can be described in terms of its period or place of origin:
contemporary / 20th century / sixties / Irish / Indian music / baroque

C Other adjectives used to describe music

| deafening | innovative | loud | peaceful | relaxing | soft | sweet |
| discordant | live | modern | recorded | rousing | soothing | tuneless |

D Things you do with music

She **plays the piano** very well, but she doesn't **read music**. She's got **a good ear**.
She can **pick out** (informal) any tune on the piano. She doesn't have to **practice** much at all.
She's a **natural**. She can **play by ear**.
He's very **musical**. He **wrote an arrangement of / arranged** a Mozart symphony for the band.
You can **play a tune** on an instrument or you can **whistle** [make a sound by pushing air
    through your lips] or **hum** [sing with lips closed]. You can **make music** in lots of ways.
I can play some **chords** [several harmonizing notes played at the same time] on my guitar.

Unit 47

Exercises

47.1 Explain the difference between

1. a track and an album.
2. an MP3 and a CD.
3. a hit and a single.
4. orchestral music and chamber music.
5. country music and folk music.

47.2 Name the styles of music you think these people might be performing.

1.
2.
3.
4.

47.3 Divide the adjectives in C on page 94 into those that have positive associations and those that have negative associations.

47.4 Fill in the blanks with words from D on page 94.

1. I started to learn the piano when I was a kid, but I always made a fuss when I was told to .... every day. Eventually I gave up the piano.
2. If you don't know the words of the song just .... along as the others sing.
3. My brother is learning the guitar, and he can already play a few basic ....
4. He can't .... music at all, but he can play almost anything by ear.
5. This music was originally written for the violin, but it has been .... quite successfully for the guitar.
6. Paul can play anything. He's got a good ....
7. I always know when my sister is home because I can hear her ....

47.5 Answer these questions about music.

1. Can you remember the name of the first single you ever bought? Who was it by?
2. Which songs are currently big hits in your native country? In the country you now live in?
3. Which of the kinds of music listed in B on page 94 do you particularly enjoy?
4. Are there any other kinds of music that are not listed that you like? What are they?
5. Are there any kinds of music listed in B on page 94 that you dislike? Why do you dislike them?
6. Do you like to have background music while you are working? If so, what kind of background music do you like?

follow-up If possible, find an online music Web site or a CD sleeve that has English on it. Note any useful vocabulary that you see.

Unit 48 Food

A Types of food

vegetables	cauliflower broccoli spinach cucumber lettuce squash
fruit	apple orange grapefruit pear strawberry banana pineapple
grains	wheat corn rice barley oats rye millet
meat	beef veal lamb pork ham bacon turkey chicken venison
fish	cod sole flounder haddock salmon herring sardine trout tuna
seafood	shrimp crab lobster mussel squid clam oyster scallop
herbs	parsley rosemary thyme chive oregano tarragon sage basil

B Flavors, tastes, and quality – adjectives and some opposites (≠)

sweet ≠ **bitter** [sharp/unpleasant]   **sour** [acid taste]   **hot, spicy** (e.g., curry) ≠ **mild bland** [very little taste]   **salty** [a lot of salt]   **sugary** [a lot of sugar]
tasty, delicious [has a good taste/flavor] ≠ **tasteless** [has no flavor at all]
greasy/oily [too much oil/fat] ≠ **dry, dried out** [no moisture or juice]
lean [has little or no fat] ≠ **fatty** [has a lot of fat]

This meat is **overcooked / overdone / undercooked / underdone**.
Do you like your steak cooked **rare / medium-rare / medium / well-done**?

C Ways of cooking food – verbs

D Courses, dishes, servings – nouns

Unit 48

Exercises

48.1 To learn long lists of words, try dividing them up into groups. You could divide these vegetable names into groups in any way you like, e.g., *vegetables that grow underground* (potatoes, carrots, etc.). Some of these words are not on page 96.

leek	cucumber	spinach	carrot	potato	cauliflower	zucchini
asparagus	corn	lettuce	onion	rice	pea	cabbage
eggplant	radish	bean	shallot	turnip	beet	celery

48.2 Use words from B on page 96 to describe these food items.

1. Indian curry
2. seawater
3. an unripe apple
4. a cup of coffee with six spoonfuls of sugar
5. strong black coffee with no sugar
6. factory-made white bread

48.3 What might you say to the person/people with you in a restaurant if . . .

1. your french fries had too much oil/fat on them?
2. your steak had obviously been cooked too much / too long?
3. your stew had too much salt in it?
4. your dish seemed to have no flavor at all?
5. your roast beef sandwich was half fat?

48.4 Explain how you would prepare the following foods. Use words from C on page 96 and any other words you know. Then discuss items in the box that you like to put on your food.

chicken	eggs	potatoes	hamburger	filet of sole
shrimp	bacon	vegetables	coffee/tea	roast beef

salt	pepper	vinegar	mustard	gravy	ketchup	hot sauce
salad	dressing	oil	mayonnaise	lemon juice	salsa	

48.5 Food quiz

1. What do we call the *meat* of these animals?

   calf   deer   cow   pig (three names)

2. Which of these fruits normally grow in your country/region? Are there others not listed here?

peach	plum	grapefruit	grape	nectarine	fig	date
orange	cherry	raspberry	melon	lime	kiwi	mango

48.6 Name your favorite fruit, vegetable, main dish, side dish, and dessert. Do you like big portions or small ones? When you are a dinner guest at someone's home, do you ever ask for seconds? Do you take seconds if offered? Compare your answers with a classmate or friend, if possible.

Unit 49 The environment

A There are many different words referring to features of the environment. Here are some arranged on a scale of small to large.

spring → brook/creek → stream → river	mound/rise → hill → mountain
cove → bay → gulf → sea → ocean	grove → woods → forest
marsh/swamp → pond → lake	trail → path → road → highway

B You have to be careful about the use of **the** and features of the environment.

Features	Use with the?	Examples
cities, countries, continents	no	Paris, Peru, Asia
countries that are in a plural form	yes	the U.S., the Philippines
individual **mountains**	no	Mount Fuji
mountain ranges	yes	the Rockies
islands	no	Easter Island
groups of islands	yes	the West Indies
rivers	yes	the Yellow River
oceans, **seas**	yes	the Pacific, the Caspian
gulfs, **bays**, and **straits**	yes	the Persian Gulf
lakes	no	Lake Michigan
general areas by compass direction	yes	the north, the southwest

C Read this encyclopedia entry about Iceland and note the words in **bold**.

> **Iceland** - An **island** republic in the North Atlantic. The **landscape** consists largely of barren **plains** and **mountains**, with large **ice fields**, particularly in the southwest. The **island** has active **volcanoes** and is known for its thermal **springs** and **geysers**. With its extensive **coastline**, Iceland has an economy that is based on fishing, which accounts for 80% of all exports. Area: 103,000 km². Population: 317,000. Capital: Reykjavik.

D Here are some other nouns that are useful when talking about the environment.

Where land meets water: **coast   shoreline   beach   estuary   cliff   peninsula**
Words connected with rivers: **source   tributary   waterfall   mouth   gorge**
Words connected with mountains: **foot   ridge   peak   summit   glacier**

E Here are some words to describe environmental problems in the world today.

air pollution   water pollution   noise pollution   overpopulation   overfishing
acid rain   radiation   oil spills   sewage   emissions
destruction of the ozone layer   greenhouse gases / the greenhouse effect
toxic/hazardous waste   groundwater or soil contamination   global warming

Unit 49

Exercises

49.1 Choose the appropriate words from page 98 to match these pictures.

1.
2.
3.
4.
5.
6.
7.
8.

49.2 Insert *the* in the paragraph below wherever it is necessary.

> Brazil is fifth largest country in world. In north, densely forested basin of Amazon River covers half country. In east, country is washed by Atlantic. Highest mountain range in South America, Andes, does not lie in Brazil. Brazil's most famous city is Rio de Janeiro, former capital. Capital of Brazil is now Brasilia.

49.3 Complete this paragraph about your own country, or any other country that interests you. Remember to use *the* if necessary.

> .... (1) is a .... (2) in .... (3). The country's economy is based on .... (4). The best-known river is .... (5). The most famous mountain range is .... (6), and the highest mountain in that range is .... (7). .... (8) and .... (9) are major environmental problems in this country today.

49.4 Give two nouns from page 98 to go with the adjectives below. Try not to repeat any of the nouns you choose.

1. sandy *beach / shore*
2. turbulent
3. steep
4. dangerous
5. shallow
6. tall
7. rocky
8. long

49.5 Answer these questions about being environmentally friendly.

1. Why do environmentalists recommend that we avoid using spray cans?
2. Why is organic farming good for the environment?
3. What is the benefit of recycling paper, cans, and bottles?
4. What are other ways to protect the environment?

Unit 50 Towns

A Read this description of Santa Fe, one of the oldest towns in the Southwestern United States. Note the words or phrases that might be useful for describing your own or another town.

Santa Fe is the most unusual town in North America. It is the only significant community that has existed through the entire recorded history of the American West. For well over three centuries, Santa Fe has been the regional capital of a succession of nations. Today, it is the capital of the state of New Mexico, a peerless repository of Southwestern lore, and a wonderfully cosmopolitan showcase for all of the arts. An astonishing assortment of museums, theaters, studios, galleries, restaurants, and nightclubs displays the artistry of residents in adobe structures that reflect the timeless beauty of Santa Fe-style architecture. Today, Santa Fe is a perfectly scaled walking town centered around the splendid centuries-old Plaza. Churches, public buildings, and historic businesses offer a picturesque treasury of Pueblo and Spanish-colonial architecture through the ages.

The town is located at the edge of the vast Rio Grande basin amid gentle pine-covered foothills of the southernmost Rocky Mountains. Although it is one of the highest towns in the country, there is a pleasant four-season climate because of the southern location and sheltering peaks.
(Adapted from *The Great Towns of the West* by David Vokac.)

B **Facilities that you might find in a town**

Sports: **swimming pool   gym   health center   golf course   tennis courts   skating rink**
Culture: **theater   opera house   concert hall   art gallery   museum**
Education: **school   university   community college   library   continuing education**
Lodging: **hotel   motel   bed & breakfast   youth hostel**
Dining and nightlife: **restaurant   coffee shop   nightclub   bar**
Transportation: **subway   train station   bus station   taxi stand   car rental agency**
Religion: **church   synagogue   mosque   temple   cathedral**
Government: **courthouse   city/town hall   police station   fire station**
Commerce: **shopping mall   department store   supermarket   drugstore**
Health: **hospital   clinic   daycare center   senior center**

C **Typical problems in modern towns**

Homelessness [when people without homes live on the streets or in temporary shelters]
Overcrowding [when too many people live in a small area]
Pollution [when the air and/or water are dirtier than in the past]
Slums [certain parts of the city where conditions are bad and dangerous for residents]
Traffic jams [when there are too many cars, so traffic is very slow or even **comes to a standstill**]
Vandalism [when pointless destruction is done to other people's property]
Crime (see Unit 61)

Unit 50

Exercises

50.1 Check that you understand the text about Santa Fe by answering these questions.

1. Where is Santa Fe?
2. What are some of the attractions you can find in Santa Fe?
3. What building material is commonly used in Santa Fe-style architecture?
4. What is the central point of the town?
5. What famous river and mountain range touch Santa Fe?
6. What is the climate like?

50.2 The description of Santa Fe comes from a travel book. Write sentences about a town of your choice. If you wish, use these questions as a guide. Some of the words and phrases from A on page 100 may also help you.

- Why is the town special?
- Where is it located?
- What features can you find in the town and nearby?
- What historic features does the town have?
- How can sightseers get around?
- What is the natural environment like?
- How is the climate?

50.3 Fill in three words that would combine well with each of the nouns below, as in the examples. Not all of the words can be found on page 100. Use a dictionary if necessary.

1. ....
   .... museum
   ....

2. ..*sports*..............
   .... center
   ....

3. ....
   ..*higher*.. education
   ....

4. ....
   .... court
   ....

5. ....
   .... club
   ....

6. ....
   .... agency
   ....

50.4 What facilities would your ideal town have? Name the most important facilities for you in each of the categories listed in B on page 100. You may choose facilities other than those listed, if you wish.

50.5 For each of the problems mentioned in C on page 100, rate them as an issue where you live. 0 means *no problem*, and 4 means *a very serious problem*. If possible, suggest some solutions for the serious problems.

crime	0	1	2	3	4
homelessness	0	1	2	3	4
overcrowding	0	1	2	3	4
pollution	0	1	2	3	4
slums	0	1	2	3	4
traffic jams	0	1	2	3	4
vandalism	0	1	2	3	4

Unit 51   The natural world

A Animals

B Specific animals

Here are the English names of some more creatures.

C Flowers and trees

D Names of trees

E Useful language associated with the natural world

Types of plants: **grass   vegetable   bush/shrub   plant   tree**
Types of animals: **mammal   reptile   fish   bird   amphibian**

Our apple tree **flowers/blossoms** in spring. Let's **pick** some flowers (not pick up).
Farmers **plant, fertilize,** and **harvest** their crops.

Unit 51

Exercises

51.1 Answer these general knowledge questions about the natural world. Use reference material to help you if necessary.

1. Is the dolphin a fish or a mammal?
2. What do bees take from flowers to make honey?
3. Can you name three animals that hibernate in winter?
4. Which is the fastest of all land animals?
5. Which bird symbolizes peace?
6. What do fish use their gills for?
7. Can you name one endangered species of plant or animal?
8. What plant or animal is the symbol of the country you currently live in?

51.2 Match the adjectives on the left with the nouns on the right.

flowing	porcupine
graceful	mane
noble	petals
prickly	eagle
rough	oak
sweet-smelling	willow
sturdy	worm
wriggly	bark

51.3 Fill in the blanks with words from page 102.

1. A tree's .... go a long way underground.
2. A cat sharpens its .... against the .... of a tree.
3. The horse is limping. It must have hurt its ....
4. A flower that is just about to open is called a ....
5. If we pick up those .... we can use them to start the fire.
6. .... move very, very slowly.

51.4 Read this description of a camel from an encyclopedia. Underline any words or phrases that you think would be found frequently in descriptions of animals.

> **Camel** - A mammal of the family Camelidae (two species): the Bactrian, from cold deserts in Central Asia and domesticated elsewhere, and the dromedary, which has one hump, not two; eats any vegetation; drinks salt water if necessary; closes slit-like nostrils to exclude sand; humps are stores of energy-rich fats. The two species may interbreed: the offspring has one hump; the males are usually sterile while the females are fertile.

51.5 Write a similar encyclopedic description for an elephant, or another animal of your own choice. Use reference material to help you if necessary.

Unit 52 Clothes

A Clothing and parts of clothing

B Materials and fabrics

Natural: **silk cotton velvet corduroy denim leather wool suede**
Synthetic: **rayon nylon polyester acrylic**

> **note** These words can be nouns or adjectives.

C Patterns

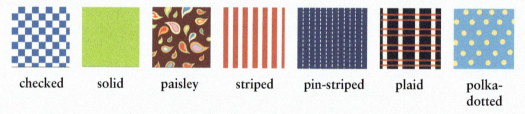

D Some verbs and phrases associated with clothing

He **undressed / got undressed**, throwing all his clothes on the floor.
I usually wear jeans, but I also like to **dress up / get dressed up** for parties.
Can I **try on** those red shoes in the window?
She **took off** her shoes and **put on** her slippers.
He **changed out** of his sports clothes and **into** his uniform.
That black bag **matches** your shoes.
Those shoes don't **fit** my son anymore. He's **grown out of** them.

E Some adjectives for describing people's clothing or appearance

Fit: **baggy loose tight**
Style: **short-sleeved / long-sleeved sleeveless V-neck turtleneck pleated
          double-breasted crew neck**
General: **casual elegant stylish trendy well dressed fashionable
          old-fashioned messy grungy** (informal) **sloppy**

104

Unit 52

Exercises

52.1 Fill in the blanks with words from A on page 104.

1. I need to get my black shoes repaired. One .... is broken and both the .... have holes in them.
2. Tie your .... or you'll trip!
3. Put your .... on; this floor is very cold.
4. I ate too much! I have to loosen my ....
5. I'm almost finished making my dress for the party, but I still have to sew up the .... and sew on some ....

52.2 Fill in the blanks with words from B on page 104. Use the correct form for any verbs you choose.

1. My blue dress .... me better now that I've lost some weight.
2. I .... ten pairs of shoes before I found a pair I liked.
3. As soon as I come home from work, I .... my work clothes and .... casual clothes.
4. The blue of his shirt .... the blue of his eyes.
5. I .... my shoes whenever I enter my house.

52.3 List the materials that these items of clothing might be made of.

1. a jacket: *denim, corduroy, leather*
2. a tie:
3. jeans:
4. socks:
5. gloves:
6. a shirt:
7. pajamas:
8. a jacket:

52.4 Describe the clothes these people are wearing, using words from page 104.

105

Unit 53 Health and medicine

A What are your symptoms?

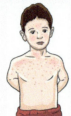   

rash   bruise   lump   a black eye

I have a **cold** / a **cough** / a **sore throat** / a **temperature** / a **fever** / a **stomachache** /
a **headache** / **chest pains** / an **earache** / a **pain** in my side / a **rash** on my chest /
a **bruise** on my leg / a **black eye** / a **lump** on my arm / **indigestion** / **diarrhea** / **insomnia** /
hives / **sunburn** / **food poisoning**.
I feel sick to my **stomach** / **nauseous** / **dizzy** / **out of breath** / **shivery** / **weak** / **stuffed
up** / **congested**.
I am **depressed** / **anxious** / **constipated** / **tense** / **hyper** (colloquial) / **tired** all the time.
I've lost my **appetite/voice**. I can't sleep, my nose **itches**, and my leg **hurts**.

B What's the diagnosis?

You have the **flu** / **pneumonia** / **bronchitis** / **rheumatism** / **arthritis** / **hepatitis** / an **ulcer** /
hypertension / **acne** / a **virus** / an **infection** / a **bug** / something that's going around.
You've **broken** your wrist and **sprained/dislocated** your ankle.
You're **pregnant** / a **hypochondriac**.
He died of lung **cancer** / a **heart attack** / a brain **hemorrhage** / a **stroke** / **AIDS**.

C What happens at the doctor's office?

First the **nurse** asks some questions and checks your **weight**. Then the nurse **takes your
temperature** and checks your **pulse** and **blood pressure**. You may have **blood tests** and an
X-ray. A **general practitioner** (**GP**) or a **family doctor** gives you a **physical** or checks for
any problems.

D What might the doctor say

Take one **pill/capsule/tablet** three times a day after meals.
Rub a little on before going to bed at night.
We'll contact the surgeon to schedule you for an **operation**.
You'll have to have your leg put in a **cast**.
You'll need some **shots** before your trip.
Rub this cream on and stay out of the sun.
Take this **prescription** to the **pharmacy** and get it filled. [receive the medicine]
You'll have to take an **antibiotic**, drink plenty of liquids, and get as much rest as possible.

E Health specialists in particular fields

allergist	dermatologist	internist	osteopath	psychiatrist
cardiologist	gastroenterologist	obstetrician	pediatrician	surgeon
chiropractor	gynecologist	ophthalmologist	podiatrist	urologist

106

Unit 53

Exercises

53.1 Find medical problems in A or B on page 106 that you might have or might get if you . . .

1. eat too fast.
2. smoke a lot.
3. play soccer or football.
4. go skiing.
5. stay out in the sun too long.
6. eat food you're allergic to.
7. run too fast to catch a bus.
8. get bitten by a mosquito.
9. eat food that has gone bad.
10. think you're sick all the time.

53.2 Match the diseases on the left with their symptoms on the right.

1. hepatitis
2. pneumonia
3. rheumatism
4. an ulcer
5. the flu

swollen, painful joints or muscles, extreme stiffness
burning pain in abdomen, pain or nausea after eating
headache, aching muscles, fever, cough, sneezing
dry cough, high fever, chest pain, rapid breathing
fever, weakened condition, yellow color of skin

53.3 State what a doctor or nurse uses these instruments for. Use a dictionary if necessary.

1. stethoscope: *to listen to a patient's chest*
2. needle:
3. tongue depressor:
4. thermometer:
5. scale:

53.4 Find the statements in D on page 106 that a doctor might say if you . . .

1. have a bad sunburn.
2. have a broken leg.
3. are about to travel to a tropical country.
4. have a bad cough.
5. need your appendix to be removed.
6. have a rash.

53.5 Name the specialist that a person would go to for the treatment of . . .

1. a skin rash that won't go away. *a dermatologist*
2. a heart condition.
3. chronic depression.
4. constant sneezing in spring or summer.
5. a pregnancy.
6. frequent back pain.
7. a painful ingrown toenail.
8. blurry vision.

follow-up Look in the health section of a magazine or newspaper or check health Web sites for other useful health vocabulary words. Add these words to your vocabulary notebook.

Unit 54

Transportation

A Types of transportation

Transportation type	Kinds of vehicle	Parts of vehicle	People working with it	Associated facilities
road	car, bus, taxi, truck, van, recreational vehicle (RV)	trunk, engine, transmission, tires, brakes, horn, hood	driver, motorist, chauffeur, mechanic	gas station, service station, garage, bus terminal
rail	commuter train, freight train, local train, express	passenger car, dining car, sleeping car, freight car	engineer, conductor, porter, ticket agent	train station, waiting room, signal, railroad crossing
water	rowboat, ferry, cruise ship, yacht, barge, containership	deck, bridge, mast, porthole, anchor, gangplank	captain, skipper, purser, first officer	dock, wharf, landing, port, lighthouse, shipyard
air	airplane, helicopter, (jumbo) jet, supersonic aircraft	cockpit, nose, tail, wings, fuselage, overhead bins, emergency exit	pilot, flight attendant, ground crew, air-traffic controller	departure lounge, duty-free shop, airport security checkpoint, runway

B Words at sea

Traditionally sailors use different words at sea: a bedroom is a **cabin**, a bed is a **bunk**, the kitchen is a **galley**, right is **starboard**, and left is **port**. The person in charge is the **captain**, and the group of people who work on the ship is called the **crew**. Many of these terms are now used in the context of an aircraft. Sailors also refer to their vessels as *she* rather than *it*.

C Some words and expressions associated with travel

Last week she **flew** to Montreal. She was **booked** on an evening flight.
The plane was scheduled to **take off** at 6 p.m. and **land** at 7 p.m. local time. The plane was **delayed** by fog, and she was **stranded** at the airport overnight.
Trains usually run **on time** here. You have to **change** trains in Philadelphia.
Our car gets 35 **miles per gallon** (mpg). It has good **pickup** and **handles** well.
A **trip** is a short **journey**. **Travel** is a general uncountable word. **Voyage** is a long **journey**, usually on board a ship.

Unit 54

Exercises

54.1 Label the pictures below with the words in the box. Use a dictionary if necessary.

deck	engine	gangplank	hood	mast	nose	porthole
steering wheel	tail	tire	trunk	wharf	wing	

54.2 Determine where these words would fit into the table in A on page 108.

fender	balloon	deck chair	metal detector
sail	gas pump	bus driver	tollbooth
glider	oar	rudder	baggage claim
check-in counter	rearview mirror	canoe	freeway

54.3 Fill in the blanks with words from page 108 or from 54.2.

Yesterday John was supposed to take a .... (1) from Washington, D.C., to New York City. He got up very early, put his luggage in the .... (2) of his car, and tried to start the engine. It wouldn't start. John lifted the .... (3), but he couldn't find anything wrong. He immediately called his local .... (4) to ask them to send a .... (5). Fortunately, the garage had someone available, and he got to John's car within 10 minutes. He quickly saw what the matter was. "You're .... (6) of gas," he said. John felt very foolish. Despite all this, he got to the airport, checked in early, and went through .... (7) and then straight to the .... (8) to read a newspaper while he waited. Soon he heard an announcement: "All flights to and from New York are .... (9) because of the weather." "If only I had decided to take the .... (10)," John thought. "It would probably have been faster, and it could have been quite pleasant having lunch in the .... (11) car, watching the scenery go by."

54.4 Write two advantages and disadvantages for each general form of travel in A on page 108.

Unit 55 Vacations

A Different places where you can spend a vacation

resort [a hotel (usually large and expensive), with leisure facilities such as tennis courts, a golf course, health spa, swimming pools, beach, etc.]
motel [a hotel for motorists, with parking spaces directly outside the rooms]
bed & breakfast (B&B) [a small hotel, inn, or private home, providing a room and breakfast the next morning for one price]
campground [an outdoor area where you can pitch a tent or park a van or an RV]
summer camp [a summer recreation area in the country, usually for children]
youth hostel [cheap lodging, mainly for young people, who share facilities (there are also **elder hostels** for traveling senior citizens)]
time-share [a house or an apartment, usually in a resort area, owned by many people and used by each owner for a specified time period (e.g., 1–2 weeks a year for vacations)]

B Activities that people like to do on vacation

sunbathe *or*
go to the beach

swim *or*
go swimming

do some
sightseeing *or*
go sightseeing

hike *or* go hiking

cycle *or* go cycling

go to an
amusement park

go shopping

camp *or* go
camping

C Useful language when you are on vacation

I'd like to **book** a **single/double room** with **two beds** / **twin beds** / a **queen-size bed** / a **king-size bed**.
Do you have a **nonsmoking room** with an **ocean view** / a **river view** available?
I'd like to guarantee my **reservation** with a credit card.
I'd like a **wake-up call** at 7 a.m., please.
We'd like **room service**, please.
What time is **check-in/checkout**? Is late checkout available?

D Common adjectives used for describing vacations

breathtaking scenery/views
exhilarating feeling/ride/moment
exotic beauty/location
glamorous surroundings/hotel

intoxicating views/air
picturesque streets/village
unspoiled charm/nature
sublime simplicity/beauty

Unit 55

Exercises

55.1 Which of the vacation places in A on page 110 have you or any of your friends stayed at? Think of at least one advantage and one disadvantage for each place, even if you have no experience staying there.

55.2 Put the eight activities shown in B on page 110 in order, based on your personal preferences. Are there any you would definitely never do? Can you think of others you would prefer to do during your vacation?

55.3 What would you say in a hotel when . . .

1. you want to reserve a room for a couple?
2. you want to reserve a room for yourself?
3. you don't like cigarette or cigar smoke?
4. you have to wake up at 6 a.m. for an important meeting?
5. you want to find out what time you must leave the room in the morning?
6. you'd rather not go to the restaurant for dinner?

55.4 Name a place that you are familiar with that fits each of these descriptions. Make a sentence for each one.

1. picturesque: *I love the picturesque villages along the Amalfi Coast in Italy.*
2. breathtaking:
3. exhilarating:
4. exotic:
5. intoxicating:
6. glamorous:
7. unspoiled:
8. sublime:

55.5 Find seven typical language mistakes in the paragraph below and fix them.

> The Smiths stayed at a camping last summer. Every day Mrs. Smith had a sunbath, and Mr. Smith made a sightseeing. The children had a cycle, and they made a travel around the island. One day the family made an excursion to a local castle. The castle had a gift shop, so they could shopping.

---

follow-up | To find useful language about vacations, get some brochures or other tourist information in English. You could try the embassies or tourist offices of English-speaking countries, or a travel agency. When you receive the information, note down any useful new words and expressions that you find.

Unit 56: Numbers and shapes

A How to say numbers in English

28%	twenty-eight percent	5'8"	five feet, eight inches (or five-foot-eight, common when describing height)
10.36 m	ten point three six meters (not point thirty-six meters)	0.702	point seven oh two or zero point seven oh two
$4/9$	four-ninths	4 ft. x 6 ft.	four feet by six feet (measuring dimensions)
4^2	four squared	$\sqrt{16}$	the square root of 16
$9/13$	nine-thirteenths or nine over thirteen	$1\ 2/3$	one and two-thirds
8^4	eight to the fourth power	7^3	seven cubed

even numbers: 2, 4, 6, . . . ; **odd numbers:** 1, 3, 5, . . . ; **prime numbers:** 1, 2, 3, 5, 7, 11 (can be divided only by 1 and itself to get a whole number)
0°C *or* 32°F   zero degrees centigrade/Celsius *or* thirty-two degrees Fahrenheit
1,623,401   one million, six hundred (and) twenty-three thousand, four hundred and one

B Two-dimensional shapes

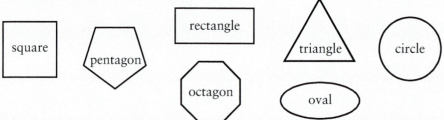

A **rectangle** has four **right angles**.
A **circle** is cut in half by its **diameter**. Its two halves can be called **semicircles**.
The **radius** of a circle is the distance from its center to the **circumference**.

C Three-dimensional shapes

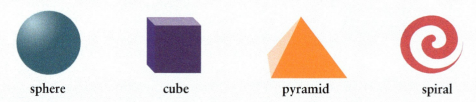

D Four basic processes of arithmetic

+ addition   – subtraction   x multiplication   ÷ division

6 x 7 = 42   Six times seven is forty-two. *Or* Six times seven equals forty-two.

$2x \times 3y - z = \dfrac{3z}{4x}$ Two *x* times three *y* minus *z* equals three *z* divided by four *x* (*or* three *z* over four *x*).

Unit 56

Exercises

56.1 Numbers quiz. Say the answers aloud.

1. What are the first four odd numbers?
2. What are the first four even numbers?
3. How much is 4^3?
4. Give an example of a decimal fraction.
5. How do you read this formula and what does it represent? $E = mc^2$
6. How do you read this formula and what does it represent? $2\pi r$

56.2 Write these symbols in words rather than in figures.

1. 79% of American women diet each year, yet 95% of those diets fail.
2. 0°C = 32°F.
3. About 15% of children under age 10 are left-handed.
4. ⅔ + ¼ × 4^2 = 14⅔ .
5. 2,769,425 people live in my city.
6. The inflation rate was 3.5% last year and 0.4% last month.

56.3 Write the adjective relating to each shape. Use a dictionary if necessary. Then notice what is different about the adjectives in the third column.

triangle: *triangular*	sphere:	square:
rectangle:	circle:	oval:
cube:	octagon:	spiral:

56.4 Read the following records aloud.

1. Oxygen makes up 46.6% of the earth's crust.
2. The highest waterfall in the world is Angel Falls, Venezuela, with a drop of 979 meters.
3. The top coffee-drinking country in the world is Finland, where 1,892 cups are consumed per person each year.
4. The longest known strike lasted 33 years. It was a strike of barbers' assistants in Copenhagen, Denmark, and it ended in 1961.
5. The smallest country in the world is Vatican City, with an area of 0.4 square kilometers.

56.5 Draw these shapes.

1. Draw a right-angled triangle with two equal sides of about 1 inch in length. Draw a small circle in the center of the triangle, and then draw lines from the circumference of the circle to each of the angles of the triangle.
2. Draw a rectangle with diagonal lines joining opposite angles.
3. Draw an octagon with equal sides. Draw an oval in the middle of the octagon.
4. Draw a cube with the dimensions of 2 by 2 by 2 centimeters.

Unit 57: Science and technology

A New fields in science

You are probably familiar with traditional branches of science, e.g., biology, botany, chemistry, physics, and zoology. Here are some newer fields.

bioclimatology [the study of how climate affects living things]
cryogenics [the study of physical systems at extremely low temperatures]
cybernetics [the study of the way information is moved and controlled by the brain or by machinery]
ergonomics [the study of the design of physical working spaces and how people interact with them]
genetic engineering [changing the genetic material (DNA) of living things]
geopolitics [the study of how geographical factors influence the politics of nations]
molecular biology [the study of organic molecules]
nanotechnology [the science of changing materials around the size of atoms and molecules]
voice technology [technology that allows machines to interpret speech]

B Fairly recent inventions that we are becoming used to

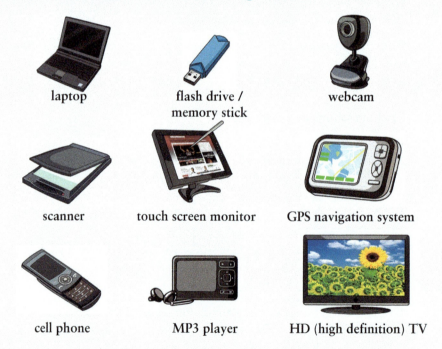

laptop   flash drive /   webcam
           memory stick

scanner   touch screen monitor   GPS navigation system

cell phone   MP3 player   HD (high definition) TV

C Useful verbs associated with science

He **experimented** with many different materials before **identifying** the right one.
The marine biologist **dissected** the animal.
When they were **combined**, the two chemicals **reacted** violently with each other.
After **analyzing** the problem, the physicist **concluded** that there was a flaw in her initial hypothesis.
James Watt **invented** the steam engine; Alexander Fleming **discovered** penicillin.
You should **patent** your invention as quickly as possible.

Unit 57

Exercises

57.1 Fill in the blanks with the type of scientist in each field. Use a dictionary if necessary.

Science	Scientist
chemistry	chemist
computer programming	....
genetic engineering	....
molecular biology	....
physics	....
zoology	....

57.2 Match the items on the left with their definitions on the right.

1. cell phone
2. MP3 player
3. scanner
4. HD (high definition) TV
5. laptop
6. memory stick
7. webcam
8. touch screen monitor

a television that has sharp images and high quality sound
a screen that responds when you touch it
a small machine that plays high quality sound from a digital file
a small camera that records moving pictures and sound onto the Internet
a phone that is small and mobile
a machine that makes electronic copies of documents and photographs
a small device that holds a large amount of information to transfer between computers
a computer that is portable

57.3 Write the noun forms for these verbs.

1. analyze: *analysis*
2. combine:
3. conclude:
4. discover:
5. dissect:
6. experiment:
7. invent:
8. patent:

57.4 Give each scientific field listed in A on page 114 a number from 0 to 5, based on your interest in the field (0 = no interest; 5 = high interest). What other fields do you feel will become important in the future and why?

> *follow-up* Increase your knowledge of scientific vocabulary by reading articles of general scientific interest in English language newspapers or magazines. If possible, find a textbook in English for schoolchildren studying a branch of science that you have studied.

Unit 58 Computers and the Internet

 Personal computers

Review Unit 57, part B, which has an illustration of a computer. Here are some other words associated with computers.

personal computer / PC / desktop computer [a computer that fits on a desk]
laptop (computer) [a lightweight portable computer that usually fits in a briefcase]
computer hardware [computer equipment or machinery]
computer software [programs that you put into a computer to make it run]
flash drive / memory stick [a portable device to store data, making it easy to move or **back up** the data]
hard drive [a device inside or outside a computer that stores large amounts of information]
CD/DVD drive [an apparatus that stores and reads information from a CD or DVD]
memory stick [a small device that holds data, often used in digital cameras]
modem [equipment that sends information between computers via telephone lines]
to download/upload [to transfer data or software between a Web site and a computer or between computers]
RAM / random access memory / memory [the memory available on a computer to store and use information temporarily, usually measured in **megabytes/gigabytes**]
spreadsheet (program) [a program or the grid you create with it to perform mathematical operations]
computer graphics [pictures, images, and symbols that you can form on a computer]
word processing [a program for writing and storing printed text on a computer]
computer virus [hidden instructions in a program designed to damage information]

 The Internet

The **Internet / "the Net"** is a network connecting millions of computer users worldwide who surf/cruise the **World Wide Web / "the Web"** [a huge portion of the Internet containing linked documents, called **pages**]. You can **access** information on the Internet by using an Internet **browser** and send and receive **e-mail** through either **wireless** (**Wi-Fi**) or **wired connectivity**.

A **Web site** is the Internet location of a group of related **Web pages**, including a **home page**.

FAQs (frequently asked questions) is a list of common questions and answers about a topic.

Chat rooms, **IM** (**instant messaging**), and **blogs** are all different ways to communicate using the Internet. You usually need to **log in** with your **username** and **password**. People interact through **social networking sites** and often have **virtual** friendships and activities.

Webcams allow you to share video across the Internet.

Search engines are online tools to seek information online. You can **google** a term to get **links** (**hotlinks/hyperlinks**) to information about it. You can **bookmark** any Web page **address** so you can return to it easily.

(See Unit 16 on abbreviations, Unit 17 on new words, and Unit 57 on technology.)

Unit 58

Exercises

58.1 Match the words in the box with the pictures below.

| flash drive | webcam | laptop | spreadsheet | desktop computer |

58.2 Fill in the blanks with appropriate words from page 116.

1. Using a .... , I just .... the term "English vocabulary" and got over 3 million results.
2. My computer is so slow lately; I wonder if it has a ....
3. Using a .... has been an effective but inexpensive way to videoconference.
4. I'm always amazed by people who carry their .... on airplanes and work on them during the flight.
5. This city is incredible! Downtown is a complete .... zone, and it's free!
6. Always be careful about .... files from the Internet.
7. I spend most of my day trying to sort through my .... Most of it is spam.
8. Don't forget to .... your data periodically.

58.3 Fill in the blanks of this text with words from the box. Use a dictionary if necessary.

| down | clicked | attachment | crashed | scanned |

The other day I .... (1) some old photos, so I could send them electronically to a friend in New Zealand. However, as I was finishing the last one, I .... (2) the mouse and suddenly the program .... (3). It was so annoying! Then, when I finally got it running again, I tried to send the photos by e-mail, as an .... (4), but the server was .... (5), and so I just gave up. I was so frustrated!

58.4 Match each verb on the left with the best phrase on the right.

1. check — the Internet
2. log in to — your hard drive
3. click on — your e-mail
4. surf — a hyperlink
5. back up — a social networking site

Unit 59: The media and the press

The term **media** (or **mass media**) usually refers to TV, radio, newspapers, and magazines – all means of communication that reach the public.

A. Radio and television

- **Types of TV programs:** documentaries   news and weather   reality shows   detective shows and mysteries   situation comedies (sitcoms)   movies   talk shows   sports   soap operas   nature shows   game shows   variety shows   dramas   commercials

- **Types of TV broadcasting:** network/commercial TV   public TV   pay-per-view   cable TV   Internet TV   satellite TV

- **Types of radio broadcasting:** AM and FM are the most common frequency bands.

- **Types of personal media equipment:**

Flat screen TV set   digital video recorder (DVR)

antenna   remote control   cable box   satellite dish

B. Newspapers and publishing

- **Parts of a newspaper:** headlines   front page   reports   editorials   sports   feature articles (e.g., fashion or social trends)   horoscopes   classified ads   cartoons/comics   crossword puzzles   letters to the editor   advice

- The **Sunday edition** of many newspapers contains additional **sections** and **supplements**, e.g., a weekly magazine, a book review section, a travel section. **Tabloid newspapers / tabloids** focus more on sensation and gossip than serious news; they have large headlines, and stories are frequently about celebrities, crimes, and UFO sightings. A **journal** is usually an academic magazine. A **comic book** is a magazine with cartoon stories, often (though not always) for children or teenagers.

C. Useful verbs associated with the media

That book was **published** by Cambridge University Press, but it was **printed** in Singapore.
The article/program was poorly **edited**.
The **documentary** was **shot/made** on location in Spain.
They government **censored** the film before showing it on TV.

(See Unit 95 for the language of newspaper headlines.)

Unit 59

Exercises

59.1 Name the type of TV program in A on page 118 that you think these might be.

1. Murder on Her Mind
2. The Amazing Underwater World
3. Baseball This Week
4. The $10,000 Question
5. Last Week in Washington
6. Late Night Talk with Joan Waters

59.2 Give the name of one TV program you know for each type listed in A on page 118. It can be in English or in your native language.

59.3 Match the media job on the left with its definition on the right.

1. A news anchor — runs the camera for a film or TV show.
2. A narrator — reads the news on television.
3. A game show host — sends news or commentary from abroad.
4. A camera operator — writes a regular feature for a newspaper or magazine.
5. A foreign correspondent — writes or broadcasts reviews of books, movies, music, etc.
6. A copy editor — tells a story while actors perform the story.
7. A columnist — hosts a show with contestants.
8. A critic — edits writing (or copy) for the media or the press.

59.4 Fill in the blanks with words from page 118.

1. He never even gets up from the sofa to change channels; he just presses the buttons on the ....
2. Although our .... was expensive, it lets us watch TV programs whenever we want to.
3. That movie on TV was .... so heavily, it didn't make sense!
4. I can't stand reading .... There's no real news, just gossip.
5. You won't find classical music on .... radio; try FM instead.
6. We subscribe to an excellent .... about gardening. It comes out once a month.
7. My favorite .... of the Sunday newspaper is sports. You can find all the scores there.
8. Do you prefer cable or .... TV? They are both expensive, but cable seems more reliable in my neighborhood.

59.5 Choose any newspaper and complete these sentences.

1. The main story on the front page is about ....
2. One editorial is about ....
3. The most interesting feature article is about ....
4. There is an advice column on page ...., a crossword puzzle on page ...., a cartoon on page ...., horoscopes on page ...., and classified ads starting on page ....

Unit 60 Politics and public institutions

A Types of government

democracy [a government elected by the people of the country]
dictatorship [a government run by one person with complete power (a dictator)]
federation [a union of political units (e.g., states) under a central government]
independence [freedom from outside control; self-governing]
monarchy [a country ruled by a king or queen (sometimes in name only)]
republic [a state governed by representatives and usually a president]

B Presidential government and parliamentary government

- A **presidential government** consists of three separate **branches** of power. There are a series of **checks and balances** that keep any one branch from becoming too powerful. The United States is an example of a presidential government. The main political parties in the U.S. are the **Republican** and **Democratic** parties. One of these parties usually has the **majority** in the two houses of Congress.

  The **Executive** Branch: The **president** and **vice president** are elected for a term of four years, and the president **appoints** officials to the executive branch, including cabinet members (who advise the president), the directors of the FBI and the CIA, Supreme Court justices, and federal **judges**.

  The **Legislative** Branch: **Congress** consists of two **houses**, the **House of Representatives** and the **Senate**. **Members of Congress** are elected for two-year terms, and **senators** are elected for six-year terms.

  The **Judicial** Branch: The **judiciary** consists of judges and courts. The **Supreme Court**, the highest court, can **limit the power of** the president and Congress. The nine **justices** on the Supreme Court are **nominated** by the president, **confirmed** by Congress, and **serve** lifetime terms.

- A **parliamentary government** consists of a **legislature** (**Parliament**) and a **Cabinet**, chosen from the majority party in Parliament. The United Kingdom is an example of a parliamentary government. The **prime minister** is the head of government and the leader of the **majority party** in the **House of Commons**, holding office while the party holds a **majority**. The prime minister selects high officials and heads the Cabinet. Parliament consists of two **chambers**, the **House of Lords** and the **House of Commons**. MPs are **members of parliament** elected to the House of Commons. The **judiciary** is independent, but it cannot overrule the prime minister or Parliament. The **Highest Court** consists of a group of Lords.

C Elections

campaign [the process of **running for office** (seeking to win an election)]
candidate [someone who **runs** (for office) in an election]
elect [choose someone or something by voting]
vote [choose in a formal way, e.g., by marking/casting a ballot in an election]

Unit 60

Exercises

60.1 Complete these sentences with the best word in parentheses.

1. India gained .... from the U.K. in 1948. (dictatorship / independence / democracy)
2. The president recently .... a Supreme Court justice. (elected / appointed / overruled)
3. She's .... for the Senate in the next election. (running / serving / nominating)
4. He was .... to Parliament last year. (voted / confirmed / elected)
5. The U.S. is a .... of 50 states. (monarchy / federation / referendum)

60.2 Fill in the blanks in this text about government in the U.S.

> The federal government in the U.S. is made up of three .... (1): the legislature, the .... (2), and the executive branch. The two main political parties are the Democrats and the .... (3). The legislature, or Congress, has two .... (4): the Senate and the House of Representatives. A presidential .... (5) takes place every four years, after a long, expensive .... (6) by the candidates. The president is not always a member of the .... (7) party in the Senate or the House. Supreme Court justices and other federal .... (8) are appointed by the president, and they may serve for life.

60.3 Complete this table.

Abstract noun	Person noun	Verb	Adjective
dictatorship	*dictator*	*dictate*	*dictatorial*
election			
politics			
presidency			
representation			

60.4 Political quiz

1. Name three monarchies.
2. Name two countries with a presidential system and two with a parliamentary system (not including the U.S. and the U.K.).
3. Name the country that has the oldest parliament in the world.
4. Name the current president of the U.S., the prime minister of the U.K., and the prime minister of Canada.
5. Name the people who represent you in local and national government.
6. Name the main political parties in the country where you are currently living.

> **follow-up** Write a paragraph about the political system in one specific country, using as much of the vocabulary on page 120 as possible.

(See Unit 63 for words dealing with types of political belief.)

Unit 61 Crime

A Common crimes

Crime	Definition	Criminal	Verb
arson	setting fire to something in a criminal way	arsonist	set fire to
burglary	breaking into a place to steal	burglar	burgle
identity theft	taking someone's personal information in order to steal from them	identify thief	steal someone's identity
kidnapping	taking a person hostage and demanding money in exchange for their freedom	kidnapper	kidnap
murder/homicide	killing someone on purpose	murderer	murder
robbery	stealing with (the threat of) violence	robber	rob
shoplifting	stealing something from a store	shoplifter	shoplift
smuggling	taking something illegally from one country to another	smuggler	smuggle

note The verbs **steal** and **rob** are different. An object is stolen (e.g., *They stole my bike*), whereas a person or place is robbed (e.g., *I was robbed last night*).

B Words associated with crime and law

Jason **committed** a crime when he robbed a bank. Several people **witnessed** the crime and notified the police. The police **charged** Jason with bank robbery. They also **accused** his wife of being an **accomplice**.

The **case went to court** and they were **tried**.
They both **pleaded not guilty** of the **charges**. Their lawyer did her best to **defend** them, but the **prosecutor presented** an **airtight case** against them.

After brief **deliberations**, the **jury delivered** their **verdict**: they **found** Jason **guilty**, but his wife was **acquitted**. The **judge sentenced** Jason to three years in prison, and he also paid a hefty **fine**. He **served** 18 months in prison but then got **time off** for good behavior and was released early. Now an **ex-convict**, Jason sees a **parole officer** every month, and he has **sworn off** crime forever.

Note: Many verbs above include specific prepositions.

C Useful nouns associated with criminal courts and the law

evidence [information presented during a trial]
felony [a very serious crime, such as murder or robbery]
misdemeanor [a crime that is less serious than a felony, such as vandalism]
proof [evidence that everyone agrees shows something to be true]
testimony [statements made by a witness under oath during a trial]
trial [a formal examination in a court of law to decide whether an accused person is guilty or not guilty]

Unit 61

Exercises

61.1 Fill in the blanks with the correct form of either *rob* or *steal*.

1. Last night a gang .... the post office. They .... $2,000.
2. My handbag .... at the theater yesterday. Four people have been .... around that area in the past two months.

61.2 Match the words and phrases on the left with the words and phrases on the right.

1. commit — a sentence of 15 months
2. accuse someone — with a crime
3. charge someone — found him guilty
4. serve — a crime
5. try — a verdict
6. find someone — for good behavior
7. time off — guilty
8. the case — a case
9. the jury — of a crime
10. deliver — went to court

61.3 Fill in the blanks in this text with verbs from page 122.

> One of the two accused men was .... (1) at yesterday's trial. Although his lawyer .... (2) him well, he was still found guilty by the jury. Because the crime was a serious .... (3), the judge .... (4) him to ten years in prison. He'll probably .... (5) less than five years of the sentence. His alleged accomplice was luckier. He was .... (6) and left the courtroom smiling.

61.4 Divide these words, connected with *law* and *crime*, into three groups: *people connected with the law*, *crimes*, and *punishments*. Use a dictionary if necessary.

prosecutor	member of a jury	parole officer	probation
prison	fine	shoplifting	homicide
detective	burglary	lethal injection	witness
smuggling	death penalty	arson	kidnapping

61.5 Write a paragraph to fit each of these newspaper headlines. Give some details about the crime and the court case, using as many words from this unit as possible.

> **Local girl's testimony gets mugger five-year sentence**

> *Singer acquitted! No evidence linking her to murder!*

123

Unit 62: Money and finances

A Banking and making purchases

When you buy something in a store, you may be asked: *How will you be paying*? You can answer: *Cash* or *In cash* / *Check* or *By Check* / *With a credit card*. When you need money from your **bank account**, you can go to an **ATM (Automated Teller Machine)** and use your **debit card, ATM card,** or **credit card** to take money out of the machine.

In a **bank** you usually have a **checking account**. You deposit money or **make deposits** [put money in] and **withdraw** money or **make withdrawals** [take money out]. You **write checks** to **pay bills**. You may also have a **savings account**, which usually pays you **interest** [money the bank pays you for keeping your savings there]. The bank sends a regular **bank statement** showing the activity in your account. If you take out more money from an account than you have in it (usually by writing checks), your account is **overdrawn**, a situation to be avoided! If you write a check but your account has **insufficient funds** to cover it, the check may **bounce** (colloquial use); that is, the bank refuses to make the payment. You can use **online banking** to access your account, **check your balance, transfer funds,** and pay bills.

If you need to **borrow** money, sometimes the bank may **lend** it to you – this is called a **bank loan**. If a bank (or a savings and loan association) lends you money to buy a home, it is called a **mortgage**. You can also take out a **car loan (auto loan)** if you want to buy a car, a **home equity loan** if you want to borrow money based on the value of your home, or a **student loan** to help pay for education. You pay back the amount of the loan – the **principal** – with **interest**.

When you use a **credit card** to make purchases, you receive a **monthly statement** from the credit card company. The **billing date** is the date the statement was prepared, the **balance** is the amount you owe, and the **due date** is the date by which you must pay. However, you can pay a part of the balance and owe the rest, but you'll incur a **finance charge**.

Money that you pay for services (e.g., to a lawyer) is usually called a **fee** or **fees**. Money paid for student courses (e.g., at a university) is called **tuition**; other costs paid by students are called **fees** (e.g., registration/laboratory fee). Money paid for a trip is a **fare** (airfare, train fare, bus fare).

B Taxes and currency

National and local governments collect money from residents through **taxes**. **Income tax** is collected on **wages** and **salaries**. **Inheritance tax** is collected on what people inherit from others upon death. **Sales tax** is a percentage of the price of goods and services, added to the total price. **Property tax** is paid based on the value of property a person owns, such as buildings, land, and vehicles.

Every country has its own **currency**. The **exchange rates** are published daily, and you can check, for example, how many Japanese yen there are currently to the U.S. dollar.

Unit 62

Exercises

62.1 Match the words on the left with their definitions on the right.

1. interest
2. mortgage
3. an overdrawn account
4. savings account
5. checking account
6. tuition
7. sales tax
8. insufficient funds
9. student loan
10. online banking

a checking account for day-to-day use
money chargeable on a loan or paid to savers
tax paid at the time of a purchase
money paid for education
a bank account with a negative balance
the reason a check bounces
a loan to purchase a home or property
using the Internet to access your accounts
an account that is used mainly for keeping money
money you borrow to pay for education

62.2 Complete these sentences with words from page 124.

1. Money that has to be paid on what you inherit is known as ....
2. When you get a bank loan, the bank .... you money.
3. How much is the .... between Vancouver and Seoul?
4. If you can't pay the entire .... on your credit card each month, you have to pay a ....
5. If you write checks for more than the amount in your checking account, your account will be .... and the checks will ....
6. Instead of going to the bank, you can use your computer to do .... It is a convenient way to .... funds between accounts.

62.3 Put a check (✓) next to the headlines that an ordinary "person on the street" might be happy to see.

62.4 Money quiz. Use reference material if necessary.

1. What kind of bank accounts pay interest? Find two banks and determine which bank pays higher interest rates.
2. What credit cards can be used worldwide? When would you use a credit card?
3. What is the process you follow to withdraw money from your account?
4. What is the exchange rate between your country's currency and the U.S. dollar? Between the U.S. dollar and the euro?
5. What are the coins and bills used in the currency of your country and one other country?

125

Unit 63

Belief and opinion

A Verbs associated with beliefs and opinions

You probably already know the verbs **think** and **believe**. Here are more verbs connected with beliefs and opinions.

I'm **convinced** [very strong feeling that you're right] we've met before.
She **maintains** [insist on believing, often against the evidence] that we're related, but I'm not convinced.
I **feel** [strong personal opinion] she isn't capable of doing the job.
I **suppose** [believe something is true / likely to happen] they'll get married sometime soon.
I **doubt** [don't believe] we'll ever see total world peace.
I **suspect** [have a belief, especially about something negative] a lot of people never even think about pollution when they're driving their own car.

B Phrases for expressing opinion

In my opinion / In my mind / In my view, we've made some progress.
If you ask me (informal), he ought to change his job.
From a teacher's **point of view** [how someone sees things, or is affected by them], the new examinations are a disaster.

C Prepositions used with belief and opinion words

What are your **views on** divorce?
What do you **think of** the new boss?
Do you **believe in** God?
I'm in favor of long prison sentences, but I'm **opposed to** the death penalty.

D Beliefs, ideologies, philosophies, and convictions

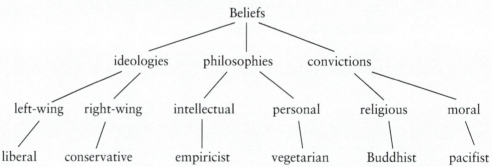

E Adjectives that describe people's beliefs and views, in pairs of similar meaning

fanatical/obsessive   eccentric/odd/peculiar   conservative/traditional
idealistic/unrealistic   middle-of-the-road/moderate   radical/revolutionary

Unit 63

Exercises

63.1 Rewrite these sentences using the verbs in parentheses.

1. I've always suspected that she doesn't really love him. (doubt)
2. Claudia is convinced that the teacher has been unfair to her. (maintain)
3. I felt strongly that I had been in that room before. (convince)
4. In his mind, we should have tried again. (feel)
5. I expect that the government will raise taxes again soon. (suppose)

63.2 Connect the left and right columns, as in the example, using the appropriate prepositions.

1. What do you think	....*of*....	the new teacher?
2. I've always been opposed	....	wasteful government spending.
3. Are you in favor	....	higher taxes?
4. I have strong views	....	educational policy
5. Do you believe	....	life after death?
6. Let's look at it	....	your parents' point of view.

63.3 Use adjectives from E on page 126 to describe the beliefs and views of these people.

1. A person who insists that the earth is flat. (a person with an ....*eccentric*.... belief)
2. Someone who believes absolutely in the power of love to solve world problems. (a/an .... believer in the power of love)
3. A politician neither on the left nor the right of the party. (a/an .... politician)
4. A vegetarian who refuses to be in the same room as people who like meat. (a/an .... vegetarian)
5. A person who is somewhat old-fashioned. (a person with a/an .... point of view)
6. Someone who believes that all taxes should be eliminated. (a/an .... thinker)

63.4 Complete these sentences with your own opinions.

1. I believe in ....
2. I'm conservative about .... but liberal when it comes to ....
3. I doubt that ....
4. If you ask me, the best way to learn English is to ....
5. It has always seemed odd to me that ....
6. I'm in favor of .... but opposed to ....

63.5 Circle the words and phrases that best describe your general character or beliefs. Use a dictionary if necessary.

a perfectionist	left-wing	a traditionalist	a moralist	middle-of-the-road
narrow-minded	dogmatic	open-minded	radical	an intellectual
pragmatic	realistic	a philosopher	dedicated	idealistic

127

Unit 64 Pleasant and unpleasant feelings

A Happiness and unhappiness

You feel...

ecstatic when you experience an intense and overpowering positive feeling.
content(ed) when you are peaceful and satisfied with what you have. **Content** is used after a verb (*He is content*), but **contented** is used before a noun (a **contented** person).
cheerful when life is looking bright and positive.
grateful when you appreciate what someone has done for you.
delighted when you feel great pleasure.
miserable when everything seems wrong in your life.
disappointed when you are unhappy about an event or action.
fed up / sick and tired (informal) when you have had enough of something disagreeable.
depressed when you are miserable over a long period of time. **Depression** is an illness, though it is used to describe sadness as well.
frustrated when you are unable to do something that you want to do.
confused / mixed up when you cannot make sense of conflicting feelings or ideas; **mixed up** is more colloquial.

B Excitement, anger, and anxiety

You feel...

excited when you are expecting something special to happen.
inspired when you are stimulated to create deeds or words. You might feel **inspired** after listening to some very powerful music or a moving speech.
enthusiastic when you have very positive feelings about doing something.
thrilled (informal) when something extremely exciting and pleasing happens.
furious/livid/seething when you are extremely angry; **in a rage/fury** are other ways of saying *violently angry*.
anxious when you are afraid and uncertain about the future. *I am so **anxious** about the results of my exams that I can't sleep.*
nervous when you are afraid or anxious about something that is or may be about to happen. Feeling **nervous** is like feeling **excited**, except that feeling nervous is negative.
apprehensive when you are nervous or anxious about something in the future.
worried when anxious thoughts are constantly going through your head.
upset when something unpleasant has happened to disturb you. It often combines feelings of sadness and anger.

> **tip** *You can use **really**, **extremely**, and **very** with most of these adjectives, though usually not with extreme adjectives (e.g., ecstatic, thrilled, livid, seething, furious).*

Unit 64

Exercises

64.1 Complete this table.

Adjective	Abstract noun	Adjective	Abstract noun
furious	....	frustrated	....
....	anxiety	....	cheerfulness
grateful	....	enthusiastic	
....	ecstasy	....	apprehension
inspired	....	excited	....

64.2 Complete the sentences below with the most appropriate words in the box.

| confused | thrilled | depressed | sick and tired |
| upset | fed up | worried | disappointed |

1. I didn't know who was telling the truth. I felt totally ....
2. Some mothers are .... for several months after the birth of a baby.
3. I think she's bad tempered because she's .... She wanted to be an actress, not a schoolteacher.
4. I was so .... when I realized he had been lying the entire time.
5. When you didn't call, we were so .... that we almost phoned the police.
6. This rainy weather has lasted too long. I'm .... with it.
7. He was terribly .... when he heard the news his grandmother had died.
8. She was .... when she heard that she had won first prize.

64.3 Add the correct ending, either *-ed* or *-ing*. Generally, *-ed* is used to describe the feeling, and *-ing* describes the thing causing the feeling.

1. She was thrill*ed* by her present. (It was a thrill*ing* present.)
2. I found the movie very excit.............. . (I felt excit.............. .)
3. The poet was inspir.............. by the sunset. (It was an inspir.............. sunset.)
4. This weather is terribly depress.............. . (I feel depress.............. .)
5. She was confus.............. by the ambiguous remarks he made to her. (He made confus.............. remarks.)
6. It is very frustrat.............. when the phones aren't working. (I feel frustrat.............. .)

64.4 Write sentences about when you or someone you know has experienced these feelings.

Example: *I felt anxious waiting for the results of my mother's medical tests.*

1. anxious
2. apprehensive
3. content
4. delighted
5. happy
6. in a rage
7. miserable
8. nervous
9. seething
10. sick and tired

Unit 65   Likes, dislikes, and desires

A   Words and expressions related to *liking*

> Dear Amy,
> I **really liked** Hui when we first met. However, I wasn't **attracted to** him at all, even though my friends thought he was handsome. He invited me out, but I must admit that I was more **tempted** by his sports car than by him at first. But it turns out that I really **enjoyed** spending time with him. He **fascinated** me with his stories of his travels around the world, and something mysterious about his past **attracted** me too. Soon I realized I had **fallen in love** with him. His sense of humor **appealed to** me, and I was also **enchanted by** his gift for poetry. Now, two years later, I'm **crazy about** him and can't understand why I didn't **fall for** him the moment we first set eyes on each other. He's a very **caring** person, **fond of** animals and children. He's always **affectionate** and **loving** toward me and **passionate about** the causes he believes in and the people he **cares for**.
> Love Mei

B   Words and expressions related to *disliking*

Loathe, detest, despise, hate, can't stand, and **can't bear** are all very strong ways of saying *dislike*, and they all can be followed by a noun or an **-ing** form.

I **loathe** everything he stands for. I **detest** pretending to like him. Most people **can't stand** to see him act this way.

Disgust, revolt, appall, and **repel** are all very strong words that describe the effect that something detested has on the person affected by it.

Those paintings **disgust** me. I was **revolted** by the way she acted. We were **appalled** by the conditions in the refugee camp. His behavior **repels** everyone.

C   Words and expressions related to *desiring*

Desire can describe attraction or it can be a formal word for **wish**.

I have a strong **desire** to see the Himalayas before I die.

Look forward to means think about something in the future with pleasant anticipation. The opposite of **look forward** to is **dread**.

I am **looking forward** to going to Fiji, but I'm **dreading** the flight. (*Note*: to is a preposition here, not part of the infinitive, so it is followed by a noun or an **-ing** form.)

Long for and **yearn for** are poetic ways to describe wishing for something very much.

After this long, cold winter, I'm **longing for** spring.
He will never stop **yearning for** his country even though he can never return.

D   Words for addressing people you have a close relationship with

honey   sweetheart   darling   dear   baby

Unit 65

Exercises

65.1 Complete this table.

Verb	Noun	Adjective	Adverb
—	affection	....	....
appeal	....	....	....
attract	....	....	....
disgust	....	....	....
hate	....	....	....
—	passion	....	....
repel	....	....	....
tempt	....	....	....

65.2 Rewrite these sentences using the word in parentheses.

1. I really like reading thrillers. (enjoy) *I enjoy reading thrillers.*
2. I despise jazz. (stand)
3. His art attracts me. (appeal)
4. Beer is disgusting to me. (revolt)
5. She longs for her true love. (yearn)
6. I'm dreading the exam. (look)
7. I was crazy about him from the start. (fall for)

65.3 In each pair of sentences, put a check (✓) next to the sentence that probably expresses the stronger feeling.

1. a) Hi Ann, how are things?   b) Sweetheart, how are things?
2. a) They've fallen in love.   b) They're very fond of each other.
3. a) I dislike her poetry.   b) I loathe her poetry.
4. a) He's crazy about her.   b) He's attracted to her.
5. a) She's looking forward to seeing him again. b) She's longing to see him.

65.4 Complete these sentences. Use a dictionary if necessary.

1. Misogynists dislike ....
2. Ornithologists are fascinated by ....
3. People who suffer from arachnophobia find .... loathsome.
4. Kleptomaniacs are constantly tempted to ....
5. Optimists look forward to ....

65.5 Answer these questions, using words from page 130.

1. What kind of food do you like?
2. What are you fascinated by?
3. What attracts you most in a loved one?
4. What do you enjoy most about your job or your studies?
5. What characteristics in people do you most despise?

Unit 66 Speaking

A Verbs describing volume of speaking and mood

These verbs may be followed by clauses beginning with **that**.

Verb	Loudness	Most likely mood
whisper	soft	secretive
murmur	soft	romantic or complaining
mumble	soft (and unclear)	nervous or insecure
mutter	soft	irritated
shout, yell	loud	angry *or* excited
scream	loud (usually without words)	frightened or excited
shriek	loud (and shrill)	frightened or amused
stutter, stammer*	neutral	nervous or excited

*Note: Stuttering and stammering may also be the result of a speech impediment.

B Verbs indicating a speaker's feelings

Verb	Patterns	Feeling	Verb	Patterns	Feeling
boast	to s.b. about s.t. / that . . .*	proud of oneself	complain whine	to s.b. about s.t. / that . . .	displeased, annoyed
insist	on s.t. / that. . .	determined	maintain	that . . .	convinced
object	that . . . / to + -ing	unhappy, in conflict	confess	that . . . / to + -ing	repentant
threaten	that . . . / to do s.t.	aggressive	urge	s.b. to do s.t.	encouraging
argue	with s.b. about s.t. / that . . .	not in agreement	beg	s.b. to do s.t. / for s.t.	desperate
groan	that . . . / about s.t.	displeased, in pain	grumble	that . . . / about s.t.	displeased

*Note: s.b. = somebody; s.t. = something.

C Adverbs to describe the way someone speaks

To describe the way someone speaks and the way someone feels, you can often use an adverb ending in **-ly**. For example: *He spoke **proudly**. She muttered **angrily**.* (This is common in written, but not in spoken English.)

If someone feels happy: **happily   cheerfully   eagerly   gladly   hopefully**
If someone feels unhappy: **dejectedly   gloomily   miserably   sadly**
If someone feels worried: **anxiously   nervously   desperately   hopelessly**
If someone feels angry: **angrily   furiously   bitterly**

Other useful adverbs are **boldly, enthusiastically, excitedly, gratefully, impatiently, passionately, reluctantly, sarcastically, shyly,** and **sincerely**.

Unit 66

Exercises

66.1 Complete each statement with the most appropriate verb from page 132.

1. "I love you," he *murmured*.
2. "I never get to be first in line," the boy ....
3. "Please, please, help me," he ....
4. "This hotel is filthy," she ....
5. "Come on, Jim, try harder," he ....
6. "Your plan will never work," he ....

66.2 Change the sentences above into reported speech using the same verbs.

Example: 1. *He murmured that he loved her.*

66.3 Complete each sentence with the correct form of the underlined word. Use a dictionary if necessary.

1. Someone who <u>boasts</u> a lot is *boastful*.
2. When you <u>object</u>, you raise an ....
3. A person who <u>begs</u> is a ....
4. If you <u>confess</u>, you make a ....
5. A person who <u>threatens</u> others is ....
6. A person who <u>insists</u> a lot is ....
7. A person who <u>argues</u> a lot is ....
8. A child who <u>whines</u> all the time is ....

66.4 Verb quiz. Look at the verbs in the table in B on page 132 if necessary.

1. Which four verbs describe speaking in a soft voice?
2. Which four verbs are used to describe speaking in a loud voice?
3. Which three verbs can be used to mean *complain*?

66.5 Complete this table.

Adverb	Adjective	Noun
bitterly		
cheerfully		
enthusiastically		
furiously		
gratefully		
miserably		
reluctantly		
sarcastically		

66.6 Write a sentence to match each of the ten adverbs listed at the end of C on page 132.

Example: *"We can easily break into the bank," she said boldly.*

Unit 67 The six senses

A The five physical senses are **sight**, **hearing**, **taste**, **touch**, and **smell**. What is sometimes called the "**sixth sense**" (or extrasensory perception) is a power to be aware of things independently of the five physical senses – a kind of supernatural sense. The five verbs referring to the senses are modified by an adjective, not an adverb.

He **looks** awful.   The trip **sounds** marvelous.   This cake **tastes** good.
It **felt** strange.   The soup **smelled** delicious.

B **Sight**

Yesterday I **glanced** out the window and **noticed** a man **observing** a house across from mine through a telescope. I thought I **glimpsed** a woman inside the house. Then I **saw** another man **peering** into the window of the same house. I **gazed** at them through my window, wondering what they were doing. Suddenly the first man stopped **staring** through his telescope. He went and hit the other man on the head with the telescope, and I realized that I had just **witnessed** a crime.

C **Hearing**

Scale of loudness: **noiseless** → **silent** → **quiet** → **noisy** → **loud** → **deafening**

D **Taste**

sweet (honey)   **salty** (potato chips)   **bitter** (strong coffee)   **sour** (vinegar)   **spicy** (salsa)

If you say something tastes **hot**, it may mean **spicy** rather than *not cold*. Food can be **tasty**, but **tasteful** refers to furnishings, architecture, or a style of dressing or behavior. The opposite of both is **tasteless**.

E **Touch**

She nervously **fingered** her collar.   He **stroked** his chin and **rubbed** his eyes.
She **tapped** him on the shoulder.   He **grasped** my hand and we ran.
It's rude to **snatch** things.   **Press** the button.
She **grabbed** her bag and ran.   Please **handle** the goods carefully.

F **Smell**

aromatic   fragrant   scented   smelly   stinking
perfumed   sweet-smelling   musty   foul   vile

G **Sixth sense (ESP)**

Here are some different phenomena that a person with sixth sense might experience.

telepathy [sharing ideas without words]   **intuition** [instinctive understanding]
déjà vu [an unusual feeling of living   **premonitions** [inexplicable knowledge of
    through an event twice]   the future]

Unit 67

Exercises

67.1 Make sentences you could say for each of these situations. Use any of these verbs – *look, sound, taste, touch,* or *smell* – followed by an adjective.

1. You see a movie about the Rocky Mountains. *Those mountains look magnificent.*
2. You wake up in the morning and smell fresh coffee.
3. A friend, an excellent cook, tries a new soup recipe.
4. A little boy asks you to listen to his first attempts on the drums.
5. Someone you are working with smells strongly of cigars.

67.2 Find the verbs in B on page 134 that suggest looking . . .

1. at a crime or accident as it occurs?
2. briefly?
3. fixedly?
4. in a scientific way?

67.3 Replace the underlined words with more precise verbs from page 134.

1. I <u>became aware</u> of a leak in the roof.
2. He <u>knocked</u> on the door <u>lightly</u>.
3. She <u>firmly took</u> my hand.
4. <u>Touch</u> the button to start.
5. He <u>touched</u> the cat <u>affectionately</u>.
6. We <u>looked gently</u> into each other's eyes.

67.4 Use the words in the box to describe the items below.

| sweet | salty | bitter | sour | spicy | hot |

1. seawater
2. chocolate cake
3. chili powder
4. lime
5. curry
6. strong, unsweetened coffee

67.5 Find the adjectives in F on page 134 that best describe the smell of these items.

1. herbs in a kitchen
2. unwashed socks
3. a hair salon
4. roses
5. a room filled with cigar smoke
6. an attic used for storage

67.6 Which of the phenomena mentioned in G on page 134 have you experienced if you . . .

1. suddenly think of someone an instant before they telephone you?
2. feel certain someone can't be trusted, even though there's no reason to believe so?
3. walk into a strange room and feel you have been there before?
4. refuse to travel on a plane because you feel something bad is going to happen?

67.7 Write a sentence about a memorable experience for each of your six senses.

Unit 68   What your body does

> **note** All the verbs on this page (except **shake** and **bite**) are regular verbs; almost all the verbs have an identical noun form: **to yawn / a yawn; to cough / a cough** (except **to breathe / a breath** and **to perspire / perspiration**).

A   Verbs associated with the mouth and breathing

I love to listen to my baby's rhythmic **breathing** as she sleeps.
If one person **yawns**, everyone else seems to do it too.
It was so smoky that he couldn't stop **coughing**.
Dust often makes me **sneeze**.
She **sighed** with relief when she heard the plane had landed safely.
Holding your breath and swallowing can help you stop **hiccupping**.
You kept me up all night with your loud **snoring**!

B   Verbs associated with eating and digestion

He patted the baby's back to make her **burp** after she ate.
My granny used to say you should **chew** every mouthful ten times.
It's embarrassing if your stomach **rumbles/growls** during class.
Drink a glass of water to help you **swallow** the pills.
You're too old to **suck** your thumb!
He **licked** the ice cream cone in the hot sun.
She always **bites** her nails when she's nervous.

C   Verbs associated with the eyes and face

She **blinked** several times to try to get the dust out of her eye.
He **winked** at me across the room to try to make me laugh.
Why are you **frowning**? What's the problem?
She was so delighted with the gift that she **grinned** from ear to ear.
He **blushed** with embarrassment when she smiled at him.
Putting weight on his injured foot made him **grimace** in pain

D   Verbs associated with the whole body

perspire/sweat   tremble   shiver   shake

Exercise makes you **sweat/perspire** (**perspire** is more formal).
My hands **tremble** when I get very upset.
Look at him! He's so cold that he's **shivering**!
She laughs so hard that her whole body **shakes**.

Unit 68

Exercises

68.1 Find the verbs on page 136 to match these definitions.

1. to draw the eyebrows together to express displeasure: *to frown*
2. to turn pink or red in the face from embarrassment:
3. to tremble, especially from cold or fear:
4. to shut and open both eyes quickly:
5. to deliberately shut and open one eye:
6. to breathe out deeply, especially to express pleasure, relief, boredom, etc.:

68.2 Write a sentence that states what could be happening in each of these situations.

1. Take your thumb out of your mouth! (*parent to child*) *A child is sucking her thumb.*
2. Listen to that! I can't sleep in the same room as him.
3. Am I boring you?
4. If you take a drink of water, it might stop!
5. Are you hungry?
6. You shouldn't eat so much so quickly!
7. You've really been exercising, haven't you?

68.3 Choose the appropriate words from page 136 to match these pictures.

1.
2.
3.
4.
5.
6.

68.4 Describe what you might do in each of these situations, using words on page 136.

1. The wind just blew dust into your face.
2. You have twisted your ankle.
3. You have a lollipop.
4. You put a piece of gum in your mouth.

68.5 Organize the words on on page 136 into one or more bubble networks. Add other words to the networks if you wish.

Unit 69

Number, quantity, degree, and intensity

A Number and quantity

Number is used for countable nouns, e.g., **a large number** of people; **amount** is used for uncountable nouns, e.g., **a large amount** of money.

Scale of adjectives useful for expressing number and quantity:

→ → → → →
tiny   small/little   average   large/considerable   gigantic / huge / vast / enormous

Add just a **tiny amount** of chili pepper, or else it may get too hot.
A **considerable number** (formal) of people have visited our Web site.
Huge amounts of money have been wasted on this project.
"Were there many people at the airport?" "Oh, about average, I'd say."

Much/many, a lot (of), lots (of), plenty (of), a number (of), a good/great deal (of)

Examples	Comments
Is there **much** work to do? No, not **much**.	mostly used in questions and negatives with uncountable nouns
You were making **a lot of** noise last night.	used in all structures, neutral
There are **lots of** nice stores on this street.	informal and usually positive
Don't worry, there's **plenty of** time.	usually positive
There are **a (great) number of / many** mistakes in this report.	more formal, used with countable nouns
There's **a good deal of / a great deal of** work to be done.	more formal, used with uncountable nouns

B Informal and colloquial words for number / quantity

I have **dozens of** (good for countables) nails in my toolbox. Why buy more?
There's **loads of** (countable or uncountable, informal) time, so slow down!
Just a **drop of** [tiny amount of any liquid] wine for me, please.
Moving is going to take **a bit of** [a small amount, usually spoken] an adjustment.
There were **tons of** (countable or uncountable – use singular verb for uncountable – informal) apples on this tree this year; last year there were hardly any.
There was **tons of** food at the party; it was way too much.

C Degree and intensity

Some adjectives, such as **tired, worried, weak**, and **hot**, can be described on a scale from weak to strong. They are modified by **a little bit / a bit / quite / rather / fairly / pretty / very / really / terribly / awfully / extremely**: e.g., *It's **really hot** today*.

Other adjectives, such as **ruined, exhausted, destroyed**, and **wrong**, are not measured on a scale, but are considered "all or nothing." They can be modified by **totally / absolutely / completely / entirely / utterly**: e.g., *That argument is **utterly wrong***.

Unit 69

Exercises

69.1 Write responses to these statements using words from A on page 138.

1. I was expecting a tax refund of $1,000 this year, but I got only $10!
   That's a tiny amount compared to what you were expecting.
2. Five billion dollars of government spending was wasted through inefficiency.
3. Over fifty people came to Dr. Nelson's lecture yesterday. She was pleasantly surprised.
4. We have 120 students most years; we'll probably have the same this year, too.

69.2 Combine these adjectives in the box with *amount*. Then divide them into two groups – *small* and *large* – in the bubble networks. Use a dictionary if necessary.

| minuscule | minute /maɪˈnuːt/ | overwhelming | excessive | insignificant |
| sizable | substantial | minimal | tremendous | tiny |

69.3 Fill in the blanks with the adjectives in 69.2. More than one answer may be possible

1. Even a/an .... amount of sand can jam a camera.
2. I've had an absolutely .... amount of work lately.
3. Oh, you've given me a/an .... amount of food here!
4. It takes a/an .... amount of money to start a business.
5. A/an .... amount of fat in your diet is dangerous.

69.4 Fill in the blanks with *much/many*; *a lot of / lots of*; *plenty of*; *a number of*; or *a good deal of / a great deal of*.

1. There's .... dust on these books. Get me a dust rag.
2. Please help yourself to more food; there's .... it.
3. There wasn't .... we could do to help, so we went home.
4. We've put .... energy into this plan. I hope it works.
5. .... young people watch action movies.

69.5 Write how you might feel in these situations, using intensifiers from C on page 138.

1. You hear that a friend is in trouble with the police. *I might feel / be pretty anxious.*
2. You've been working nonstop for 18 hours.
3. Three people give you different directions to get to the same place.
4. You pass an exam you had expected to fail.
5. Your best friend is going abroad for two years.

Unit 70 Duration of time

A Periods of time

the Ice Age   the Stone Age   the Middle Ages   the digital age
      (major historical/geological periods)

After the war, a new **era** [long period, perhaps decades] of peace and stability began.
The happiest I've ever felt was during that **period** [general length of time] of my life.
We've had a **spell** [indefinite but short time] of hot weather.
During the 1980s, I lived in Hong Kong **for a time**. (vague, indefinite)
Do you want to borrow this book **for a while**? [indefinite but not very long time]

B Useful phrases with time

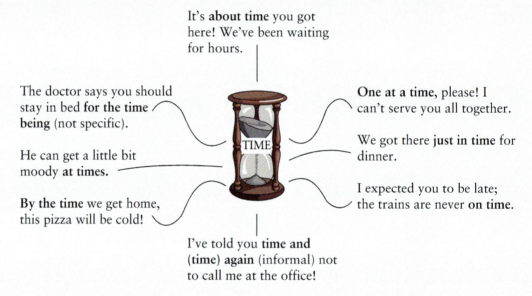

It's **about time** you got here! We've been waiting for hours.

The doctor says you should stay in bed **for the time being** (not specific).

He can get a little bit moody **at times**.

By the time we get home, this pizza will be cold!

One at a time, please! I can't serve you all together.

We got there **just in time** for dinner.

I expected you to be late; the trains are never **on time**.

I've told you **time and (time) again** (informal) not to call me at the office!

C Verbs associated with time passing

1998 → 2008   Ten years had **passed/elapsed** before I heard from her again.
Don't worry. The time will **pass** quickly. Time **passes** slowly when you're bored.
Elapse is more formal and is normally used in the perfect or past, without adverbs.
Pass can be used in any tense and with adverbs.

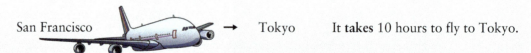

San Francisco   Tokyo   It **takes** 10 hours to fly to Tokyo.

The batteries in this cell phone should **last** three or four days.
This movie **lasts/runs** for three hours. Do we have time to watch it?
The meeting **dragged on** [longer than expected or necessary] for two hours.

Note also: **Take your time**; you don't have to hurry.

Unit 70

Exercises

70.1 Fill in the blanks with *age, era, period, spell,* or *time*.

1. During the tax amnesty, there will be a .... of six months when people can pay the taxes they owe from previous years without a penalty.
2. The twentieth century will be seen by historians as the .... of the automobile.
3. These factories mark the beginning of a new .... of industrial development for the country.
4. For a .... I thought I would never find a job, but then I got lucky.
5. We had a very cold .... in February: All the pipes in our house froze.

70.2 Match the questions on the left with the responses on the right.

1. Was your train on time?   Just in time to catch the last train!
2. When did you arrive at the station?   No, by the time I left work, it was too late.
3. The train is finally leaving the station. No, it wasn't. In fact, it's always late.
4. Did you go to the movies last night?   At times.
5. Do you ever miss your country?   It's about time!

70.3 Write what you might say in these situations, using phrases from B on page 140.

1. A child repeatedly leaves the refrigerator door open despite being told not to many times.
   I've told you time and again not to leave that refrigerator door open!
2. Someone you're happy to see arrives just as you are serving tea/coffee.
3. You write on a postcard that you expect it to arrive at someone's house after you do.
4. A large group of people want to talk to you, but you'd prefer to see them individually.
5. You ask someone to use an old printer while the new one is being repaired.
6. You explain to someone that the weather occasionally gets very cold in your country.
7. You tell someone you'll do your best to arrive punctually for a meeting.
8. Your friend just got a job. You think she should have gotten one long ago.

70.4 Complete these sentences using verbs from C on page 140.

1. The train to Washington ....
2. Use this DVD to record. It will ....
3. These shoes have been great; they've ....
4. Everyone got bored because the speeches ....
5. The disaster occurred in 1932. Many years ....
6. I'll miss you terribly. I only hope the weeks ....
7. There's no hurry at all; just ....
8. It was a long movie. It ....

> *follow-up*   Your native culture or country may have names for important periods in history. Describe these periods in English, using vocabulary from this unit.

Unit 71

Distances and dimensions

A Wide, broad, tall, high, deep, shallow

Wide is more common than **broad**, e.g., *It's a very **wide** road/aisle/doorway.*
Make a note of typical collocations for **broad** as you meet them, e.g., *This book covers a **broad** range of subjects; We came to a **broad** [big area] expanse of grassland.*
Note the word order for talking about dimensions, e.g., *The room is **five meters long** and **four meters wide**.*

Tall is used for people, but it can also be used for things like buildings and trees when they are **high** and **thin** in some way. Otherwise, use **high** for things.

She's very **tall** for a five-year-old.
His office is in that **tall** building on the square.
There are some **high** mountains in the north.

deep ≠ **shallow**

B Derived words, phrases, and compounds

long: Let's measure the **length** of this rope.
I swam twenty **lengths** (of the swimming pool).
I've **lengthened** her skirt for her.
Getting a visa can be a **lengthy** (usually refers to time) process.
Can I make a **long-distance** phone call?
short: The new road will **shorten** our trip by 10 minutes.
There's a **shortcut** [quick way] to the station.
We will arrive **shortly** [very soon].
wide: Let's measure the **width** of the room.
They're **widening** the road.
broad: I want to **broaden** (usually abstract contexts) my experience.
She's very **broad-minded** and tolerant of others.
high: The **height** of the ceiling is nine feet.
I think very **highly** [respect someone] of them.
low: You can **lower** your cholesterol by changing your diet.
far: He loves traveling to **faraway** places.
deep: The **depth** of the river here is about 10 feet (3 meters).
His death so soon after hers **deepened** our sadness even further.

C Other verbs for dimensions and for changing them

Our property **stretches** down to the river, with plenty of room to **extend** the house.
The cities are **spreading** and the countryside is **shrinking**.

Unit 71

Exercises

71.1 Complete B's replies using a form of the distance/dimension words on page 142.

1. A: These pants I bought are too long.
   B: Well, why don't you get them .... ?
2. A: He's a big boy, isn't he? Almost six feet!
   B: Yes, he's ....
3. A: Why are we taking this side street?
   B: Just to get there a little bit quicker; it's ....
4. A: The traffic seems to move faster on this road since I was last here.
   B: That's because they ....
5. A: Do you think it's safe to dive here?
   B: I wouldn't. At this end of the pool, it's only three feet ....

71.2 Write the opposites of the underlined words.

1. the <u>length</u> of the room ≠
2. to <u>shorten</u> ≠
3. a <u>narrow</u> range of goods ≠
4. a <u>local</u> call ≠
5. <u>deep</u> water ≠
6. <u>nearby</u> places ≠

71.3 Complete these sentences by matching the clauses on the left with the ones on the right.

1. The city's spread out a lot;   for miles along the river.
2. It takes 10 weeks;   you should broaden it.
3. We extended the house   it's much bigger now.
4. You can choose;   there's a wide range available.
5. Your experience is too narrow;   it's a lengthy procedure.
6. The forest stretches   to give us more room.

71.4 Fill in the blanks with prepositions of distance. Use a dictionary if necessary.

1. The car was parked .... a distance .... about 150 yards (137 meters) from the robbery.
2. I saw you .... the distance yesterday, but I didn't call out your name because I could see you were with someone.
3. She's a great shot with a bow and arrow. She can hit an empty can .... a distance of about 100 feet (30.5 meters), which I can't do.
4. What's the total distance .... here .... Paris?

71.5 Complete these sentences using verbs from C on page 142. Use the correct form for each verb.

1. AIDS .... rapidly in several areas of the world.
2. Our land .... as far as the river.
3. They want to .... the parking lot another 40 feet (12.2 meters) behind the building.
4. Because of smaller families and decreased immigration, the population is ....

143

Unit 72 — Obligation, need, possibility, and probability

A Obligation

Have to says that circumstances oblige you to do something, e.g., *I **have to** leave early*. **Have got to** has the same meaning and is often used in spoken English and informal situations, e.g., *I've **got to** run.* (informally spoken as *I **gotta** run*)

Must is an instruction or command; it is often found in signs, notices, and "official language," e.g., *All those entering **must** have a valid passport*. It is sometimes used to show urgency, e.g., *It's an emergency; I **must** see the doctor now.*

I've **got to** get my hair cut.
I have an interview tomorrow.

There's no bus service, so
I **have to** walk to work.

RIGHT LANE MUST EXIT

The company **is required to / obliged to** refund your money if the tour is canceled.
You **are liable** (formal/legalistic) for any damages when you rent a car.
The bank robbers **forced** him at gunpoint to open the safe.
We **had no choice/alternative but** to sell our house; we owed the bank $100,000.
A prison sentence is **mandatory** [automatic; no alternative] for drug trafficking.
"Were sports **compulsory/obligatory** at your school?" "No, they were **optional** [you can choose]."
Nonprofit organizations are usually **exempt** [free from usual obligation] from taxes.

The negative of **must** and **have (got) to** are formed with **need to** and **have to** when we mean something is not necessary / not obligatory, e.g., *You **don't need to / don't have to** wash the dishes; we have a dishwasher.*

> **Must not** shows prohibition, e.g., *Passengers **must not** stand in the aisles.*

B Need

The grass **needs** cutting.
The house is **in need of** (more formal than **needs**) some major repairs.
There is a **shortage** [not enough] of doctors.
There is a **need** (formal: we feel a need) for more discussion on this issue.
Some claim that students show a **lack** of intellectual curiosity.

C Scale of probability: from cannot happen to will definitely happen

impossible → unlikely → possible → probable → certain → inevitable

Economists have been talking about the **possibility** of a recession. Does this mean there is a **chance** that I might lose my job?

Unit 72

Exercises

72.1 Complete these sentences using the words in parentheses and obligation words and phrases from A on page 144.

1. They were losing $10 million a year, so the company . . . (close down)
   was forced to / had to / had no choice but to / close down.
2. You can rent a car, but you . . . (put down a deposit)
3. In some countries, military service . . . (for young people)
4. This jacket has ketchup stains on it; I . . . (the cleaners)
5. He didn't want to give them the money, but they had guns; they . . . (hand it over)
6. I didn't want to take math, but I had to. It's . . . (in high school)

72.2 List something that you feel . . .

1. regularly needs cutting. *my hair, the lawn*
2. there is a lack of.
3. is compulsory in schools.
4. people are in need of.
5. is inevitable.
6. you no longer have to do.
7. is exempt from some rules.
8. you were once forced to do.

72.3 Circle the words in each line that might be used with the *probability* word in the last column.

1. (quite)   (very)   absolutely   **possible**
2. very   absolutely   highly   **impossible**
3. absolutely   highly   quite   **probable**
4. highly   absolutely   extremely   **unlikely**
5. very   extremely   absolutely   **inevitable**
6. absolutely   highly   quite   **certain**

72.4 Use the combinations in 72.3 to say how probable these statements are.

1. Petroleum will become obsolete within the next 50 years.
2. There will be rain in the Amazon forest within the next eight days.
3. A human being will live to be 150 years old someday.
4. You will be a professional musician.

> **follow-up** Look at the editorial page of an English language newspaper and circle the obligation / need / possibility / probability words you see.

Unit 73: Sound and light

A General words to describe sound

I could hear the **sound** (neutral) of voices / music coming from the next room.
The **noise** [loud, unpleasant sounds] of the traffic here is pretty bad.
I tried to hear her voice above the **din** [very loud, irritating noise] of the machines.
The children are making a terrible **racket** [very loud, unbearable noise, often of human activity] upstairs. Could you tell them to be quiet?

Noise and **sound** are both countable when they are of short duration or when they are different sounds/noises. They are uncountable when they are continual or continuous.

Their lawnmower makes **a lot of noise**, doesn't it? The **sound** of the ocean is very soothing. (both uncountable)
I heard **some** strange **noises/sounds** during the night. (both countable)

B Types of sounds and things that typically make them

These words can be used as nouns or verbs: I could hear the rain **pattering** on the roof. We heard the **patter** of a child's feet.

Verb / Noun	Example of what makes the sound
bang	a door closing heavily in the wind
clang	a big bell ringing; a hollow metal object being struck
crash	a heavy object falling onto a hard floor or hitting something
creak	stepping on a wooden stair; sitting on a bed with noisy springs
hiss	gas/steam escaping through a small hole
pop	a balloon bursting
ring	the sound of a small bell, a chime, a telephone
roar	the noise of heavy traffic; the noise of a huge waterfall
rumble	the distant noise of thunder; the noise of traffic far away
rustle	opening a paper/plastic bag; dry leaves underfoot
thud	a heavy object falling onto a carpeted floor

C Darkness and types of light

These brown walls are kind of **gloomy**. We should paint them white.
This flashlight gives a **dim** light. I think it needs new batteries.
It was a **somber** [serious, dark, gloomy] room, with dark, heavy curtains.
The sun **shines** and gives out **rays** of light.
A flashlight gives out a **beam** of light.
In the distance we saw a **flash** of lightning.
Stars **twinkle**.
A flame **flickers** in the breeze.
White-hot coals in a fire **glow**.
A diamond necklace **sparkles**, and a gold object **glitters**.
The **glare** of the sun in the window hurts my eyes.

Unit 73

Exercises

73.1 Fill in the blanks with *sound(s)*, *noise(s)*, *din*, or *racket*.

1. There was a terrible .... outside our apartment building last night; it was a fight involving about six people.
2. I could sit and listen to the .... of the river all day.
3. My car's been making some strange .... I'll have to have it checked.
4. I hold my hands over my ears when I walk by that construction site because of the .... !
5. I can't sleep if there's .... of any kind, so I use earplugs.

73.2 Write the sound that you think each of these items might make. Use words from the table in B on page 146.

1. a bottle of fizzy mineral water being opened:
2. a typewriter being dropped down an iron staircase:
3. a mouse moving among dead grass and leaves:
4. a heavy object falling on the floor:
5. a starting gun for a sporting event:
6. a slow train passing, heard through the walls of a house:
7. an engine starting up on a jumbo jet:
8. a rusty old gate opening slowly:

73.3 Match each sentence on the left with a sentence on the right.

1. I saw a beam of light coming through the window.
2. The jewels sparkled in the sunlight.
3. The candle began to flicker in the breeze.
4. The first rays of the sun shone into the room.
5. The glare of the truck's headlights momentarily blinded me.

Then it died, leaving us in complete darkness.

It was a police officer holding a flashlight.

It was clearly time to wake up and start the day.

I pulled over to the side of the road.

I'd never seen such a beautiful bracelet.

73.4 Circle the correct meaning of each underlined word.

1. She beamed at him.
   a) smiled   b) shouted   c) attacked
2. After a day of skiing, our faces glowed.
   a) were frozen   b) were dried up   c) were full of color
3. He has a twinkle in his eyes.
   a) a piece of grit   b) a sign of humor   c) a sign of anger
4. He flashed a look of surprise.
   a) briefly showed   b) hid   c) repeatedly showed

Unit 74
Possession, giving, and lending

A Possession

All his **possessions** [things a person owns] were destroyed in the terrible fire.
Don't leave any of your **belongings** [small things a person owns, e.g., bag, laptop, cell phone, coat; always plural] here; we've had a few thefts recently.

Estate in the singular can mean a big area of private land and the buildings on it, or all of someone's wealth upon death.

   She owns a huge **estate** in the country.
   After his death, his **estate** was calculated at $3 million.

Property (uncountable) is used in a general sense for houses, land, etc. A **property** (countable) is a building, e.g., house, office building.

   They went bankrupt and lost all their **property**.
   This **property** would be ideal for developing a resort.

B Words for people connected with ownership

The **proprietor** (used for stores, businesses, etc.; **owner** is less formal) of this restaurant is a friend of mine.
The **landlord/landlady** [owner of rented property] is raising the rent.
Do you own this house? No, we're just **tenants/renters**.

C Giving

It gives me great pleasure to **present** you **with** this clock from all of us.
Would you like to **contribute/donate** something to the children's hospital fund?
The river **provides** the village **with** water / **provides** water **for** the village.
Thompson Dairy **supplies** (often used for "selling" contexts) the supermarket **with** milk.
When she died, she **donated** her books to the library. She also **left** $5,000 **to** her dog!
You've been **assigned** to Room 24. Here's your key.

D Lending, borrowing, and renting

Remember that ladder you **lent** me last week? Can I **borrow** it again?
I'm trying to get a **loan** from the bank to buy a boat.
We've decided to **rent** a car. Can you recommend a good **car rental** agency?

> *note*   When you **lend** or **loan**, you give; when you **borrow**, you receive.

Unit 74

Exercises

74.1 Fill in the blanks with the correct verbs in the box.

| left | lent | donated | presented |

1. A millionaire .... his entire library to the school.
2. My grandmother .... me $10,000 in her will.
3. My landlord .... me $100 until payday.
4. When I retired, the company .... me with a gold watch.

74.2 The phrasal verbs in the box are associated with *giving*. Check their meanings in a dictionary and then fill in the blanks below.

| hand over | hand out | let go of | give away | hand down |

1. That bed has been .... from one generation to the next. It originally belonged to my great-grandparents.
2. Would you help us .... some flyers at the meeting?
3. I won't .... that old painting. It might be valuable someday.
4. When Tim got bigger, we .... his bike; it wasn't worth selling it.
5. If a mugger attacked me, I'd .... my wallet.

74.3 Think of something that . . .

1. you would hand over to a mugger if threatened.
2. has been handed down in your family.
3. is often handed out in classrooms.
4. you value and would not want to let go of.

74.4 Write questions that match these answers. Use words from page 148.

1. Oh no, we own it. Most houses here are owner occupied.
2. I'm sorry, but I need it to take photos myself.
3. No, you have to buy textbooks yourself.
4. Sorry, but I've already given money at the office.
5. Compact cars start at $30 a day; bigger cars are more expensive.

74.5 Complete this story by choosing the most appropriate words from page 148.

Horatio Fatcat began his career by buying up old .... (1) in the city when prices were low. He got .... (2) from several banks to finance his deals, and soon he was one of the biggest .... (3) in the city, with some 50,000 .... (4) renting houses and apartments from him. He was also the .... (5) of many stores and businesses. He became very rich and bought himself a huge .... (6) in the country, but he .... (7) more and more money from the banks and soon the bubble burst. Recession came and he had to sell all his .... (8) and .... (9) – everything. He was left with just a few personal .... (10), and when he died he was penniless.

Unit 75 Movement and speed

A Types of movement

Move refers to motion but also to changing where you live (*move* to a new apartment).
Cars, trucks, buses, etc., **travel/drive** along roads.
Trains **travel** along rails.
Planes **fly** in the sky.
Boats/ships sail on rivers / across the ocean.
Rivers/streams **flow/run** through cities/towns/villages.

Some things often have specific verbs associated with their types of movement.

White clouds **drifted** across the sky.
The flag **fluttered** in the wind.
The leaves **stirred** in the light breeze.
The trees **swayed** back and forth as the gale grew fiercer.
The car **swerved** to avoid a dog running across the road.

B Verbs to describe fast and slow movement

The traffic was **crawling** because of the construction.

Stop **dawdling**! We'll be late!

The car **tore/sped** (informal) along the road at high speed.
Everyone was **hurrying/rushing** to get their shopping done before the holidays.
The train was **creeping/plodding** along at 30 miles an hour. I knew we'd be late.

C Verbs to describe walking

She **paced** [take regular steps back and forth] up and down as she waited.
I enjoy **strolling** [walk slowly in a relaxed manner] in the park.
He **tiptoed** [walk quietly with your heels off the ground] around so he wouldn't wake anyone.
He **marched/stormed** [walk fast and forcefully] out of her office and slammed the door.
Don't **shuffle** [walk slowly without lifting your feet] around like that! Pick up your feet!
Since breaking her leg, she **limps / walks with a limp**. [walk slowly with difficulty]

D Some nouns describing speed and their typical contexts

Speed is a general word used for vehicles, e.g., *We drove at breakneck* **speed**.
Rate is often used in statistics, e.g., *The birth* **rate** *is declining/increasing*.
Pace shows how you experience something as happening, fast or slow, e.g.,
    The lesson was moving at a very slow **pace**.
Velocity is used in technical/scientific contexts, e.g., *the* **velocity** *of a bullet*.

Unit 75

Exercises

75.1 Write the things that are probably being described by these sentences.

1. It sails at dawn. *a ship or a boat*
2. It flows through the capital city.
3. I had to swerve hard to avoid it and nearly ended up in the river.
4. It was traveling at 80 miles per hour when it derailed.
5. It was swaying back and forth in the wind. In fact, I thought it might break.
6. It flew from branch to branch looking for a place to build its nest.

75.2 List other things that can be described by each of these movement verbs.

1. sway: a tree, *a person dancing, a drunk person, a boat*
2. flow: a river, ...
3. crawl: traffic, ...
4. flutter: a flag, ...
5. drift: a cloud, ...
6. run: a stream, ...

75.3 In what situations might you . . .

1. tear out of the house? *If you were very late for something*
2. deliberately dawdle?
3. plod along at a steady pace?
4. not even dare to stir?
5. storm out of a place?
6. walk with a limp?
7. tiptoe around the house?
8. pace up and down?
9. stroll (around) somewhere?
10. rush to get somewhere?

75.4 Fill in the blanks with *speed*, *rate*, *pace*, or *velocity*. Use the guidelines in D on page 150 to help you.

1. The increase in the .... of inflation is alarming.
2. I just couldn't stand the .... of life in the city, so I moved to a small town.
3. High- .... winds destroyed several homes.
4. A: What .... were you going at the time?
   B: Oh, about 60 miles an hour, I'd say.
5. The lecturer spoke at a snail's .... , so people started falling asleep.
6. The crime .... in this city has decreased since the mayor hired a new police chief.
7. I enjoy riding my bicycle down steep hills at a high .... It makes me feel as free as a bird.

Unit 76 Texture, brightness, density, and weight

A Texture – how something feels when you touch it

Adjective	Typical examples
coarse	sand, sandpaper
downy	a newborn baby's hair
fluffy	a soft pillow
furry	a thick sheepskin rug
jagged	sharp, irregular edges of broken glass or metal
polished	varnished wood / a shiny metal surface
prickly	a thistle / a cactus / thorns on a rose
rough	new, unwashed denim jeans / bark of a tree
silky	silk itself / fine, expensive stockings
sleek	the outside of a highly polished, new car
slippery	a fish just out of the water
smooth	the cover of this book
sticky	jam or glue left on a surface

Here are some other words used with adjectives of texture.

Your hair has a silky **feel**.
The ground is rough **underfoot**.
The old table has a beautiful polished **surface**.
This cotton is very smooth **to the touch**.

B Brightness

shiny leather shoes

a **dazzling** light

a **shady** corner of the garden

costumes full of **vivid** colors

You wear such **dull** colors; why not get some **brighter** clothes?
A **dim** light came through the living room curtain.
I wear sunglasses because of the **glare** of the sun.

C Density and weight

a solid ≠ **hollow** object
an area with **dense** ≠ **sparse** vegetation
She has **thick** ≠ **thin/fine** hair.
Your bag's **as light as a feather**! Have you brought enough clothes for the trip?
Your bag's **as heavy as lead**! What's in it, bricks?
This suitcase is very **bulky**. [difficult to carry or store]

Unit 76

Exercises

76.1 Write words that describe how you would expect these items to feel.

1. honey or syrup: *sticky*
2. the surface of a mirror:
3. a wet bar of soap:
4. the branches of a rosebush:
5. a gravel driveway:
6. the inside of a pair of sheepskin gloves:
7. the edge of a piece of broken, rusty metal:
8. heavy, stone-ground wholegrain flour:
9. the feathers in a pillow or quilt:
10. A plastic CD case:

76.2 Look around your own home and find . . .

1. something sleek to the touch.
2. something rough underfoot.
3. something with a smooth surface.
4. something furry.
5. something silky.

76.3 Write answers to the questions below, using these common U.S. weights and their metric equivalents. Then say the questions out loud.

Weight	Written as	Metric equivalent
ounce	oz.	28.35 grams
pound (16 oz.)	lb.	453.6 grams (0.454 kilogram)
fluid ounce	fl. oz.	29.69 milliliters
pint (16 fl. oz.)	pt.	0.473 liter
quart (2 pts.)	qt.	0.946 liter
gallon (4 qts.)	gal.	3.79 liters

1. A friend tells you her new baby weighed 7 pounds at birth. Is this a big, tiny, or more or less average baby?
2. If you drink a half liter of milk a day, is a gallon of milk enough for a week?
3. Make a (private!) note of your approximate weight both in pounds and kilograms.
4. Would 16 oz. of cheese be sufficient if you were making two cheese sandwiches?

76.4 Animal Quiz.
Name the animals being described. Each description could be more than one animal.

1. a creature with a sleek coat
2. a slippery creature
3. a creature with a furry coat
4. a prickly creature

76.5 Pair puzzles. Fill in the letters to make a pair of related words from page 152.

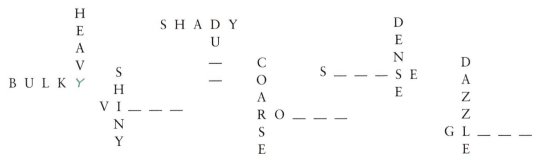

Unit 77 Success, failure, and difficulty

A Succeeding

We **succeeded in** persuading (in + -ing) a lot of people to vote.
I **managed** to contact him just before he left his office.
We've **achieved/accomplished** (both can be used with quantity phrases such as
   a lot / a little) a great deal in the past three years.
The company has **attained** all its **goals/aims/objectives** for this year.
We fully expect to **reach** our sales **targets/goals** in the next fiscal year.
She **fulfilled** a lifelong **ambition** when she learned to fly an airplane.
Your performance has not only **met**, but **surpassed/exceeded expectations**.
We've finally **realized** our **dream** of buying our own home.

Here are some typical collocations with "succeeding" verbs.

	achieve	fulfill	meet	reach	realize
an agreement				✓	
an ambition	✓	✓			✓
a dream	✓				✓
an obligation		✓	✓		
a target			✓	✓	

B Failing and difficulty

Plans and projects sometimes **go wrong** or **misfire**. [don't turn out as intended]
Companies or clubs may **fold / go under** [close down] because of lack of success.
A project may **falter** [go through a series of ups and downs], even if it finally succeeds.
All your plans and hard work/efforts may **come to nothing**.
I'm afraid I **missed** my **chance**. I'll have to try again.
I have great **difficulty (in)** getting up in the morning.
I **find it difficult/hard** to remember people's names.
It's **hard/difficult** to hear what she's saying.
We've **had some trouble/problems with** (**trouble** is uncountable; **problems** is countable)
   the neighbors lately.
I have a **hard time** starting my car on cold winter mornings.
I have no money and my girlfriend left me. I need help; I just can't **cope** anymore.
I can't **cope with** our living situation: I'm leaving!

C Parts of speech

Verb	Noun	Adjective	Adverb
accomplish	accomplishment	accomplished	—
achieve	achievement	achievable	—
attain	attainment	attainable	—
fulfill	fulfillment	fulfilling	—
succeed	success	successful	successfully

Unit 77

Exercises

77.1 Fill in the blanks with appropriate words from page 154. There may be more than one possible answer for each sentence.

1. The charity drive failed to .... its goal of $100,000.
2. I never thought I would .... my ambition, but now I have.
3. Very few people .... all their hopes and dreams in life.
4. A: Did you .... to get there on time?
   B: Yes, just barely.
5. A: Did you .... in getting a loan from the bank?
   B: No, they turned me down. I'm still not sure what .... wrong.
6. Unfortunately, our marketing plans .... ; no one wanted to buy chocolate-covered pickles.
7. Our earnings increased by 20%. We .... our target of 10%!
8. Some people can't .... with a lot of stress.

77.2 Use the context to figure out the meanings of the underlined words. Explain the words by using the expressions in B on page 154.

Verb	Noun	Adjective	Adverb
------	ambition		
------	difficulty		------
expect			
fail			------
realize			------
	target		------
	trouble		------

77.3 Correct the underlined mistakes in these sentences.

1. I'm amazed that you can cope <u>for</u> all the work they give you.
2. She succeeded <u>to rise</u> to the highest rank in the company.
3. Do you ever have trouble <u>to use</u> this photocopier? I always find it difficult.
4. I've <u>accomplished</u> to get all my work done this week, so I'm taking a long weekend!
5. I have <u>the</u> hard time driving to work with all the traffic.
6. We've <u>succeeded</u> a great deal during this past year.

77.4 What might happen if . . . / What would you do if . . .

1. a plan misfired? *I'd abandon it / look for an alternative.*
2. an organization had only two members left out of fifty?
3. you were having a lot of problems with your car?
4. you were taking a class but faltered halfway through?
5. you started a small business but it came to nothing?
6. you surpassed all your goals for English study?

(See also Unit 26 for words connected with problems.)

Unit 78 Idioms and fixed expressions: general

Idioms are fixed expressions with meanings that are not always clear or obvious. For example, the expression **to feel under the weather**, which means to feel sick, is a typical idiom. The words do not tell us what it means, but the context usually helps.

A Tips for remembering idioms

Think of idioms as units, just like single words. Always record the whole phrase in your notebook, along with information on grammar and collocation.

> This can opener **has seen better days.** [it is fairly old and broken down (usually about things, always perfect tense form)]

Idioms are often informal and include a personal comment on the situation. They are sometimes humorous or ironic. As with any informal words, be careful how you use them. Never use idioms just to sound fluent or "good at English," or you might seem to be too intimate or informal when you don't mean to be.

Idioms can be grouped in a variety of ways. Use whichever way you find most useful to help you remember them. Here are some possible ways to group idioms.

- **By grammar**

  pull a fast one [trick/deceive somebody]
  stick/poke your nose in(to) [interfere] } verb + object

  be in seventh heaven [extremely happy / elated]
  feel down in the dumps [depressed/low] } verb + prepositional phrase

- **By meaning** (e.g., idioms describing people's character/intellect)

  He **takes the cake** [is the extreme / the worst of all].
  You're **a pain in the neck.** [a nuisance / difficult person]

- **By verb or other key word** (e.g., idioms with **make**)

  Don't **make a mountain out of a molehill**. [exaggerate the importance]
  Since losing my job, I can barely **make ends meet**. [manage to live on one's income]

B The grammar of idioms

It is important when using idioms to know just how flexible their grammar is. Some are more fixed than others. For instance, **barking up the wrong tree** [be mistaken] is always used in continuous, not simple, form: *I think you're **barking up the wrong tree***. A good dictionary may help, but it is best to observe the grammar in real examples.

(See Units 82–87 to note how idioms are grouped in different ways.)

Unit 78

Exercises

78.1 Complete the idioms in each sentence below with one of the key words in the box. Use a dictionary to look up the key word if necessary.

| shot | bucket | plate | block | handle | pie |

1. All the promises these politicians make! It's just ....*pie*........ in the sky. [big promises that will never happen]
2. The tiny amount donated is just a drop in the .... compared with the huge amount needed. [tiny amount compared with a large amount]
3. I have enough on my .... [have more than enough work] as it is; I can't do that job too.
4. When I told her what I thought, she just flew off the .... [lost her temper] and shouted at me.
5. His father was a gambler too. He's a real chip off the old .... [just like one's parents/grandparents]
6. I wasn't really sure of the answer, so I guessed it; it was just a .... in the dark. [a wild guess]

78.2 Organize these idioms into different groups. Use some of the ways suggested on page 156, plus any other ways you can think of. Use a dictionary if necessary.

be in a bind	child's play	rough and ready	be up to it
hold your tongue	be out of sorts	hold your horses	a fool's errand
odds and ends	keep mum	give or take	sink or swim

78.3 Circle the correct verb form for the underlined idioms. Use a good dictionary or a dictionary of idioms if necessary.

1. You bark / are barking up the wrong tree if you think I dented your car.
2. Holland is springing / springs to mind as a good place for a bicycle trip; its land is nice and flat.
3. That remark is flying / flies in the face of everything you've ever said before on the subject.
4. He was innocent after all. It just goes / is just going to show that you shouldn't believe what you read in the papers.
5. You sit / 're sitting pretty! Look at you – an easy job, a fantastic salary, a free car!
6. His attitude is leaving / leaves a lot to be desired. I wish he would try to be more responsible.

78.4 Guess the meaning of these underlined idioms without using a dictionary.

1. It's midnight. Time to hit the sack.
2. This is just kid's stuff. I want something challenging!
3. He was down and out for two years, but eventually he got a job and found a home for himself.
4. Why is she giving me the cold shoulder? She's usually so friendly.
5. I haven't seen Mario in ages. We only get together once in a blue moon.

Unit 79

Everyday expressions

Everyday spoken language is full of fixed expressions that are not necessarily difficult to understand but have a fixed form that does not change. These should be learned as whole expressions. These expressions are sometimes hard to find in dictionaries, so it is important to be on the lookout for them.

A Conversation-building expressions

Here are some common expressions that help to modify or organize what we are saying. There are many more expressions like these. (See also Units 27 and 28.)

Expression	Meaning/function
As I was saying, I haven't seen her for years.	→ takes the conversation back to an earlier point
Speaking of politics, who do you think will be the next president?	→ moving from the current topic to a new but related topic
If you ask me, she's heading for trouble.	→ giving your opinion (even if no one has asked for it)
That reminds me, I haven't called my parents in weeks.	→ something in the conversation makes you think of something else
Come to think of it, I do know someone you could contact for a job.	→ remembering something you had forgotten earlier in your conversation.

B Key words

This and **that** are examples of key words that occur in several expressions.

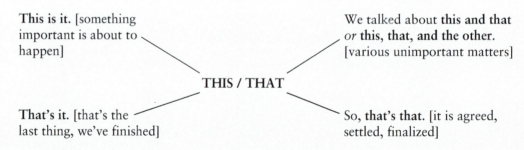

This is it. [something important is about to happen]

We talked about **this and that** or **this, that, and the other.** [various unimportant matters]

THIS / THAT

That's it. [that's the last thing, we've finished]

So, **that's that.** [it is agreed, settled, finalized]

C Common expressions for modifying statements

If worst comes to worst [if the situation gets really bad], we'll have to cancel the trip.
If all else fails [if nothing else succeeds], suggest that she contact a lawyer.
What with one thing after another [because of a lot of different circumstances], I haven't had time to reply to her letter.
When it comes to [as for] restaurants, this town's not that good.
As far as I'm concerned [as far as it affects me / from my point of view], we can eat at any time.
As luck would have it [by chance], she was out when I called.

Unit 79

Exercises

79.1 Complete the fixed expressions in these sentences without looking at A on page 158.

1. Come .... I don't remember giving her the key. I'd better call her and check, just in case.
2. If you .... , the economy's going to get much worse before it gets any better.
3. .... of vacations, what are you planning to do on yours?
4. That .... , I have a message for you from Maria.
5. As .... before we were interrupted, I'm planning to take a long vacation next summer.

79.2 Complete these mini-dialogs with *this/that* expressions from B on page 158.

1. KEN: What were you and Mike talking about?
   MARA: Oh, ...

2. LIZ: How many more?
   JUN: No more, actually, ...

3. JUAN: Here comes the big announcement we've been waiting for.
   PEDRO: Yes, ...

4. TIM: OK, I'll take our final decision to the committee.
   CHEN: All right, so .... Thanks.

79.3 Find the expressions in C on page 158 that contain these key words.

1. come(s)
2. luck
3. fails
4. worst
5. far
6. thing

79.4 Complete this network of everyday expressions with *now*. Use a dictionary if necessary. Then use the expressions with *now* to rewrite the sentences below.

1. Do you want me to do it right away, or can it wait?
2. So, everybody, listen carefully. I have news for you.
3. I bump into her in town occasionally, but not that often.
4. I know you are upset, but everything will be better soon.

Unit 80 Similes

Similes are expressions that use **as . . . as . . .** or **like . . .** to compare one thing with another.

A **As . . . as . . .** similes are easy to understand. If you see the phrase **as dead as a doornail**, you don't need to know what a *doornail* is. In this case, the whole phrase means *completely dead*. But remember, fixed similes are usually informal/colloquial and often humorous, so use them with caution. Here are some tips to help you remember similes.

- Create a picture in your mind.

as **bl**ind as a **b**at   as **strong** as an **ox**   as **qu**iet as a **m**ouse

- Some can be remembered as pairs of opposites.

  as **heavy** as **lead** ≠ as **light** as a **feather**
  as **black** as **night** ≠ as **white** as **snow**

- Some can be remembered by sound patterns.

  as **b**usy as a **b**ee   as **g**ood as **g**old   as **c**ool as a **c**ucumber

Here are some other useful **as . . . as . . .** similes.

When it comes to business, he's **as hard as nails**. [tough, cold, and cruel]
I'll give this plant some water. The soil's **as dry as a bone**.
The fish must have been spoiled. After dinner, I was **as sick as a dog**.
Don't worry. Installing this new software is **as easy as falling off a log**.
She gave the answer **as quick as a wink**.
When I told him, his face went **as red as a beet**.

Sometimes the second part can change the meaning of the first.

The new carpet was **as white as snow**. [beautifully white]
When he saw it, his face went **as white as a sheet**. [pale with fear/horror]

B *Like . . .* similes

My plan **worked like a charm**, and the problem was soon solved.
Be careful the boss doesn't see you; she has **eyes like a hawk**.
No wonder he's overweight. He **eats like a horse**.
Did you sleep well? Yes, **like a log**. [very well]
Oh, no! I forgot to call him again. I've got **a brain like a sieve**!
She walks around **like a bull in a china shop**. [very clumsily]
Instead of helping us out, she sat there **like a bump on a log**. [immobile]
Dick and Jane are so much alike; they're **like two peas in a pod**.
He just stood there **like a statue**. [without moving or without emotion]

Unit 80

Exercises

80.1 Complete the *as ... as ...* similes without looking at A on page 160.

1. My throat is as dry as a/an .... ; I need a drink of water.
2. Jack always does the heavy lifting; he's as strong as a/an ....
3. He never says a thing; he's as quiet as a/an ....
4. After eating that bad cheese, I was as sick as a/an ....
5. I can't read this small print; I'm as blind as a/an .... without my glasses.

80.2 Match the words on the left with the words on the right to complete the similes. Two of the similes are not on page 160. Try and guess them.

1. *as* quick *as a/an*   daisy
2. *as* busy *as a/an*   beet
3. *as* flat *as a/an*   wink
4. *as* fresh *as a/an*   bee
5. *as* red *as a/an*   pancake

80.3 Fill in the blanks to complete these similes that use the same word.

1. a) I feel great now. I .... like a log.
   b) It's as easy as .... off a log.
2. a) The old man's hair was as white as ....
   b) Her face suddenly went as white as a/an ....

80.4 Complete this simile word puzzle by finding a related word for each clue. Two of the similes are not on page 160.

Across
2. dry
3. heavy
6. white
8. cold
9. blind
10. log
11. nails
12. cool

Down
1. quiet
4. fresh
5. light
7. red

80.5 Use a simile from page 160 to describe ...

1. a person who sees everything and never misses a thing.
2. a plan or course of action that worked very well.
3. a person who eats a great deal.
4. a person with a very bad memory.
5. a person who stays still and shows no emotion.

Unit 81 Binomials

Binomials are expressions (often idiomatic) in which two words are joined by a conjunction (usually **and**). The order of the words is usually fixed. For example:

odds and ends [small, unimportant things], e.g., *Let's get the main things packed; we can do the **odds and ends** later.*

give and take [a spirit of compromise], e.g., *Every relationship needs some **give and take** to be successful.*

A Binomials and sound patterns

Entertainment has become **part and parcel** [part of (formal)] of reporting the news.
The boss was **ranting and raving** [shouting / very angry] at us.
He's so **prim and proper** [rather formal and fussy] at work.

B Binomials and synonyms

You can **pick and choose** [have a wide choice]; it's up to you.
My English is progressing in **leaps and bounds**. [big jumps]
It's nice to have some **peace and quiet**. [peace/calm]
The doctor recommended some **rest and relaxation / R&R**. (informal)
First and foremost [first / most importantly], you have to work hard in life.
What we need to combat crime is **law and order**. [police enforcement of the law]

C Binomials with prepositions and adverbs

In this part of town you'll find cafés **here and there**. [scattered around]
He stayed at my house **on and off / off and on** [occasionally] for several years.
I've been running **back and forth** [to and from somewhere] all day.
He's been **down and out** [without a home or money / in difficult circumstances] ever since he lost his job.
She's recovered from the accident and is **out and about** [active] again.
My dog ran **up and down** [in both directions] the street.

D Binomials linked with words other than *and*

Her boss won't help her; she'll have to **sink or swim**. [survive or fail]
Slowly but surely [gradually], I realized the boat was sinking.
You may not think so now, but **sooner or later** [sometime/someday], you'll learn your lesson.
She didn't want to get half of the reward; it had to be **all or nothing**.
Well, I'm sorry, that's all I can offer you; **take it or leave it**.
It's about the same distance as from here to Boston, **give or take** [a little more than or a little less than] a few miles.
This package weighs two pounds, **more or less**. [approximately]

Unit 81

Exercises

81.1 Create binomials by pairing words in the box with the words below, without looking at page 162. Pair words that are either near synonyms or near antonyms (opposites) of each other.

| raving | clean | tired | out | bounds | order |
| then | quiet | there | choose | parcel | foremost |

1. law and ..*order*..........................
2. part and ....
3. neat and ....
4. first and ....
5. sick and ....
6. ranting and ....
7. pick and ....
8. down and ....
9. peace and ....
10. leaps and ....
11. now and ....
12. here and ....

81.2 Rewrite these sentences using some of the binomials you formed in 81.1. Note that the new sentences will often sound more informal than the original sentences.

1. The new mayor promised that efficient policing would be a priority.
2. The house looks orderly and spotless now for our visitors.
3. I have had enough of traffic jams. I'm going to start using the train.
4. My command of English vocabulary has improved rapidly since I've been using this book.
5. There are lots of courses in this university, so you can make your own selection.
6. I've seen her occasionally, taking her dog for a walk.

81.3 Combine the words in the box to form binomials. Some are from page 162 and some are new. Then use the binomials to complete the sentences below. Use a dictionary if necessary.

| prim | able | high | give | sound |
| ready | take | dry | proper | safe |

1. I was left .... and .... with no one to help me.
2. I'm glad you're .... and .... after such a dangerous trip.
3. I am .... and .... to handle new responsibilities in my job.
4. The administrative assistant is always so .... and .... , which makes the whole atmosphere always seem very formal.
5. If we're ever going to reach a compromise, there must be some .... and ....

81.4 Fill in the blanks with words other than *and*. Then check D on page 162 or a dictionary if necessary.

1. sooner .... later
2. all .... nothing
3. head .... toe
4. sink .... swim
5. slowly .... surely
6. last .... not least

Unit 82 Idioms describing people

A Positive and negative qualities

Positive	Negative
She has **a heart of gold**. [very kind, generous]	He's **as hard as nails**. [no sympathy for others]
He's **as good as gold**. [generous, helpful, well-behaved; often used for children]	She's kind of **a cold fish**. [distant, unfriendly]
He has **a good head for** numbers/figures. [good at math]	She **gets on everyone's nerves**. [irritates everybody]
She's **got her head screwed on** (right). [sensible]	I don't trust him. He's **a real back stabber**. [betrays trust]
	He's **a pain in the neck**. [a nuisance, difficult] Nobody likes him.

B People's fast and slow qualities

Fast	Slow
He's **a quick study**. He'll learn how to do the job in no time.	Come on! Hurry up! You're such **a slowpoke!**
You've asked him to marry you? You're **a fast worker!** You only met him three weeks ago!	She's a little **slow on the uptake**. It takes her a while to understand things.

C Describing people's social skills

He's a real **straight arrow**. [serious and honest]
Her ideas are **off the wall**. [eccentric, bizarre (informal)]
He's a bit of **an oddball**. [peculiar, strange]
He's (gone) **around the bend** [absolutely crazy/mad], if you ask me.
He's really **over the top**. [very exaggerated in behavior]
My politics are **middle-of-the-road**. [moderate; neither left- nor right-wing]

D Idioms for people in the classroom

She's the **teacher's pet**.

Olga's at the **head of the class**.

He's a **know-it-all**.

He's a **big mouth**.

She's a **slacker**.

note The last three idioms are also said of people outside of the classroom.

Unit 82

Exercises

82.1 Complete these idioms without looking at page 164.

1. He does a lot of volunteer work; he has a heart ....
2. Don't expect any sympathy from the boss; she's as hard ....
3. I'm sure Andre will help you; he's as good ....
4. She learned all the office procedures the first day at work. She's a quick ....
5. Tell him to hurry up! He is such a ....

82.2 Use idioms from page 164 to describe . . .

1. an irritating person who thinks he/she knows everything.
2. the person who is the teacher's favorite.
3. someone who never breaks the rules.
4. the person who gets the best marks.
5. a person who is very lazy.

82.3 Some idioms have a key word. For example, two idioms on page 164 have *gold* in them. Use these expressions with the key word *heart* to complete the sentences below. Then look for other sets of idioms based on key words.

to have
- a change of heart [change in attitude]
- your heart in the right place [good intentions, despite bad judgment]
- your heart set on something [wish for intensely]
- a heart [show compassion]
- a heart of stone [unsympathetic]

1. The boss isn't likely to give you a raise. He has ....
2. Come on, ... ! Make a donation to the children's fund.
3. Don't be angry with him. He has ....
4. At first she didn't want to live in a big city, but she's had ....
5. I really want to take a vacation next month. In fact, I ....

82.4 Idioms quiz. Fill in the blanks with a part of the body in order to express what a difficult person might do.

get on ....   be a pain in ....   stab you in ....

82.5 Write the idioms that these drawings represent.

1.   2.   3.

Unit 83 — Idioms describing feelings and mood

A Positive feelings, moods, and states

Mary seems to be **on cloud nine** [extremely pleased/happy] these days.
After he heard the good news, he was **walking on air**. [joyful, thrilled]
She seems to be **keeping her chin up** [happy despite bad things] after being fired.
Everyone in the office seems to be **in high spirits**. [lively, enjoying things]

B Negative feelings, moods, and states

His **heart sank** when he heard the bad news. [felt sad very quickly]
Kim is **in a bad/foul mood**. [a bad frame of mind / temper]
You **haven't been yourself** [seem slightly ill or upset] lately. Is anything wrong?
What's the matter? Why the **long face**? [looking unhappy]

C Physical feelings and states

I'm so hungry **I could eat a horse**! [very hungry]
I'm **feeling dead tired / dead on my feet**. [exhausted]
You're looking a little bit **under the weather**. [not very well / ill]
I was almost **at death's door** [very sick or ill] last week!

D Fear / fright

She was **scared stiff**. [very scared]
You **scared/frightened him to death**. [frightened him a lot]
We were all **shaking in our boots** [trembling with fear], waiting for our test results.
The poor kid! You **frightened/scared him out of his wits**. [extremely scared]
I **jumped out of my skin** [was startled/surprised] when I heard the loud bang.

> **note** There is an element of exaggeration in these idioms; they make comments on the situation and lighten the tone, so use them only informally.

E

Horoscopes can be a good place to find idioms about moods and states since a horoscope usually tries to tell you how you are going to feel during the coming day/week/month. Look at these horoscopes and note the idioms in boldface. Collect more idioms from horoscopes if you can.

Capricorn
(Dec. 22–Jan. 19)
Don't **get carried away** (1) with expensive plans you can't afford. **Keep a cool head** (2) and take everything as it comes. On the work front, things are looking better.

Taurus
(April 20–May 20)
Someone will say something that will **make you swell with pride** (3) and you may **be on top of the world** (4) for a while, but your evening won't be so easy.

(1) get excited; lose control
(2) stay calm
(3) feel very proud
(4) extremely happy

Unit 83

Exercises

83.1 Group these idioms as expressing either *positive* or *negative* feelings. Use a dictionary if necessary.

to be in seventh heaven
to feel/be a bit down
to feel blue
to be head over heels

83.2 Using the idioms from 83.1 and from A on page 166, say how you would probably feel if . . .

1. you were told you had just won a huge sum of money.
    I would feel/be on cloud nine.
2. your boss told you to redo a piece of work you'd already done three times.
3. you were told you'd gotten a very high mark on an exam.
4. you had a bad headache and your neighbor was making a lot of noise late at night.
5. nothing seemed to have gone right for you today.
6. someone you were secretly in love with told you they were in love with you.

83.3 Complete these idioms without looking at page 166.

1. Don't sneak up behind me like that! You scared me ....
2. I don't need a doctor, I just feel a little bit under ....
3. Last year, when I won that medal, I really was on ....
4. I wasn't expecting such a loud noise; I nearly jumped ....
5. I've had nothing since breakfast; I could ....

83.4 Look for idioms about feelings, moods, and states in these horoscopes. Underline them, and then check their meanings in a dictionary.

Scorpio
(Oct. 24–Nov. 21)
You may be itching to travel today, but be patient; this is not a good time to take a trip. Events at work will keep you on the edge of your seat for most of the day. Altogether an anxious time for Scorpios.

Leo
(July 23–Aug. 22)
You'll be up in arms over something someone close to you says rather thoughtlessly today, but don't let it spoil things. Something you thought special you will discover really is just a dime a dozen.

83.5 Use the idioms you underlined in 83.4 to rewrite these sentences.

1. This new MP3 player is really just like all the other ones.
2. I've been in suspense all day. What happened? Tell me!
3. We enjoyed our vacation, but by the end of it, we were restless to go home.
4. Everyone protested loudly when they canceled the outing.

83.6 Find the idioms on page 166 that include the words *boots*, *swell*, *weather*, and *carried*. Write a sentence in your notebook for each of the idioms you find.

Unit 84: Idioms connected with problematic situations

A Problems and difficulties

Idiom		Literal phrase
to **be in a fix**	=	be in difficulty
to **be in a bind**	=	be in a dilemma or predicament
to be **in a (tight) spot**	=	be in a situation that is hard to get out of

B Reacting in situations

to **take a back seat** [not do anything; let others act instead]	≠	to **take the bull by the horns** [act positively to face and attack the problem]
to **stir things up** [do/say things that make matters worse]	≠	to **straighten things out** [do/say things that clarify or calm the situation]
to **play one's cards close to one's chest** [hold back information]	≠	to **lay one's cards on the table** [be very open, state exactly what your position is]

C Idioms with *get*

This has to be done by next week; we'd better **get our act together** [organize ourselves to respond (informal)] before it's too late.

We need a thorough investigation to **get to the bottom of** [find the true explanation or reason for the state of affairs] things.

It's difficult to **get** people **to sit up and take notice**. [make them pay attention]

I'm trying to **get a grasp of** [understand] what's happening, but it's not easy.

(See Unit 91 for more idioms with *get*.)

D Changes and stages in situations

We can see **the light at the end of the tunnel** [the solution seems close] at last.
I'm afraid we've **come to a dead end** [cannot continue] with this project.
I think I've reached a **turning point** [a major change] in my career.
You should say "Sorry." **It would go a long way** [help a lot] in resolving the problem.

The government and the unions have **buried the hatchet** [stopped fighting each other], at least for the time being.

All that trouble last year was just **swept under the rug** [deliberately ignored or forgotten, without solving it] in the end.

Unit 84

Exercises

84.1 Fill in the blanks with appropriate idioms from page 168.

1. I think I'll just .... and let the others work this out.
2. No, please don't say anything; you'll only ....
3. It's been a long, hard struggle, but I think at last we can see ....
4. The police are trying their best to get to ...., but the case is a real mystery at the moment.
5. We're in a tight .... financially; we probably won't be able to make our payments this month.
6. At last I've managed to get him to sit ....; maybe now he will do something.
7. I find it hard to get a .... the causes of global warming, don't you?
8. I'm going to lay .... so you'll know exactly what my intentions are.

84.2 Look up these idioms in a dictionary, using the underlined words as your key word. Then see what other idioms or useful phrases you can find listed near them.

1. take the <u>bull</u> by the horns: *(to be/act) like a bull in a china shop [be very clumsy]*
2. come to a <u>dead</u> end
3. play your <u>cards</u> close to one's chest
4. <u>straighten</u> things out
5. <u>stir</u> things up

84.3 Paraphrase the meanings of these idioms. Use a dictionary if necessary.

1. It's not working; we'll have to <u>go back to square one</u>. *go back to the beginning again*
2. The teachers want one thing, the students want the exact opposite. But I'm sure we can find a <u>happy medium</u>.
3. We were on <u>pins and needles</u> all night waiting for news from the hospital. They finally called us at 6:30 a.m.
4. Poverty and crime <u>go hand in hand</u> in this part of town.
5. Things are better, but problems remain. We're not <u>out of the woods</u> just yet.

84.4 Write questions that match these answers.

1. Well, we've buried the hatchet for the moment, but I'm not sure it's permanent.
2. Yes, it's been a real turning point in my career.
3. Yes, I think it would go a long way. You know how sensitive he is, and how much he appreciates little gestures.

Unit 85   Idioms connected with praise and criticism

A Praise

- **Saying people are good at something**

  He's a really **first-rate / top-notch** programmer – the very best!
  When it comes to contracts, she's really **on the ball**. [knows a lot]
  Tareq really **has a way with** [good at establishing good relations] children.
  Sandra really **has a green thumb** [good at gardening]; just look at those flowers!

- **Saying people/things are better than the rest**

  Mary is **head and shoulders above** [much better than] the other students in the class.
  Our Olympic team is **the cream of the crop**. [the best (usually said of a group of people)]
  When it comes to electronics, our company is **miles / light years ahead** (used for people or things) of the competition.
  That meal was just **out of this world**. [outstanding/superb (usually said of things)]
  Your garden **puts** the others in the neighborhood **to shame**. [surpasses, is far better]

B Criticism

Note that in common use, there are far more idioms connected with criticism than there are idioms connected with praise.

- **Idioms with animal words**

  Don't be **(a) chicken / a scaredy cat**. [easily frightened, cowardly (informal)]
  He's always **crowing** [boasting] about his accomplishments.
  I don't trust her; she's a **snake in the grass**. [not to be trusted]
  Some people **worm their way** [accomplish something dishonestly] into good positions.

- **Idioms with food words**

  When it comes to unreliability, he really **takes the cake**. [is the epitome / most striking example of some negative quality]
  Anne-Marie **wants to have her cake and eat it, too**! [wants everything without any contribution from her side]
  I think he's just trying to **butter me up**. [give false praise]

- **Idiomatic synonyms of the verb *to criticize***

  Must you always **put me down** in front of other people?
  You shouldn't **run down / knock** your own country when you're traveling.
  Why do you always **pick apart** everything I say?

Unit 85

Exercises

85.1 Rewrite these sentences without changing their meanings. Use idioms from A on page 170.

1. The hotel we were staying in was fantastic.
2. Joe is far ahead of the other kids when it comes to arithmetic.
3. This restaurant is much, much better than all the other restaurants in town.
4. You're way ahead of me in understanding all this technology; I'm impressed.
5. The very best graduates from our university went on to business school.

85.2 Write the idioms from page 170 that these pictures might help you to remember.

1. 　2. 　3. 　4.

85.3 Which of the expressions in 85.2 is most appropriate for . . .

1. praising someone's knowledge/ability in their profession?
2. saying that someone is praising you just to gain an advantage?
3. saying someone is scared for no good reason?
4. praising someone's gardening skills?

85.4 Express the *opposite* meaning of these sentences using idioms from page 170.

1. She's a <u>third-rate</u> athlete. *She's a first-rate (or top-notch) athlete.*
2. Al is <u>extremely trustworthy</u>.
3. Steve <u>doesn't get along with</u> babies; just look at how they react when they see him.
4. He often <u>says how wonderful</u> his school is.
5. She <u>praises</u> everything I say.
6. She wants a promotion, a company car, and a raise, yet she can't even get to work on time. She <u>doesn't ask for much, does she</u>?
7. Your dinner parties <u>are the same as mine</u>.
8. She is always <u>so quiet and modest</u> about her high grades.

85.5 Using a good dictionary or a dictionary of idioms, find more idioms that include the food words below for praising or criticizing people/things/actions. Make sentences in your notebook with the idioms you find.

1. ham　　2. tea　　3. icing　　4. nut　　5. bacon

Unit 86 Idioms connected with using language

A Idioms connected with communication problems

She **can't get a word in edgewise**.   I **can't make heads or tails of** what she's saying.

B Good talk, bad talk

I hate how the boss always **talks down** [talks as if the other person(s) were inferior] to us.
My friends are always **talking behind my back**. [saying negative things about a person when that person is not there]
It was just **small talk** [social talk, not talk on serious matters], nothing more, honestly.
It's gone too far this time. I'll just have to **give him a talking** to. [scold/warn someone]
They always **talk shop** [talk about work] over lunch; they can't get enough of it!
Don't listen to her; she's **talking through her hat**. [talking ignorantly; telling lies]
OK, you **talked me into** [persuaded someone] it. I'll go to the movies with you.
I don't recall his number **off the top of my head** [remember something immediately], but I will get it for you.

C Talk in discussions, meetings, etc.

Unit 86

Exercises

86.1 Read these dialogs and provide comments about them.

1. MARY: Well, clearly I don't expect someone with your intelligence to understand this document.
   ERIC: Gee, thanks.

   It seems that ...*Mary is talking down to Eric*............... .

2. JOE: So that's what I'm going to do – take it all away.
   DANA: What about . . .
   JOE: And if they don't like it, they can just go and do what they like.
   DANA: But if they . . .
   JOE: Not that I have to consult them; after all, I'm in charge around here.
   DANA: I wonder if it . . .
   JOE: You see, I'm the kind of person who can make tough decisions.

   It seems that Dana can't get ....

3. MEG: So, area-wise the down-matching sales-profile commitment would seem to be high-staked on double-par.
   BING: Huh? Could you say that again? You've got me there.

   It seems that Bing can't make ....

4. SAM: So then George tells me that he never said it.
   LISA: You mean he actually denied saying it? Can you believe that guy?
   SAM: That's right! Can you imagine – oh, George, I didn't see you standing there.

   It seems that Sam and Lisa are talking ....

86.2 Write the idioms from page 172 that these drawings represent.

1. .... the discussion

3. get ....

2. ....

4. get to / come to ....

86.3 Fill in the blanks to complete the idioms.

1. She is very direct and always .... her mind.
2. I get bored with small .... ; let's talk about the economy.
3. The boss gave me a real .... to after that stupid mistake I made. I admit it though, I was wrong.
4. He is always talking .... his hat. He really should check his facts.

173

Unit 87 Miscellaneous idioms

A Idioms associated with paying, buying, and selling

He did $600 worth of damage to the car, and his parents had to **foot the bill**. [pay the bill, usually a large amount]

That restaurant was a **real rip-off**. *or* That taxi driver really **ripped us off**. [made someone pay too much for something (very informal)]

She **drives a hard bargain**. [negotiates a very good deal] She knew I was desperate to buy an apartment, so she charged as much as she could get.

If you want the fastest laptop, you'll have to pay **top dollar**. [a very high price]

He bought a real **lemon** [a machine with many problems] when he got that car.

B Idioms based on parts of the body

He's **made quite a bit of headway** [made progress] lately with algebra.

If I seem preoccupied, it's because I have a lot **on my mind** [a lot to worry about] these days.

We had to pay **through the nose** [pay a very high price] for that new video-game system.

I can't remember the name . . . but it's on **the tip of my tongue**. [something you know but can't remember immediately]

With this project, I've finally got something to really **sink my teeth into**. [really enjoy doing]

You've really got to **hand it to her** [acknowledge or admit]: she's an incredible singer.

Please don't be angry, but I really had to **get that off my chest**. [say something that has been bothering you]

C Idioms associated with daily routine

Come on! **Rise and shine!** [a command to someone to get up, often said to someone who doesn't want to and at a very early hour] Time to leave! There's no time for breakfast. We can **get a bite to eat** [have a snack or meal] on the highway. I'll drive and you can **take a nap** [sleep for a short period] in the back seat. When we get there, there'll just be time to **freshen up** [wash and clean oneself up] before the meeting. It's going to be a long day; I'm sure I'm going to **crash** [be very tired / quickly go to sleep (informal)] pretty early. Still, we can just **hang out** [relax] at home tomorrow, **put our feet up** [relax], and watch TV like **couch potatoes!** [people who sit or lie around, e.g., on a couch, watching TV, and who do not have a very active life]

Unit 87

Exercises

87.1 Read these mini-dialogs and answer the questions, using idioms from page 174.

1. LEE: I'll give you $85.
   YOKO: No, $100 or nothing.
   LEE: Oh, come on. Make it $90, OK?
   YOKO: No, I said $100 and I mean $100.

   What's Yoko doing? ....

2. HENRY: I'm so upset with Mark.
   NAN: What happened?
   HENRY: He really hurt my feelings and he doesn't even realize it. I'm so angry!

   What should Henry do? ....

3. JULIE: La-da-da-di . . .
   BETH: What's that song you're singing?
   JULIE: Oh, it's . . . um, uh . . . I'm sure I know the title. It'll come to me.

   Does Julie know the name of the song or not? ....

87.2 Rewrite these sentences, replacing the underlined words with idioms from page 174.

1. Can I tell you about a problem I have? I just have to <u>tell somebody</u>. It's been <u>bothering</u> me for a while now.
2. They charged us $200 for a tiny room without a TV. They <u>robbed</u> us!
3. We'll have just enough time <u>to get a quick snack</u> before the show.
4. I <u>must admit</u>, Maria handled the situation admirably.
5. I think I'll just go upstairs and <u>sleep for a little while</u>, if nobody minds.
6. We had to <u>pay a very high price</u> for the apartment, but we had no choice.

87.3 Think of a situation where you might. . .

1. be willing to pay through the nose for something.
2. foot the bill for a large group.
3. hang out with people you don't really like.

87.4 Write the idioms from page 174 that these drawings represent.

1.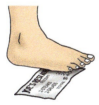
2.
3.

> **follow-up** Look up idioms in a dictionary for other parts of the body, e.g., *thumb*, *tongue*, *heels*, *toe*, *palm*, *back*, and make a list of examples in your notebook.

175

Unit 88 Proverbs

Speakers tend to use proverbs to comment on a situation, often at the end of a true story someone has told, or in response to some event. Like all idioms, proverbs are useful and enjoyable to know and understand, but they should be used with caution.

A Warnings / advice / morals

Proverb	Paraphrase
Don't count your chickens before they're hatched.	→ Don't plan how to use the good results of something before the results have happened.
Don't put all your eggs in one basket.	→ Don't invest all your efforts, money, or attention in just one thing.
Never judge a book by its cover.	→ Don't judge people/things by their outward appearance.
Never look a gift horse in the mouth.	→ Don't complain about a gift even if it's not perfect.

B Key elements

Proverbs can be grouped by key elements, e.g., animals and birds.

When the **cat's** away, the **mice** will play. [People will take advantage of an authority figure's absence to behave more freely.]
You can lead a **horse** to water, but you can't make it drink. [You can try to persuade someone, but you can't force him/her.]
A **bird** in the hand is worth two in the bush. [Keeping what is definite is better than trying to get more and losing everything.]

C Visualizing

As with learning all vocabulary, visualizing some element often helps.

Where there's smoke, there's fire.
[Rumors are usually based on some degree of truth.]

Too many cooks spoil the broth.
[Too many people interfering is a bad way of doing things.]

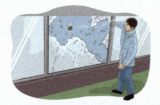

People who live in glass houses shouldn't throw stones.
[Don't criticize others' faults if you have the same faults yourself.]

It's no use crying over spilled milk.
[It doesn't help to keep feeling sad / keep complaining about something bad that has already happened.]

Unit 88

Exercises

88.1 **Find proverbs on page 176 that fit these situations.**

1. A friend says she has just been offered a free two-week vacation, but she doesn't like the place where it is offered.
2. Your brother says he can't be bothered applying to different universities and will apply to just one, even though it is very difficult to be accepted to.
3. You have lost a lot of money after investing in a restaurant with several partners, and you keep complaining about how terrible your partners were.

88.2 **People often refer to proverbs by saying only half and leaving the rest for the listener to fill in. Complete the proverbs in these mini dialogs.**

1. TOSHI: Jin is always criticizing people who are stingy, yet he's the cheapest person I know.
   JAE: Yes, well, people who live in glass houses ....
   TOSHI: Exactly.

2. SUE: The people in the office have been playing computer games and surfing the Web all day since the boss left on vacation.
   MIN: Well, you know what they say, "When the cat's away, ..."
   SUE: Well, they're certainly doing that.

3. ARI: I didn't believe those rumors about Nick and Sue, but apparently they are seeing each other.
   BINA: You're so naive; you know what they say, "Where there's smoke, ..."
   ARI: Well, I suppose you're right.

4. KIM: You know, I am paying for my daughter's tuition, apartment, a car, everything! And she still can't manage to get to class on time.
   JOHN: Really? Well, you know, you can lead a horse to water, ...
   KIM: I'm afraid that's true, isn't it?

88.3 **Match the proverbs on the left with ones on the right that have a similar meaning. Then say what they have in common in terms of meaning.**

1. A bird in the hand is worth two in the bush.
2. Don't count your chickens before they're hatched.
3. All that glitters is not gold.
4. Absence makes the heart grow fonder.

Never judge a book by its cover.
Familiarity breeds contempt.
Never look a gift horse in the mouth.
Don't cross your bridges before you come to them.

> *follow-up* Try translating some proverbs from your native language, word for word, into English. Then, if you can, ask native speakers of English if they know of any English proverb that has the same or similar meaning.

Unit 89   Expressions with *do* and *make*

A Phrasal verbs

The next six units deal with phrasal verbs and other expressions based on common verbs. Phrasal verbs are verbs that combine with different prepositions or adverbs to make two- or three-word verbs that have completely new meanings and are often difficult to guess. Phrasal verbs are more common in spoken English than in written English.

B Common phrasal verbs with *do* and *make*

Phrasal verb	Meaning	Example
do away with	abolish	There is a growing movement in this country to do away with income tax.
do something over	redo	You need to do this resume over; it is full of mistakes.
do without	manage without	You'll have to do without a cigarette for a while. Smoking isn't allowed here.
make of	think (opinion)	What do you make of his remarks?
make off with	take or steal	The gang made off with more than $200,000.
make up for	compensate for	The superb food at the hotel made up for the uncomfortable rooms.

C Phrasal verbs that have many different meanings

Do up can mean not only *fasten* but also *tie* and *put into a bundle*. Similarly, **make out** can mean *manage to see*, *succeed or progress*, and *understand* as well as *write* or *complete*. **Make up** can mean *compose* or *invent*; it can also mean *constitute* or *form*, *put cosmetics on*, *prepare by mixing together various ingredients*, and *make something complete*.

D Other common expressions with *do* and *make*

Note that **do** emphasizes the action itself while **make** often emphasizes the result of the action.

You **do** your best / a disservice / a favor / a good job / nothing / aerobics / exercises / laps / sit-ups / sprints / weightlifting / yoga / chores / the cooking / the dishes / (the) gardening / homework / (the) housework / (the) laundry / paperwork / the shopping.

You **make** money / (a) noise / sense / sure / trouble / war / an agreement / arrangements / an attempt / a choice / a decision / a difference / an effort / an excuse / a good or bad impression / a mistake / a promise / a suggestion / a bed / a cup of coffee / a delivery / a living / a meal / a phone call / (photo) copies / a profit / allowances for . . . / the best of . . . / fun of . . . / a fuss about . . . / the most of . . . / a point of . . .

Unit 89

Exercises

89.1 Write the meanings for each of these underlined phrasal verbs using *do* and *make*.

1. Can you <u>make out</u> that little house in the distance? *manage to see*
2. A human being <u>is made up</u> of many, often conflicting, desires.
3. Would you <u>do up</u> these buttons for me?
4. Those children are always <u>making up</u> silly stories.
5. How are you <u>making out</u> at your new job?
6. I like the way you've <u>done up</u> your hair.
7. I'll <u>make out</u> a check to you and you can cash it.

89.2 Fill in the blanks with the necessary prepositions or adverbs to complete this story.

> Last weekend we decided to start doing ....*over*............ (1) our cabin in the country. We agreed that we could really do .... (2) the ugly old fireplace in the bedroom. As we began to tear it down, we found a small box behind a loose brick, and we didn't know what to make .... (3) it. When we opened it, there were some old pictures. At first we could not make .... (4) what was in the pictures, but we wiped them clean and realized they all depicted the same young man. We spent an enjoyable evening making .... (5) stories to explain why the pictures had been hidden.

89.3 Correct the mistakes in these sentences. Either the wrong word order or the wrong preposition or adverb has been used.

1. I don't know what to make that statement of.
2. Try to make the most off a bad situation.
3. Your shoelaces are untied. Do up them or you'll trip on them.
4. They like to make away that they are terribly important.

89.4 Divide the expressions in D on page 178 into groups that will help you learn them.

89.5 Complete these sentences using an appropriate expression from D on page 178.

1. It doesn't matter if you pass or not as long as you do ....
2. Companies that once made a huge .... are now going bankrupt.
3. If you make a .... the game is over.
4. You should dress formally for an interview if you want to make ....
5. I don't like doing .... , but someone has to clean, wash, iron, and cook!
6. Could you do me a .... by lending me your car?
7. The hurricane really did some .... to the area, destroying over fifty homes.

89.6 Choose ten phrasal verbs or expressions with *do* or *make* that you want to learn. Make a list of them in your notebook, and then use them to write a paragraph.

Unit 90

Expressions with *bring* and *take*

A Common phrasal verbs with *bring*

Technology has **brought about** [caused to happen] many changes in the way we live.
Keep talking to him, and you'll **bring** him **around** [persuade] to your point of view.
I wish they'd **bring back** [reintroduce] record players.
This scandal will surely **bring down** [destroy, remove from power] the government.
This bad cough was **brought on** [caused by something bad] by the wet weather.
Several companies are **bringing out** [introducing] a new line of cell phones this year.
The seasoning really **brings out** [reveals or exposes] the flavor of this dish.
I was **brought up** [raised] on a farm.
Please don't **bring up** [introduce] the subject of taxes; you know it annoys me.

B Common phrasal *verbs* with *take*

He **takes after** [resembles or has similar traits] his father in more ways than one!
I wish I could **take back** [withdraw] that e-mail I just sent her.
She was completely **taken in** [deceived] by him.
Sales have really **taken off** [started to improve] since we started the new ads.
The plane **took off** [left the ground] right on time.
We'll have to **take on** [increase] more staff if we're going to **take on** more work.
I'm **taking** my mother **out** [escorting, inviting to a restaurant, etc.] for her birthday.
Can you **take over** [do something that someone else was doing] for me? I need to leave.
When did you **take up** [start a hobby, etc.] golf?
Our company was **taken over** [taken control of] by a larger company.

C Other common expressions with *bring* and *take*

Her research **brought** some very interesting facts **to light**. [revealed]
Matters were **brought to a head** [reached a point where changes had to be made] when Pat was fired.
It's best that the negotiations be **brought out into the open**. [made public]
The government was **brought to its knees** [made weak or helpless] by the crisis.
His new wife has **brought out the best/worst in** [be good/bad for someone] him.
Don't let him **take advantage of** [use superiority unfairly] you.
Just because you're having a bad day, don't **take it out on** [cause somebody else to suffer because you are angry or unhappy] me!
The gorgeous sunset **took my breath away**. [surprised, amazed]
She loves **taking care of** [looking after, caring for] small children.
We **took part in** [participated in] a demonstration last Saturday.
The story **takes place** [happens] in South Korea.
He doesn't seem to **take pride in** [get satisfaction from] his work.
The boss always **takes** everything **in (her) stride**. [deals with things calmly]

Unit 90

Exercises

90.1 Fill in the blanks with the appropriate prepositions or adverbs.

1. Looking at these photos really brings .... memories.
2. How can you bring .... change if you won't even talk with each other?
3. Do you think our company will be taken .... by a corporate giant?
4. Maybe you're taking .... more work than you can handle.
5. This time it's my treat: I'm taking *you* .... to dinner!
6. After her husband died, she brought .... six children all by herself.

90.2 Complete this bubble network for *take* (see Unit 2). Then make one for phrasal verbs with *bring*.

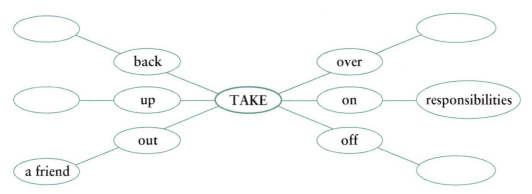

90.3 Answer these questions, using one of the phrasal verbs in A or B on page 180.

1. What caused your rash? *It was brought on by strong sunlight.*
2. Who does that little girl act like – her mother or her father?
3. Do you have any special hobbies?
4. How's your new business doing?
5. Do you think you'll manage to persuade him to let you come on the trip?
6. Why do you suppose our plane is landing two hours late?
7. What do politicians often promise before an election?

90.4 Replace the underlined words with expressions from C on page 180.

1. The story of the movie <u>happens</u> in Casablanca during the war.
2. Today's newspaper <u>reveals</u> some fascinating information about the president.
3. How does he always manage to <u>be so calm about things</u>?
4. The view from the top of the hill <u>was astonishing</u>.
5. He <u>capitalized on</u> her weakness at the time and she sold the car to him.
6. The main function of a nurse is <u>to care</u> for the sick.
7. Whenever you're upset, you always <u>make the children suffer</u>.

90.5 Find the expressions in C on page 180 that mean the opposite of these expressions.

1. to become upset
2. to look on
3. to disregard
4. to avoid confrontation
5. to be careless about
6. to be bored by something

181

Unit 91: Expressions with *get*

A. The basic meanings of *get* in spoken English

- to buy, receive, or obtain something, e.g., *Please **get** me a newspaper when you're in town. I **got** a letter from John today. She **got** high marks on her exam.*
- to change one's position – move or be moved, e.g., *How are you **getting** home tonight?*
- to change one's state of being – become or make, e.g., *We are all **getting** older if not wiser.*

B. Some specific meanings of *get*

I don't **get** [understand] it. Why did he say that?
Her arrogant behavior really **gets** [annoys, irritates] me sometimes.
I'll **get the phone / the door**. [answer]
Once we **got to know** [began to know] each other, we became great friends.

C. Common phrasal verbs with *get*

Phrasal verb	Meaning	Example
get along	have a good relationship with	He gets along well with his roommates.
get along	manage	How will we ever get along without you?
get at	reach, find	I hope the investigation will get at the truth.
get away with	do something wrong without being caught	The robbers got away with several thousand dollars.
get behind	fail to produce something at the right time	I've gotten really far behind with my work.
get by	manage (financially)	We couldn't get by on my salary alone.
get down	become depressed	This rain is really getting me down.
get down to	direct your attention to	It's about time we got down to work.
get off	finish, leave	I get off work at 5:00 p.m.
get out	leave	Get out and don't come back!
get out of	avoid a responsibility	I'll try to get out of that appointment.
get over	recover from	She's just getting over the flu.
get through	come to a successful end	It's a relief to get through all my exams!
get up	wake up	Get up, you're late for work!

D. Other common expressions with *get*

The meeting **got off to a good/bad start** [began well/badly] with her speech.
I'm having a little **get-together** [informal social gathering]. I hope you can come.
When we moved, **I got rid of** [threw away, destroyed] half the things in the attic.
I'm going to **get back at** [take revenge on] her somehow.
After two days of meetings, we've **gotten nowhere**. [made no progress, wasted time]
You must have **gotten out of the wrong side of the bed** [be in a bad mood] today.

Unit 91

Exercises

91.1 Replace the underlined expressions using *get* with other expressions that mean the same thing. Notice that you will be changing the text from informal to slightly more formal language.

> I don't <u>get</u> interesting offers through e-mail very often. However, an unusual one came this morning. It was titled "Are little things <u>getting you down</u>?" It went on, "If so, <u>get</u> some of our special pills today. Taking just one in the morning will help you <u>get along well</u> at work, at home, or at school. It will stop the feeling that you're <u>getting nowhere</u> in life and will ensure that you <u>get</u> rich and successful with little effort on your part. Go to our Web site and pay just $25 online today, and you will <u>get</u> your tablets and your key to success within 10 days."

91.2 Fill in the blanks with words from page 182.

1. Just get .... all your exams and then you can relax.
2. You're still sneezing! Haven't you gotten .... that cold yet?
3. It's so difficult to get .... on a teacher's salary.
4. He doesn't get .... well with his co-workers. No one likes him.
5. It takes time to get to .... your teachers and classmates.

91.3 Match the situations on the left with the appropriate expressions on the right.

1. You are very late in completing a critical project.
2. Someone is about to throw something away.
3. Your roommate is still asleep and has an important meeting in 30 minutes.
4. Someone has done something very cruel to you.
5. Some people have stolen your money.

They'll never get away with this.

Just you wait! I'll get back at you one of these days!

Don't get rid of that yet!

Get up! You're going to be late!

How did I get so far behind?

91.4 Complete these sentences in any appropriate way.

1. I would hate to get rid of ....
2. The job interview got off to a bad start when ....
3. I find it very hard to get down to ....
4. I wish I could get out of ....
5. .... is really getting me down.

91.5 There are other phrasal verbs and expressions based on *get* not listed on page 182. Write example sentences in your notebook using any that you can think of. Use a dictionary if necessary

Unit 92 — Expressions with *set* and *put*

A Common phrasal verbs with *set*

You should **set aside** [reserve, save] some money for the future.
He tried to **set aside** [ignore, not think about] their differences.
Set your clock **back/ahead** [change to an earlier/later time] one hour.
The damage from the fire **set** us **back** [cost] more than $10,000.
The new law **set off** [caused, incited] protests throughout the country.
We should **set out** [depart, begin to do something] before dawn to get there on time.
The bank helps people who want to **set up** [start, establish] a business.

B Common phrasal verbs with *put*

She's good at **putting** her ideas **across**. [communicating to others]
Please **put away** [pick up and put in the right place] your toys now.
He is always **putting** her **down**. [criticizing]
He **put** his own name **forward** [proposed] to head the committee.
We had a new air-conditioning unit **put in** [installed] last year.
I'm going to **put in** [submit] an application for that job.
You're **putting** me **on**! [deceiving or teasing someone as a joke (informal)]
They've **put off** [postponed] making their decision for another week.
Your bad attitude really **puts** me **off**. [discourages, irritates; also **turn off** (informal)]
He's good at **putting on** [pretending to have] all kinds of accents.
The firefighters quickly **put out** [extinguished] the fire.
Please don't let me **put** you **out**. [inconvenience]
You're not allowed to **put up** [hang, mount] posters here.
I can **put** you **up** [give accommodations to] for the weekend.
I can't believe you stole a car! Who **put you up to** [instigated, incited] this?
Why do you **put up with** [tolerate] such rudeness from your wife's family?

C Other common expressions with *set* and *put*

He has **set his heart/sights on** [desires] becoming a dancer.
Did someone **set fire to** [ignite] the house / **set** the house **on fire** deliberately?
Diane had never **set foot in** [been to] Italy before.
Jill is very **set in her ways**. [fixed in one's habits]
Try to **set a good example**. [be a good model for others]
His humorous remarks **set the tone** [influenced the mood] for the meeting.
You really need to **put your foot down** [be firm about something] with teenagers.
You can succeed if **you put your mind to it**. [focus all your energy on]
It was easy to **put two and two together**. [draw an obvious conclusion]
I'll **put in a good word** [speak favorably] for you with the boss
We're behind on this project, so we have to work late. **To put it another way** [restate an idea], we'll get fired if we don't finish by tomorrow.

Unit 92

Exercises

92.1 Replace these underlined phrasal verbs from A on page 184 with their more formal English equivalents.

1. They have recently set up a committee on neighborhood crime.
2. We try to set aside some money for our summer vacation every week.
3. The new ad campaign set us back over two million dollars.
4. If we hadn't set out so late, we would have arrived on time.
5. The government's unpopular new taxes set off a wave of protests.
6. When we cross the International Date Line, should we set our clocks back?

92.2 Write two nouns that could follow each phrasal verb from B on page 184. Remember that their meanings might change depending on the noun that follows.

1. put out   *a fire, a host*
2. put forward
3. put off
4. put across
5. put up
6. put on
7. put away
8. put up with

92.3 Write responses to these statements or questions, using any appropriate phrasal verb from A or B on page 184.

1. How should we publicize our play? *We could put up posters.*
2. That high definition TV must have cost a fortune.
3. This room is in a terrible mess.
4. Do you have room for one more guest this weekend?
5. Guess what? I won the lottery! I'm rich!
6. What happened when he started the meeting with bad news about the company's finances?

92.4 Rewrite these sentences without changing their meanings, using the expressions in B and C on page 184.

1. He never wants to do anything in a new or different way.
2. Why do you always criticize him? Don't you realize how sensitive he is?
3. Her aim is to become president of the company.
4. Please concentrate on the problem at hand.
5. She threw lighter fluid on the trash and lit it with a match.
6. This is the first time I've ever been in the southern hemisphere.
7. You really should be firm with the children or there'll be trouble later.
8. If Ms. Martin doesn't show the behavior she wants, the children certainly won't behave.
9. In other words, I won't do it at any price.

92.5 Choose ten of the phrasal verbs and other expressions with *set* and *put* that you particularly want to learn and write your own example sentences in your notebook.

185

Unit 93   Expressions with *come* and *go*

A   Common phrasal verbs with *come*

I **came across** [found by chance] a beautiful old vase in that junk shop.
He **comes across** [appears] as very serious, but he's really friendly.
Nothing can **come between** [separate; be a barrier between] him
   and soccer.
The movie **comes on** [starts to be shown or broadcast] at six.
Come on [express disbelief], you can't be serious!
Come on [encourage], you can do it – I know you can!
Has that new photo software **come out** [been
   published, made public] yet?
The stain on the carpet won't **come out**. [be removed]
She was knocked unconscious, but she **came to** [became
   conscious] quickly.
Your bill **comes to** [amounts to, totals] $55.
Our new Web site is finally **coming together**! [working successfully]
I've **come up with** [invented, created] a great idea.

B   Common expressions with *come to* and *come into*

Come to an agreement / a conclusion / a halt / a standstill [stop] / an end / a decision /
   mind [enter one's thoughts] / blows [start fighting] / grips with / terms with
   [acknowledge and accept psychologically] / one's senses [become sensible again after
   behaving foolishly]
Come into bloom / contact / a fortune / money / operation [start working] / sight / view /
   power [a political party or a ruler] / existence / fashion / use / possession of

C   Common phrasal verbs with *go*

What is **going on** [happening] next door? They **went on** [continued] working despite the
   noise. As the weeks **went on** [time passed], things improved. You **go on** [go in
   advance / go ahead of someone], we'll catch up with you later.
I wouldn't like to **go through** [experience, endure] that again. Let's **go through** [check]
   the plans again. Unfortunately, the business deal we were hoping for did not **go
   through** [be completed or approved]. He **went through** [spent, used] his entire
   paycheck in one night.
He **goes for** [is attracted by] taller women. Whichever job you **go for** [choose], I'm sure
   you'll make the best of it. I think you should **go for it**. [take a risk]
Those shoes don't **go with** [suit, match] that dress.
The alarm **went off** [rang] when the burglars tried to open the door.
She would never **go back on** [break a promise] her word.

D   Other common expressions with *go*

He's been **on the go** [very busy, on the move] all day and he's exhausted.
It **goes without saying** [is clear without being said] that we'll all support you.
Your work is good, **as far as it goes**. [but is limited or insufficient]
I'm sure she'll **go far**. [be very successful]
They **went to great lengths** [took a lot of trouble] to keep it a secret.
Unfortunately, the business **went bankrupt**. [declared a state of financial ruin]

Unit 93

Exercises

93.1 Complete these sentences with one of the expressions in B on page 186.

1. I found it hard to make up my mind, but finally I came ....
2. No ideas come .... , but I'll tell you if I think of any.
3. I love it in spring when my cherry tree comes ....
4. Halfway up the hill, the bus came ....
5. All good things must come ....
6. The telephone first came .... in the 19th century.
7. They disagreed so fiercely that they actually came ....
8. As we turned the corner the house came ....

93.2 Rephrase these underlined phrasal verbs.

1. He <u>went on</u> composing music until he was in his eighties. *continued*
2. She <u>went through</u> all her pockets looking for her keys.
3. She has a new book <u>coming out</u> in June.
4. I was sure he'd <u>go for</u> a sports car.
5. I <u>went through</u> three pairs of running shoes training for the race.
6. After the surgery, it took the patient several hours to <u>come to</u>.

93.3 Replace the underlined expressions with ones from D on page 186.

1. <u>I don't need to say that</u> we wish you all the best in the future.
2. They <u>took great pains</u> to avoid meeting each other.
3. I've been <u>running around</u> all day, and now I'm ready to relax.
4. His teachers always said that he would <u>be a success</u> in life.
5. The book is good <u>up to a point</u>, but it doesn't tackle the most important issue.

93.4 Match the questions on the left with the answers on the right.

1. Why is she looking so miserable?   Right after the news.
2. What's going on over there?   Everything is finally coming together.
3. When does your alarm clock usually go off?   It's a fight, I think.
4. How much did the hotel bill come to?   Seven-thirty, normally.
5. When does the game come on TV tonight?   Her firm went bankrupt.
6. Why are you so happy?   Over $1,000!

93.5 Complete these sentences in any appropriate way.

1. I recently came across ....
2. I would never want to go through ....
3. It's easy to come to the conclusion that ....
4. It is difficult to come to terms with ....
5. Nothing could come between my friends and me except ....

Unit 94 Miscellaneous expressions

Here are some expressions formed with **look, see, run, turn, let,** and **break**.

A Look

Look up [search for] new words in the dictionary.
I'm really **looking forward to** [anticipating] meeting your parents.
Look out [be careful]! You could fall from there if you're not careful.
You shouldn't **look down on** [view as less important] him because he's not well educated.

B See

I'd better **see about/to** [deal with, attend to] arrangements for the conference.
They went to **see** Jim **off** [say goodbye at an airport, station, etc.] at the airport.
It's not hard to **see through** [not be deceived by] his behavior.
I must be **seeing things**. [hallucinating]
They **don't** always **see eye to eye**. [disagree]
Pat has been **seeing someone** [dating, having a romance with] for a few months.
It's sometimes hard to **see the forest for the trees**. [see the big picture instead of focusing on details]

C Run

I **ran into** [met unexpectedly] an old friend yesterday.
Her patience has **run out**. [come to an end]
Let's **run through** [review, rehearse] the presentation again.
Red hair **runs in my family**. [a characteristic that appears in many family members]
She **runs** [manages / has overall responsibility for] the business.

D Turn

She **turned down** [refused] the job offer.
Who do you think **turned up** [made an (unexpected) appearance] last night at the party?
I'm going to **turn over a new leaf** [start again, with good intentions] this year.
It's your turn to do the laundry. [It's your duty because I did it last time.]
It's late. I think I'll **turn in**. [go to bed]

E Let

He has been **let down** [disappointed] by college rejection letters.
She won't **let us in on** [tell something secret] her plan.
I hope the rain **lets up** [becomes less strong] soon.
Let go of [stop holding] the rope.
Please **let me be**. [stop bothering someone]
She **let it slip** [mentioned accidentally, casually] that she had been given a pay raise.

F Break

The car **broke down** [stopped working] again this morning.
They've **broken off** [ended] their engagement, so there won't be a wedding.
Burglars **broke into** [forcibly entered] our house while we were on vacation.
He **broke her heart**. [made someone deeply unhappy]
The runner **broke the record** [was better than anything before] for the 10-kilometer race.

Unit 94

Exercises

94.1 Fill in the blanks to create expressions from page 188. Use only one word in each blank.

> OK, let's run .... (1) the plans for tomorrow's party one more time. First, I have to see .... (2) the food arrangements while you make sure that none of the karaoke equipment is likely to break .... (3). I don't suppose many people will turn .... (4) until later, but Nick and Jill promised to come early to help us. I'm sure they won't let us .... (5). I'm really looking .... (6) to it!

94.2 Rewrite the underlined phrases using the words in parentheses.

1. Why can't she <u>realize he is deceiving her</u>? (see)
2. I <u>met</u> Jack <u>by chance</u> at the library yesterday. (run)
3. I cooked dinner yesterday. It's <u>up to you</u> to do it today. (turn)
4. I thought I was <u>hallucinating</u> when I saw a monkey in the garden. (see)
5. I wish you'd <u>stop bothering me</u>. (let)
6. When she left him, she <u>made him utterly miserable</u>. (break)

94.3 Complete these sentences in any appropriate way.

1. If the snow doesn't let up soon, ...
2. Halfway up the mountain, he let go ....
3. She turned over a new leaf by ....
4. He felt terribly let down when ....
5. She let it slip that ....
6. I'm afraid we've run out of ....

94.4 Answer these questions.

1. Have you ever turned down an offer or invitation that you later regretted?
2. Have you ever had problems because of something (a vehicle or a piece of equipment, perhaps) breaking down at an inconvenient time? What happened?
3. Is there someone you don't see eye to eye with? Why not?
4. Is there a skill, quality, or physical trait that runs in your family?
5. Have you ever resolved to turn over a new leaf? In what way(s)?
6. Do you have anything you have to see to today? If so, what?
7. Has your home ever been broken into? What happened?
8. What time do you usually turn in?

94.5 The expressions on page 188 are only some of the many expressions using *look*, *see*, *run*, *turn*, *let*, and *break*. In your notebook, write two other phrasal verbs or expressions using each of these verbs. Use a dictionary if necessary.

Unit 95

Headline English

A Newspaper headlines try to catch the reader's eye by using as few words as possible. Therefore, the language of headlines is unusual in a number of ways.

- Grammar words, such as articles or auxiliary verbs, are often left out, e.g.:
  EARLY CUT FORECAST IN INTEREST RATES
- The simple present form of the verb is used, e.g.:
  MAYOR OPENS HOSPITAL
- The infinitive is used to describe something that is going to happen in the future, e.g.:
  PRESIDENT TO VISIT FLOOD AREA

B Newspaper headlines use a lot of distinctive vocabulary that is shorter and sounds dramatic. The words marked * can be used either as nouns or verbs in headlines.

Newspaper word	Meaning	Newspaper word	Meaning
aid*	help	link*	connect
ax*	cut, remove	loom	is likely to happen
back	support	move*	step toward a desired end
bar*	exclude, forbid	OK*	approve, endorse
bid*	attempt	ordeal	painful experience
blast*	explode, criticize	oust	push out
blaze*	fire	pact	agreement
boost*	to increase or encourage	plea*	request
boss* chief head*	manager, director	pledge*	promise
		plunge*	go down sharply
clash*	dispute	poll*	public opinion survey
combat*	fight	probe*	investigate
curb*	restrain, limit	quit	leave, resign
cut*	reduce	seek	look for, pursue
deny	contradict	soar	do well
dive*	go down sharply	stall	stop temporarily
drive*	campaign, effort	talks	discussions
edge*	get closer	threat	danger
flat	no change	vow*	promise
go-ahead, nod	approval	wed	marry
hike*	increase		
key	essential, vital		

Newspaper headlines often use abbreviations, e.g., **Gov't** for *Government*, **House** for *United States House of Representatives*, **FDA** for *Food and Drug Administration*. (See Unit 16 for more abbreviations.)

Unit 95

Exercises

95.1 Match the headlines on the left with the appropriate topics on the right.

1. FDA OKS HIV HOME SCREENING
2. STUDENTS BLAST MOVE TO OUST TEACHER
3. FAT LINKED TO HEART DISEASE
4. STAR WEDS SECRETLY
5. GOV'T PROBE STALLS
6. MIDDAY NAPS GET NOD FROM RESEARCHERS, WORKERS

investigation about government is stopped
marriage of a famous person
new medical test for home use
complaint at a school
study involving work and sleep
research about diet and health

95.2 Explain what the following headlines mean in ordinary English.

1. STORE BLAZE – 5 DEAD   *Five people died in a fire in a store*
2. MOVE TO CREATE MORE JOBS
3. GO-AHEAD FOR WATER CURBS
4. MAN QUITS AFTER JOB ORDEAL
5. POLL PROBES SPENDING HABITS
6. ELECTRIC COMPANY SEEKS RATE HIKE

95.3 These headlines contain verbs from the table in B on page 190. Look at the underlined verbs and explain what they mean. You may need to use more than one word in your explanation.

1. CITY TO <u>CURB</u> SPENDING   *to limit*
2. GOV'T TO <u>PROBE</u> AIRLINE SAFETY
3. UNION BOSS <u>BLASTS</u> JOB CUTS
4. HOUSING CHIEF <u>PLEAS</u> FOR HOMELESS AID
5. PRESIDENT <u>COMBATS</u> STOCK PLUNGE
6. TRADE PACT <u>BOOSTS</u> EXPORTS

95.4 Look at these headlines and think about the stories they might tell. Which ones would interest you? Explain why or why not.

WOMEN BARRED FROM KEY JOBS

GOV'T BACKS RAIL TAKEOVER BID

INFECTIOUS DISEASE CRISIS LOOMS

AIRFARES SOAR, TOURISM DOWN

MAYOR DENIES DRUG USE

LIONS EDGE STEELERS IN OVERTIME

follow-up   Look through some English language newspapers and find some examples of headlines that use the words and grammar noted on page 190.

Unit 96 The language of signs and notices

Signs and notices in English often use words and expressions that are rarely seen in other contexts. Look at these signs and notices with their "translations" into more everyday English.

1. **No trespassing or soliciting. Violators will be prosecuted.**

   If you walk on this private property, ask for donations (especially money), or try to sell things, you may be taken to court.

2. **Feeding the animals strictly prohibited**

   You are not allowed to feed the animals.

3. **Reduced speed ahead**

   Start driving more slowly soon.

4. **Limit: 5 garments per customer**

   You may only take five pieces of clothing into the fitting room.

5. **Post no bills**

   You may not put up any posters or signs here.

6. **PLEASE DEPOSIT REFUSE IN PROPER RECEPTACLES**

   Please put trash in the trash container or bin.

7. **Smoking is hazardous to your health**

   This is a warning that smoking causes serious physical damage.

8. **No cell phone use at counter**

   You must turn off your cell phone before coming to the teller or salesperson.

9. **This area is a smoke-free environment**

   There is no smoking allowed. (Usually any smoking areas will be clearly marked.)

10. **Reserved parking. Violators subject to tow away at vehicle owner's expense.**

    You may not park without permission. If you do, your car might be towed away, and you will have to pay for the towing.

11. **Prohibited: Bicycles, skateboards, rollerblades, playing ball. Monetary fine will be imposed**

    You may not use bicycles, skateboards, or rollerblades, or play ball here. If you do, you must pay money as a penalty.

12. **Federal law prohibits tampering with, disabling, or destroying any smoke detector in any aircraft lavatory.**

    On an airplane, you may not touch the smoke detector in the bathroom/lavatory.

Unit 96

Exercises

96.1 State where you would expect to see each of the notices on page 192.

Example: 1. *near private homes, apartments, or businesses*

96.2 Match the words on the left with their more everyday translations on the right.

1. to prosecute
2. a receptacle
3. a trespasser
4. a monetary fine
5. to solicit
6. to prohibit
7. a violator
8. to tamper
9. a vehicle
10. smoke-free

money paid as a punishment
someone who disobeys the rules/law
to bring a legal case against
to damage, misuse, or alter something improperly
a means of transportation, such as a car
no smoking allowed
a container, can, or bin
to forbid something
someone who goes on private property without permission
to ask for something (usually money) or try to sell something

96.3 Explain these signs and notices in everyday English. Then state where you would expect to see each of them.

1. Nothing to declare
2. Any spectator throwing objects onto the playing field will be ejected.
3. REFUNDS ONLY WITHIN 14 DAYS.
4. Unlawful to litter on city streets.
5. Right lane ends, merge left.
6. Shoplifters will be prosecuted to the full extent of the law.
7. CAUTION: WORKERS AHEAD. REDUCE SPEED. FINES DOUBLED.
8. No vacancies

96.4 What signs would a store manager put up in order to . . .

1. let customers know that they cannot eat or drink while in the store?
2. ask people not to put notices on the walls?
3. warn people not to come into the store to ask for money or do other business?

96.5 Sometimes signs have a humorous or ironic tone, rather than a formal one. Explain what these signs might mean and where you might see them.

1. If you break it, you've bought it.
2. Don't even think about parking here.
3. In God we trust, all others pay cash.

193

Unit 97 Words and gender

Here are some ways to avoid sexist or gender-biased language.

A Words and expressions with -man

Some words contain the generic **man** even though they refer to both sexes. Below are some suggestions for replacing such words with gender-neutral words.

Traditional word / expression	Gender-neutral substitute
man, mankind	human being(s), human(s), humanity, people
manpower	work force, staff, labor
to man	to staff
man-made	synthetic, artificial, manufactured
man on the street	average/typical/ordinary person

B -man, -woman, and -person

Here are some gender-neutral words to replace traditional job titles and roles that use **-man**, **-woman**, or **-ess**. Sometimes, however, there is no neutral word (e.g., **fisherman**, **repairman**).

Gender neutral	Traditional male	Traditional female
businessperson, executive	businessman	businesswoman
chair(person)	chairman	chairwoman
camera operator	cameraman	–
crew member	crewman	–
firefighter	fireman	–
flight attendant	steward	stewardess
member of congress	congressman	congresswoman
police officer	policeman	policewoman
postal worker	mailman/postman	–
salesperson, sales representative	salesman	saleswoman
spouse	husband	wife
worker	workman	–

C Social marking of roles

Some words, particularly the names of jobs, are "socially marked" as belonging to one gender even though the words are neutral in form. For example, **nurse** has been thought of as a female job for so long that if a nurse is a man, some people say **male nurse**. Try to avoid using such gender-biased language as **girl**, **woman**, **lady**, **male**, etc., before the names of jobs, e.g., **male nurse, woman doctor, female taxi driver, male secretary**. In general, these modifiers give the impression that there is something strange about one gender having this particular job or role. In addition, the use of **girl** or **boy** should be used only to refer to children, not to adults.

Exercises

97.1 Read this gender-biased advertisement for an airline. Change the wording to make it more gender neutral.

> **Now Eagle Airlines offers even more to the businessman who needs comfort!**
>
> Let us fly you to your destination in first-class comfort, served by the best-trained stewardesses in the world. The successful businessman knows that he must arrive fresh and ready for work no matter how long the journey. With Eagle Diplomat-Class you can do just that. And, what's more, your wife can travel with you on all international flights for half the regular fare! Your secretary can book you on any of our flights 24 hours a day. All she has to do is book online at eagleair.com or pick up the phone and call 800-555-1234.

97.2 Match the words on the left with their gender-neutral substitutes on the right. Use a dictionary if necessary.

1. mankind
2. unmanned
3. forefathers
4. foreman
5. cleaning lady

supervisor
housekeeper
unstaffed
ancestors
human beings

97.3 Change the underlined gender-biased words into neutral ones.

1. We'll have to elect a new <u>chairman</u> next month.
2. Several <u>firemen</u> and <u>policemen</u> were hurt in the riots.
3. The airline reports that its <u>stewardesses</u> are on strike.
4. I wonder what time the <u>mailman</u> comes every day.
5. Is this fabric natural or <u>man-made</u>?
6. Her brother's a <u>male nurse</u>, and she's a <u>lady doctor</u>.
7. TV news reporters and <u>cameramen</u> rushed to the scene of the accident.
8. If you don't like the new tax system, write to your <u>congressman</u>.
9. A <u>salesman</u> for the company will stop by and leave samples.
10. This radio program likes to conduct <u>man-on-the-street</u> interviews.
11. Be careful! There are <u>workmen</u> working on the side of the road.
12. We'll be meeting a group of <u>businessmen</u> from overseas.

97.4 Put an *F* next to any of these occupations that you think are socially marked as typically *female* and an *M* next to the ones that you think are typically *male*. How are these occupations translated into your native language – by neutral or by socially marked words?

1. barber
2. secretary
3. farmer
4. dressmaker
5. hairdresser
6. teacher
7. detective
8. dancer
9. burglar
10. butcher

Unit 98   Formal and informal words

The degree of formality in the words you use depends on your relationship with the person you're communicating with. Using formal words demonstrates that you want to be polite, show respect, or keep yourself at a distance (e.g., by using "official" language). Using informal words demonstrates that you are friendly towards and feel equal to or close with the person. You should try to match your words with the formality of each situation.

A Scales of formality

Some groups of words can be put on a scale from very formal to very informal.

Very formal	Neutral	Very informal
abode/residence	house/apartment	place
offspring	children	kids

B Short, monosyllabic slang words

Informal versions of words are often short and monosyllabic, as we can see in the right-hand column in the table above. These include slang words.

It cost me ten **bucks**. [dollars]
I'm going to have to really **cram** [study hard] for tomorrow's test.
I'm **beat** [tired] after studying all day, so I'm just going home.
Come and meet my **folks**. [mother and father]

C Clipped words

Shortening a word tends to make it less formal.

I'll meet you in the **lab**(oratory).
Our company needs a stronger presence on the (Inter)**Net**.
We should put an **ad**(vertisement) in the (news)**paper**.
Are you still on the (tele)**phone**?
My sister's a **vet**(erinarian).

D Formality in signs, instructions, etc.

You will often see formal words in signs, notices, and directions.

We regret we cannot accept checks.	Smoking permitted in designated areas only.	*Do not leave children unattended.*
[Sorry, we don't take checks.]	[No smoking except in smoking sections.]	[Don't leave your children alone.]

(See Unit 96 for more signs and notices.)

Unit 98

Exercises

98.1 Use an English-English dictionary to find neutral or more formal words for these words.

1. kid: *a child or young person*
2. a pal
3. snooze
4. a cop
5. brainy
6. a nerd

98.2 Make these mini-dialogs more *informal* by changing the underlined words. Refer to page 196 if necessary.

1. JIM: Ann, can you lend me 50 <u>dollars</u>?
   ANN: What for?
   JIM: To pay the rent on my <u>abode</u>.

2. MOM: Where's today's <u>newspaper</u>?
   DAD: Mary might have it. She was looking at the <u>advertisements</u>.
   MOM: Well, where is she?
   DAD: In her room, talking on the <u>telephone</u>.

98.3 Change the formality of these remarks/sentences for each situation described.

1. Should we go to your residence or mine to work on our assignment? (*said by one classmate to another classmate*)

2. How many offspring do you have in school? (*said by one parent to another parent at a school parents' meeting*)

3. Will there be lab classes next week? (*said by a student to a university professor*)

4. Dear .... :
   Thank you for your inquiry regarding our new line of clothing for kids. (*a business letter written to a customer*)

98.4 Find words on page 196 that have the same meaning as these words or phrases.

1. to be sorry
2. alone
3. feeling exhausted
4. allowed
5. parents
6. to study a great deal

98.5 Explain these notices in less formal language and where you might see them.

1. Payment is expected at the time services are rendered.

2. These seats must be vacated for seniors and disabled persons.

Unit 99

Varieties of English

This unit is a brief introduction to some of the many varieties of English used in different English-speaking regions of the world. You may come across many of the words covered in this unit in your own reading, listening, or travel.

A Canadian English

In Canada, the two official languages are English and French. Canadian English has a great deal in common with American English, although it is sometimes similar to British English, especially in spelling. There are also many words and expressions that are unique to Canadian English.

Some distinctive Canadian words are **Mountie** for *member of the Royal Canadian Mounted Police*, **chesterfield** for *sofa* or *couch*, **riding** for *political constituency*, **reeve** for *mayor*, **first nations** for *indigenous peoples*, and **loonie** (informal) for the Canadian one-dollar coin with an image of a loon [water bird] on one side. The terms **Anglophone/Francophone** are used to describe a person who speaks English/French. Canadian English spellings are sometimes the same as in American English, e.g., *tire* and *radio program*, compared with the British *tyre* and *radio programme*. In other cases, Canadian spellings are the same as in British English, e.g., *centre* and *colour*, compared with the American English *center* and *color*.

B Australian English

Australian English is particularly interesting for its rich store of highly colloquial words and expressions. Australian colloquialisms often involve shortening a word. Sometimes the ending -ie, -o, or -oh is then added, e.g., a **truckie** is a truck driver, and a **milko** delivers the milk; **beaut**, short for *beautiful*, means *great*, and **biggie** is *a big one*. **Oz** is short for *Australia*, and **Aussie** for *Australian*. **G'day**, short for *Good day*, is a common greeting, pronounced guh-DAY, with the first syllable said very quickly.

C Indian English

Indian English, on the other hand, is characterized by sounding more formal than other varieties of English. It has retained in everyday usage words that are found more in the classics of 19th century literature than in contemporary TV programs, e.g., The **bereaved** are **condoled**, and the Prime Minister is **felicitated** on his or her birthday. An Indian might complain of a pain in his **bosom** (rather than in his chest), and an Indian thief or bandit is referred to as a **miscreant**.

Unit 99

Exercises

99.1 Rewrite these sentences so they are more typical of Canadian English.

1. We were driving down the Trans-Canada Highway when we saw a Royal Canadian Mounted Police officer in the rearview mirror.
2. Let's meet at the Eaton Center.
3. The mayor of this city is a speaker of French.
4. All I've got is a 1-dollar coin.
5. I don't like the color of paint that you've chosen for the front door.

99.2 Write what you think these examples of Australian colloquialisms mean. They are all formed by abbreviating an English word that you probably already know.

1. She wants to be a <u>journo</u> when she leaves <u>uni</u>.
2. He's planning to do a bit of farming <u>bizzo</u> while he's in the States.
3. What are you doing this <u>arvo</u>?
4. We decided to have a party, as the <u>oldies</u> had gone away for the weekend.
5. Let's play a game of <u>footy</u>.
6. This weekend I'm going to take a <u>walkabout</u> for two days outside the city.

99.3 Match the Indian English word on the left with its American English equivalent on the right.

1. undertrials — someone with extreme views
2. wearunders — the Mumbai (Bombay) film industry
3. issueless — underwear
4. the common man — the general public
5. ultra — people awaiting trial
6. Bollywood — have no children

99.4 Name the variety of English that each of these statements or questions represents. Then rewrite each statement or question in American English.

1. We got really bitten by mozzies at yesterday's barbie.
2. That's a nice chesterfield.
3. The police nabbed the miscreant.
4. My brother is a truckie.
5. We took my father to the hospital last night because he had a pain in his bosom.
6. At my university, I am studying the culture of first nations.

> **follow-up** Do an Internet search of English varieties that you are interested in (e.g., Singaporean English, Jamaican English). Find information about their different vocabularies.

Unit 100: American English and British English

A American English differs considerably from British English. Pronunciation is the most striking difference, but there are also a number of differences in vocabulary and spelling as well as slight differences in grammar. Yet on the whole, speakers of American and British English have little or no difficulty understanding each other.

B American English words ending in **-or**, **-er**, and **-ize** usually end in **our**, **-re**, and **-ise** in British English, e.g., color/colour; center/centre; criticize/criticise.

C Common American English words and their British English equivalents

Travel and on the street		In the home	
American English	British English	American English	British English
gasoline	petrol	antenna	aerial
truck	lorry	elevator	lift
sidewalk	pavement	eraser	rubber
crosswalk	zebra crossing	apartment	flat
line (of people)	queue	apartment building	block of flats
vacation	holiday	closet	wardrobe
national holiday	bank holiday	to call (by telephone)	to ring
parking lot	car park	faucet	tap
trunk (of car)	boot	kerosene	paraffin
hood (of car)	bonnet	(Scotch) tape	sellotape
freeway/highway	motorway	cookie	biscuit
round trip	return	candy	sweets
one-way	single	garbage	rubbish
engineer (on train)	engine driver	diaper	nappy
subway	underground	pantyhose	tights
baby carriage	pram	flashlight	torch
shopping bag	carrier bag	bathroom	toilet, WC
cell phone	mobile (phone)	French fries	chips

D Different meanings in American English and British English

Here are some words and phrases that can cause confusion because they mean something different in American English and British English.

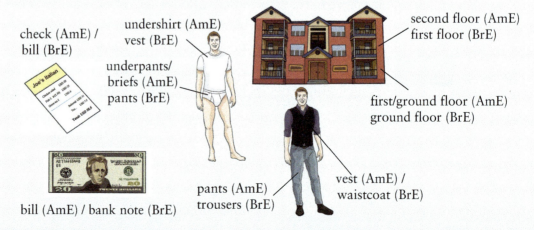

check (AmE) / bill (BrE)

undershirt (AmE) / vest (BrE)

underpants/ briefs (AmE) / pants (BrE)

second floor (AmE) / first floor (BrE)

first/ground floor (AmE) / ground floor (BrE)

vest (AmE) / waistcoat (BrE)

pants (AmE) / trousers (BrE)

bill (AmE) / bank note (BrE)

200

Unit 100

Exercises

100.1 Circle all the words that would be written by an American English writer.

1. labor
2. centre
3. realize
4. movie theater
5. neighbour
6. industrialise

100.2 Write *(A)* the American and *(B)* the British words for these items.

1.
3.
5.
7.
9.

A = cell phone
B = mobile

2.
4.
6.
8.
10.

100.3 Put the following in British English

1. Let's take the subway.
2. Please pass the cookies.
3. It's in the closet.
4. Would you like French fries with that?
5. I'll call you tonight.
6. It's in the trunk.
7. Let's check under the hood.
8. One-way or round-trip?
9. He left the faucet on.
10. Excuse me, where's the bathroom?

100.4 American and British English quiz.

1. Which would surprise you more – an American or a British man telling you that he wanted to go and change his pants?
2. You have walked into an office building. If the office you need is on the second floor, how many flights of stairs do you need to climb (a) in the U.K.? (b) in the U.S.?
3. If a British English speaker asks for a bill, is that person more likely to be in a bank or a café?
4. Would a man wear a vest over or under his shirt (a) in the U.S.? (b) in the U.K.?

100.5 Imagine you are going on a vacation to the U.K. List the words from C and D on page 200 that would be the most important words for you to know. List the words that would be important to know for someone who is traveling with a baby.

(See also Unit 99 for English in different parts of the world.)

Pronunciation symbols

/ . . . /	Pronunciations are shown between slashes in the International Phonetic Alphabet (IPA).
/ ' /	Primary stress: A raised stress mark appears before the syllable of a word with the strongest stress.
/ ˌ /	Secondary stress: A lowered stress mark appears before a stressed syllable with less than primary stress.
/ · /	A raised dot separates syllables.
/ (. . .) /	Parentheses enclose sounds that may or may not be heard in any given utterance of the word.

Vowel sounds

Symbol	Examples
/ə/	*in unstressed syllables:* alone, sofa, label, habit, connect, suppose
/ər/	*in unstressed syllables:* under, adviser, solar
	in stressed syllables: bird, fur, earn, sunburn
	An /r/ noticeably changes the sound of a preceding /ə/.
/i:/	feet, sea, gladly
/ʌ/	cut, love
/ɪ/	fit, bid
/eɪ/	fate, bay

Symbol	Examples
/e/	bet, bed
/æ/	bat, ban
/ɑ/	hot, bond, barn
/ɔ:/	bought, saw, author
/oʊ/	go, boat, know
/ʊ/	put, good
/u:/	blue, boot, shoe, lose
/aɪ/	bite, ride, height, sky
/aʊ/	house, now
/ɔɪ/	boy, join

Consonant sounds

Symbol	Examples
/b/	bid, robe
/d/	did, ladder
/ð/	this, bother, breathe
/dʒ/	judge, gentle
/f/	foot, safe
/g/	go, rug
/h/	house, behind, whole
/j/	yes, onion
/k/	kick, cook
/l/	look, ball, feel, pool
/əl/	settle, middle – *a syllabic consonant*
/m/	many, some
/n/	none, sunny, sent
/ən/	kitten, button, botany – *a syllabic consonant*
/ŋ/	ring, think, longer
/p/	peel, soap, pepper

Symbol	Examples
/r/	read, carry, far, card – *In some regions of North America -r is not always pronounced at the end of words or before consonants.*
/θ/	think, both
/s/	see, mouse, recent
/ʃ/	shoe, ash, nation
/t/	team, meet, sent
/t̬/	meeting, matter – *In North American English, -t- or -tt- is usually voiced between vowels; the result is similar to /d/, but /t/ is also correct.*
/tʃ/	church, rich, catch
/v/	visit, save
/w/	watch, away, witch
/(h)w/	which, where – *Many North American English speakers pronounce /hw/ in such words and many pronounced /w/.*
/z/	zoo, has, these
/ʒ/	measure, beige, azure

Index

Unit 1

adaptability
alongside
Anglo-Saxon
associate
attain
classical music
coin
common sense
contact
core
element
express (an opinion)
fame
flexibility
formal
French
grammar
hibernate
in touch with
informal
kingly
Latin
level
life span
longevity
loss for words
luggage
neutral
opportunity
period
plural
range
readiness
regal
register
remarkable
reptile
royal
sense of humor
shade of meaning
shell
subtle
take sides
tend
thanks to you
tortoise

Unit 2

beach
big day
big race
bubble
camping
cat
collocation
draw a line
enjoy
give me a hand
handy
heart
highly complex
hotel
intestines
kidneys
liver
look forward to
lungs
network
overpriced
package
point a finger/gun
price
priceless
receipt
relaxing
sightseeing
single-handed
skeleton
skinny
spend
stomach
sunbathing
tent
touring
triangle
utter nonsense
youth hostel

Unit 3

air
antonym
armchair
balcony
bedroom
bubble network
cast
cease
commuter flight
cruise ship
diagram
director
dresser
economy class
electronically
ferry
first class
furniture
highway
kitchen
lamp
living room
meaning
mezzanine
orchestra
performance
producer
rail
reservation
road
rural
sea
sofa
stool
stop
subway
synonym
table
train
travel
tree diagram
urban

Unit 4

apostrophe
beat
capital letter
chat

colloquial style
colon
comma
confident
converse
countable noun
cunning
dash
determined
eloquent
exclamation point
exhausted
fat
hang out
hyphen
infinitive
intransitive (verb)
irregular verb
irregularity
main verb
opposite
parentheses
past participle
past tense
pejorative
period
phrase
pigheaded
prefix
put up with
question mark
quotation marks
regular verb
root
scheme
semicolon
sentence
shred
skinny
slang
slim
smug
stingy
stress
subject
suffix
syllable
thin
thrifty
tolerate
transitive (verb)

uncountable noun
word family

Unit 5

bird
church
cost of living
dated
enemy
escape
expectancy
foe
form
friend
get worse
guide words
hairy
jam
make a living
mislay
misplace
mistake
part of speech
piece of paper
pleasure
put
ring
sales slip
slide
slip (behind/into/off/on/
   through)
slip (one's) mind
standard of living
taboo
technical
thick
top
underneath
underwear

Unit 6

active
advantage
alternative
appropriate
association
automatic
calendar

context
diary
employ
employable
employee
employer
encounter
entail
expression
extract
heart
heart of the matter
heart-broken
highlight
interval
link
memory
paragraph
phonetic symbol
recombine
review
self-employed
spiral
strategy
target
technique
unemployed

Unit 7

aspect
background
broadcast
buzzard
cement-mixer
chisel
clambered
clear
combination
cranky
crystal
debilitating
earthquake
echidnas
failure
false friend
film footage
Germanic
gingerly
gladiolus
grammatical

headscarf
hypertension
identification
infer
it must/could be
it's (a bit) like
it's a kind of / sort of / type of
it's something you use for
Latin
malady
medication
monitoring
ongoing
remedy
similarity
sphygmomanometer
structure
sugar-free
superstitious
tiptoe
tree-lined
tureen
unfamiliar
up to (one's) eyes
visual
warm-hearted

Unit 8

addressee
admission
alphabetize
angry
arrival
artist
beautify
bottle opener
breakable
brutal
Buddhism
Buddhist
complication
computer
curiously
delicious
digitize
doctor
donation
edible
employee
employer
enjoyment
environmentalism
erasable
excitement
flexibility
flexible
forgetful
friendliness
furious
goodness
governor
happiness
harmless
homeless
hopeful
industrialize
journalism
journalist
laziness
legal
liberalism
outrageous
passive
payee
payor
pencil sharpener
physicist
pianist
pollution
popularize
productive
profitable
programmer
projector
promotion
purify
racism
reduction
refusal
reliable
replacement
rewritable
sadness
scarcity
sender
supervisor
teacher
terrify
thoughtfulness
variable
wealthy
wildly
worker
writer

Unit 9

anti-
appear
autobiography
autograph
autopilot
bicycle
bilateral
bilingual
comfortable
convenient
disagree
disappear
disapprove
disconnect
discredit
dislike
disloyal
disprove
disqualify
dissimilar
ex-
excommunicate
exhale
extract
illegal
illegible
illiterate
immature
impartial
impatient
import
improbable
income
inconvenient
inedible
insert
internal
irreplaceable
irreversible
micro-
mis-
misbehave
monogamous
monologue

monotonous
multi-
overdo
overdose
overqualified
oversleep
overwork
postdated
postgraduate
postwar
precaution
preconceived
prerequisite
preschool
pro-
proponent
pseudo-intellectual
pseudonym
refill
replace
reread
retype
semi-
semicolon
similar
subconscious
submarine
subway
tie
un-
unbend
uncomfortable
undercooked
underestimate
underpay
underused

Unit 10

advertise
advertisement
advertiser
advertising
compose
composer
composite
composition
conduct
convert
deport

deportation
deported
deportee
depose
depress
divert
educate
exports
express
imports
impose
impress
inspect
inspecting
inspection
inspector
introduce
introducer
introduction
introductory
oppress
oppression
oppressive
oppressor
postpone
produce
prospect
respect
revert
root
support
suspect
transport

Unit 11

abstract noun
absurdity
achievement
action
adjustment
adulthood
aggressiveness
amazement
anger
anonymity
apprenticeship
attractiveness
belief
bitterness

boredom
breadth
brotherhood
calm
carelessness
chance
childhood
collection
combination
companionship
complexity
consciousness
curiosity
depth
discouragement
faith
fear
freedom
friendliness
generosity
happiness
hope
hostility
idea
illusion
imagination
improvement
intention
investment
kindness
kingdom
length
luck
manhood
martyrdom
membership
motherhood
neighborhood
originality
ownership
partnership
principle
production
rage
reason
recognition
reduction
relationship
replacement
resentment
sense

sensitivity
shock
sight
speed
stardom
strength
tenderness
thought
warmth
width
wisdom
womanhood

Unit 12

absent-minded
air-conditioned
all-out
blue-eyed
brand-new
broad-shouldered
broken-down
built-in
built-up
burned-out
curly-haired
duty-free
easygoing
first-class
flatfooted
good-natured
handmade
interest-free
last-minute
left-handed
long-distance
long-haired
long legged
longstanding
nearsighted
off-peak
open-toed
part-time
pigheaded
quick-tempered
quick-witted
red-haired
rosy-cheeked
rundown
self-absorbed
self-centered

self-reliant
self-righteous
self-taught
slim-hipped
so-called
straight-haired
stuck-up
sugar-free
suntanned
thin-lipped
tight-fitting
time-consuming
top-secret
two-faced
warmhearted
well-known
world-famous
worn-out

Unit 13

address book
air-traffic control
alarm clock/system
assembly line
baby-sitter
bank account
bedroom
birth control
blood donor/pressure
brain drain
bus driver/stop
business class
computer technology
credit card
data processing
death penalty
family planning
food poisoning
football
gas station
generation gap
grass roots
greenhouse effect
hay fever
health care
heart attack
human being
human rights
income tax
Internet banking

junk food
labor force
light year
luxury goods
mother tongue
notebook
phone book
public works
race relations
raincoat
reference book
sound barrier
status symbol
sunglasses
touch screen
trademark
waste basket
windmill
windshield wiper
youth hostel

Unit 14

backup
breakdown
break-in
breakout
breakthrough
breakup
cover-up
crackdown
cutbacks
downturn
drawback
dropout
feedback
getaway
holdup
input
layoffs
layout
lookout
outbreak
outcome
outlay
outlets
outlook
pinups
printout
setback
setup

shakeup
standoff
takeover
tryout
turnover

Unit 15

academy
alarm
alcove
algebra
alphabet
avant-garde
balcony
ballerina
bandit
bankrupt
bazaar
blitz
bonanza
bonsai
boutique
bungalow
caftan
carafe
caravan
casino
catastrophe
cemetery
chauffeur
cobra
confetti
cosmonaut
coup
cruise
cuisine
cul-de-sac
dachshund
delicatessen
democracy
drama
easel
elite
embargo
fiasco
fjord
frankfurter
futon
ghetto

gimmick
guerrilla
guitar
hamburger
harem
holocaust
igloo
jackal
judo
junta
karate
kayak
kindergarten
kiosk
kumquat
kung fu
landscape
lasso
lemming
lexicon
macho
mammoth
marmalade
mattress
molasses
mosquito
mystery
ombudsman
origami
pajamas
patio
piano
poodle
pseudonym
psychology
résumé
sauna
sauté
seminar
shampoo
shawl
siesta
ski
slalom
snorkel
soprano
spaghetti
steppe
synonym
taffeta
tea

theory
tofu
tsar
tulip
tundra
tycoon
vanilla
vendetta
verve
waltz
wanderlust
yacht
yogurt

Unit 16

acronym
a.m./p.m.
ASAP (as soon as possible)
ATM (automated teller machine)
cc
dorm
Dr.
e.g.
enc.
etc.
fax
FYI (for your information)
ID (identification)
i.e.
initials
IRS (Internal Revenue Service)
lab
laser
memo
Mr.
Mrs.
Ms.
OPEC (Organization of Petroleum Exporting Countries)
phone
PIN (personal identification number)
P.O. Box (Post Office Box)
P.S. (postscript)
R&D (research and development)

radar
Rd. (Road)
re:
RSVP
St. (Saint or Street)
typo
UN (United Nations)
U.S.A. (United States of America)
yuppie

Unit 17

attention deficit disorder (ADD)
audio book
blended family
cybercafé
cyberphobia
cyberspace
DNA fingerprinting
downsizing
eating disorder
e-commerce
ecotourist
family leave
freeware
greening
infomercial
information overload
keyboarding
managed care
MP3
netiquette
outsourcing
plus-size
reality TV
repetitive strain injury (RSI)
road rage
sick building syndrome
snail mail
snowboarding
sound bite
spam
spin doctor
surfing the Net
technophobe
telecommuting
texting
wannabe
webcast

Unit 18

apostrophe
castle
Christmas
climb
comb
compound
conduct
conflict
contest
contract
convict
debt
decrease
defect
desert
detail
doubt
dumb
export
fasten
heir
honest
honor/honorable
import
increase
industry
insult
interesting
knee
knob
knock
knot
knowledge
library
listen
muscle
object
photograph / photographic / photographically / photography
pneumonia
pseudonym
psychiatry
psychic
psychology
receipt
recipe
record
reject
salmon
should
soften
subject
subtle
suspect
sword
upset
vegetable
whistle
whole
wreck
wrist
wrong

Unit 19

bash
clang
clank
clash
click
clink
crackle
crash
creak
dash
drizzle
gargle
giggle
groan
growl
grumble
grumpy
mash
meow
moo
mumble
onomatopoeic word
sizzle
smash
spit
splash
spray
sprinkle
spurt
tinkle
trickle
whack
wheeze
whip
whirr

whisper
whistle
whiz
wriggle

Unit 20

air
allowed
aloud
bow
brake
break
doe
dough
fair
fare
faze
flew
flu
grate
great
groan
grown
heir
hoarse
homograph
homonym
homophone
horse
hour
house
lead
live
mail
male
meat
meet
minute
moan
mown
pail
pain
pair
pale
pane
pare
peal
pear
peel

phase
pray
prey
raise
rays
reed
resume
right
sail
sale
scene
scent
seen
sent
sew
sight
site
sole
some
soul
stake
streak
sum
tea
tear
tee
their
threw
through
toe
tow
use
waist
wait
waste
weak
week
weight
wind
wood
would
wound
write

Unit 21

after (that)
afterward
as soon as
at an earlier time

at that time
before (that)/(then)
by the time
during
earlier
first
following
formerly
in the meantime
interchangeable
it used to be
just as
meanwhile
once
precisely
previously
prior to
ration
retire
sentimental
simultaneously
since then
the minute
the moment
throughout
till then
until then
when
whenever
while

Unit 22

admission
applicant
as long as
clean energy
condition
dial
driver's license
emergency
helmet
however
in case (of)
motorcycle
no matter how/which/who
on condition that
peace talks
prerequisite
proficiency

provided (that)
recipe
requirement
source
supervisor
suppose
supposing
turn up
under any/the/what circumstance
unless
vice versa
what if
wherever
whichever
whoever

Unit 23

aim
allegation
arise (from)
as a consequence
as a result
because of
bitter
bring about
cause
ceasefire
collide
consequence
consequently
decline
due to
generate
give rise (to)
grounds
ignite
lead to
motive
outcome
prompted
provoke
purpose
reason
result
spark
stem (from)
therefore
upshot (of)

Unit 24

acknowledge
admit/admittedly
after all
agree (that)
all very well
although
bossy
concede
concession
conservative
content
criticism
despite
even though
gloomy
great divide
huge discrepancy
ideals
in contrast
in spite of
liability
liberal
method
nevertheless
nonetheless
on the contrary
on the other hand
poles apart
quite the opposite
reverse
rude
sensible
though
to the contrary
world of difference

Unit 25

along with
also
ambition
and so forth
and so on
anyway
apart from
as well as
besides
catering
certificate

consideration
consultant
emphatic
enormous
excessive
exhaust
fortune
further to
furthermore
hospitality
in addition
interchangeable
likewise
moreover
on top of (all) that
plus
pursuant to
qualification
similarly
to boot
tourism
what is more

Unit 26

animal rights
appraisal
approach
argument
aspect
assessment
circumstance
claim
controversy
debate
difficulty
dilemma
economy
efforts
evaluation (of)
information
isolation
issue
key (to)
middle class
overpopulation
private sector
problem
proposal (to)
question
reason

response
ridiculous
situation
solution
text-referring word
topic
traffic
urban
way out (of)

Unit 27

after all
afterthought
anyway
conclusion
discourse marker
distant
exhausted
fine
good
great
hang on
hesitation
hold on
interruption
let me see
listen
look
monologue
now then
of course
ragged
right of way
scowl
sort of
still
uncomfortable
well (then)
you know
you see

Unit 28

above
actually
apparently
below
briefly
earlier

especially
finally
first
first of all
firstly
for example
for instance
further
in conclusion
in fact
in other words
in particular
in reference to
in sum
in summary
lastly
leaving aside
next
particularly
refer you to
regarding
second
secondly
see page
specifically
that is to say
the following
third
thirdly
to conclude
to sum up
with reference to

Unit 29

advice
baggage
butter
cash
cement
coal
concrete
cotton
countable noun
detergent
electricity
equipment
flour
furniture
gas/gasoline
glass

immigration
knowledge
leather
luggage
meat
money
oil
paper
plastic
polyester
progress
research
rice
silk
soap
solar power
soup
sugar
toothpaste
traffic
travel
uncountable noun
wind power
wood
wool
work

Unit 30

acoustics
aerobics
arts
athletics
authorities
billiards
binoculars
blues
cards
checkers
classics
clothes
contents
darts
dominoes
economics
fireworks
glasses
goods
gymnastics
handcuffs
headphones

jeans
looks
means
news
outskirts
overalls
pajamas
pants
physics
pliers
premises
proceeds
scissors
series
shorts
spaghetti
sports
stairs
sunglasses
suspenders
tights
tongs
tweezers
underpants
whereabouts

Unit 31

basement
bland
Can I have/borrow . . . ?
chocolate
cloth
coffee
countable nouns
fish
frying pan
glass
hair
home
institution
iron
kitchen
land
laundry room
light
material
milk
(news)paper
noise
painting

paper
people
pepper
relax
stuff
tea
thread
trade
turkey
uncountable nouns
waiter
wine

Unit 32

allegation
barrage
bonfire
bunch
bundle
cast
clump
company
complaint
couple
crew
crowd
demonstration
dissatisfied
flock
gang
group
heap
herd
host
journalist
marine life
pack
pair
people
pile
public
row
school
series
set
stack
staff
string
swarm
team

Unit 33

(a little) bit (of)
(a) piece (of)
article
bar
blade
breath
carton
clap
cloud
confusion
disrepair
drop
emergency
flash
flux
groceries
gust
health
item
kilo
loaf
means
mind
package
panic
pound
poverty
rumble
shock
siege
slice
spell
state
stroke
tube
uncertainty

Unit 34

aluminum
bag
bamboo
barrel
basket
bottle
bowl
box
bucket
can

Index 213

cane
canned goods
cardboard
carton
case
china
container
contents
crate
(eye)glasses
glass
jar
jug
liquids
liquor store
metal
mug
pack
package
pot
pottery
sack
six-pack
supermarket
tin
tube
wicker
wood

Unit 35

African
African American
American
Antarctic
Arab
Arabic
Arctic
Asia
Asian
Atlantic Ocean
Australia
Bangladeshi
bilingual
Brazilian
British
Briton
Canadian
Caribbean
Chinese
Congolese
Dane
Danish
dialect
Dutch
English
ethnic group
Europe
Far East
Filipino
fluently
French
German
Greek
Icelandic
Indian Ocean
Iraqi
Irish
Israeli
Italian
Japanese
Korean
Kuwaiti
Latin (America)
Lebanese
Mediterranean
Mexican
Middle East
multilingual
native language
North America
North/Central/Southern
 Africa
Pacific Ocean
Pakistani
Polish
Portuguese
regional group
Saudi
Scandinavia
Spaniard
Spanish
Swede
Swiss
Thai
Turk
Turkish
Venezuelan
Vietnamese

Unit 36

autumn
blizzard
blustery
boiling
breeze
chilly
damp
downpour
drizzle
drought
flood
foggy
freezing
frost
gale
hailstone
hazy
heat wave
humid
hurricane
icy
melt
mild
misty
muggy
overcast
pour
scorching
shower
sleet
slush
smog
snowdrift
stifling
storm
sweltering
thaw
thunderstorm
tornado
torrential rain

Unit 37

Afro
athletic
bald
beard
beautiful
black

blond
brunette
bushy eyebrows
chubby
complexion
crew cut
curly
dark
dark-haired
dark-skinned
double chin
early fifties
elderly
elegant
fair
fat
fortyish
freckles
good looking
gray
handsome
heavy
heavyset
in his teens
late fifties
long
messy
middle-aged
mid-fifties
muscular
mustache
obese
overweight
plump
receding hairline
red-haired
redhead
round
scrawny
scruffy
senior (citizen)
skinny
slim
sloppy looking
stocky
straight
stylish
teenager
thin
thirty-something
unattractive

wavy
well built
well dressed
white
wrinkles

Unit 38

able
abrupt
affable
aggressive
ambitious
anxious
argumentative
arrogant
assertive
blunt
bossy
brainless
brainy
bright
broad-minded
brusque
cheap
clever
clueless
cocky
confident
congenial
crafty
cruel
cunning
curt
cynical
determined
direct
down-to-earth
dumb
easygoing
eccentric
economical
envious
even-tempered
excessive
extravagant
extroverted
foolish
frank
generous
gifted

gregarious
honest
hopeful
ill-mannered
impolite
innocent
inquiring
intelligent
introverted
jealous
miserly
naive
nosy
obstinate
odd
One person's meat is another one's poison
open
optimistic
original
outgoing
peculiar
permissive
pessimistic
pigheaded
prying
pushy
quarrelsome
relaxed
reliable
rude
sadistic
self-assured
self-important
sensible
sensitive
shrewd
shy
silly
simple
sincere
sly
smart
smug
sociable
stingy
stubborn
stupid
talented
tense
thin-skinned

thrifty
tight-fisted
trustworthy
unconventional
unprincipled
weird

Unit 39

acquaintance
admire
adore
be attracted to
best friend
break up
can't stand
classmate
colleague
companion
co-worker
crush on
despise
detest
disgust
dislike
ex-
friend
get along (well)
hate
honor
idolize
junior
loathe
look down on
look up to
love
love-hate relationship
make up
mate
partner
put down
roommate
see eye to eye
senior (to)
significant other
split up
teammate
turn (someone) off
turn (someone) on
worship

Unit 40

apartment (building/
  complex)
attic
basement
bucket
can opener
carport
condo
condominium
corkscrew
cutting board
den
dental floss
driveway
electrical outlet
foyer
front hall
garage
grater
hall
hallway
ironing board
landing
laundry room
master bedroom
microwave
mobile home
mop
patio
plug
porch
remote control
single-family house
spatula
stepladder
studio (apartment)
study
townhouse
trailer
walk-in closet

Unit 41

bang
battery
break (down)
bruise
bump
come off

crack
dead
dent
doorknob
dripping
fall down
fast
flat tire
flood
knock over
leaking
lock (someone) out
lose
misplace
plumber
power failure
power outage
recharge
rip
run out
slow
smash
spill
sprain
stain
stopped
twist
wear out
won't start

Unit 42

break out
casualty
cholera
civil war
damage
destroy
disaster
drought
earthquake
epidemic
erupt
explosion
famine
fire
flood
hurricane
injure
major accident
malaria

pandemic
plane crash
rabies
refugee
shake
spread
starve
suffering
survivor
tornado
tragedy
typhoid
typhoon
unrest
victim
volcano
war

Unit 43

ace
associate's degree
Bachelor of Arts (B.A.)
Bachelor of Science (B.S.)
bachelor's degree
college
community college
compulsory
cram
dental school
Doctor of Philosophy (Ph.D.)
drop out (of)
elementary school
faculty
fail
financial aid
flunk
grade
graduate (from)
grant
high school
home-school
instructor
junior college
junior high school
kindergarten
law school
lecturer
major
Master of Arts (M.A.)

medical school
middle school
nursery school
parochial school
pass
postgraduate
Pre-K
preschool
primary school
private school
professional school
professor
public school
scholarship
score
secondary school
start (school/college)
state college/university
tuition
undergraduate
university

Unit 44

(a) living
accountant
actor/actress
administrative assistant
aerospace engineer
apply for
artist
blue-collar worker
boss
camera operator
carpenter
chemical engineer
chief executive officer (CEO)
civil engineer
collect
computer engineer
computer programmer
construction worker
correspondent
database manager
dayshift
dietitian
director
doctor
editor
electrician
entertainment

entry-level employee
executive
field
fired
flextime
give notice
health care
home improvement
industrial engineer
journalism
lab technician
laid off
manager
moonlight
nightshift
occupation
offered
(on) strike
painter
photographer
physical therapist
physician
playwright
plumber
promoted
promotion
quit
(registered) nurse
reporter
resign
secretary
skilled worker
supervisor
systems analyst
telecommute
unemployed
unemployment
union representative
unskilled worker
white-collar worker
workaholic
writer

Unit 45

archer
archery
auto racing
badminton
baseball (player)
bat

Index 217

beat
billiards
bow
bowling
break (a record)
canoeing
club
cross-country skiing
cue
cyclist
discus
fencing
fishing
goals
golf
golfer
gymnast
high jump
hockey
hold (the record)
horseback riding
javelin
jockey
jogging
line
long jump
long-distance runner
lose (by/to)
marathon
mountaineer
oar
paddle
Ping-Pong
points
pole vault
pool (player)
racquet
rod
rowing
runs
scuba diving
set (a record)
skater
sprinter
squash
stick
surfer
swimmer
table tennis
take up

tennis (player)
track and field
win (by)
windsurfing

Unit 46

architecture
art lover
ballet
biography
bomb
cast
ceramics
concert
costume
dance
direction
drama
edition
exhibit
exhibition
film
fine art(s)
literature
marvelous performance
movie
music
musical
novel
opera
painting
performing arts
playing (at)
play
poetry
production
publish
rave review
sculpture
set
short story
theater
work(s) of

Unit 47

(a) natural
album

arrange/arrangement
baroque
be musical
big band music
blues
CD
chamber music
chord
classical
contemporary
country and western
dance music
deafening
discordant
download
electronic music
folk
good ear
guitar music
heavy metal
hit single
hum
innovative
instrumental music
jazz
live
loud
make music
modern
MP3 player
orchestral music
peaceful
piano music
pick out
play by ear
playlist
pop
recorded
relaxing
rousing
soft
song
soothing
soul
soundtrack
sweet
track
tune
tuneless
vocals
whistle

Unit 48

appetizer
bake
barbecue
bitter
bland
boil
broil
casserole
delicious
dessert
dried out
dry
entrée
fatty
fish
fruit
fry
grain
grill
helping
lean
main dish
medium
mild
overdone
portion
rare
roast
salty
seafood
sour
spicy
tasteless
tasty
undercooked
vegetable
well-done

Unit 49

acid rain
air pollution
barren
bay
beach
brook
city
cliff
coast
coastline
compass
contamination
continent
country
cove
creek
destruction
emissions
estuary
export
foot
forest
geyser
glacier
global warming
gorge
greenhouse effect/gases
grove
gulf
hazardous waste
highway
hill
ice field
island
lake
landscape
marsh
mound
mountain
mouth
noise pollution
ocean
oil spill
overfishing
overpopulation
ozone layer
path
peak
peninsula
plain
pond
radiation
range
ridge
rise
river
sewage
shoreline
soil
source
spring
strait
stream
summit
swamp
thermal spring
toxic waste
trail
tributary
volcano
water pollution
waterfall
woods

Unit 50

adobe
art gallery
bar
basin
bed & breakfast
capital
car rental agency
cathedral
church
city hall
clinic
community college
concert hall
continuing education
courthouse
crime
daycare center
department store
drugstore
fire station
golf course
gym
health center
homelessness
hospital
hotel
library
mosque
motel
museum
nightclub
opera house
overcrowding
picturesque
police station

Index 219

pollution
restaurant
school
senior center
shelter
shopping mall
skating rink
slums
standstill
subway
supermarket
swimming pool
synagogue
taxi stand
temple
tennis court
theater
town hall
traffic jam
train station
university
vandalism
youth hostel

Unit 51

amphibian
bark
bat
beak
bee
bird
blossom
bough
branch
breast
bud
bus
claws
crag
dolphin
eagle
egg
fertilize
fish
flower
frog
gills
grass
groundhog
harvest
hoof
leaf
mammal
mane
maple
nest
oak
palm
parrot
paw
petal
pick (flowers)
pigeon
pine
plant
pollen
porcupine
reptile
root
scales
seal
shark
shrub
snail
snake
stalk
tail
thorn
tree
trunk
twig
vegetable
whiskers
willow
wing
worm

Unit 52

acrylic
baggy
belt
buckle
button
cap
casual
change into / out of
checked
collar
corduroy
cotton
crew neck
cuff
denim
double-breasted
elegant
fashionable
fit
grow out of
grungy
hem
(high) heel
leather
long-sleeved
loose
match
messy
nylon
old-fashioned
paisley
pinstriped
plaid
pleated
polka-dotted
polyester
rayon
seam
shoelaces
short-sleeved
silk
sleeve
sleeveless
slippers
sloppy
sneak
sole
solid
striped
stylish
suede
take off
tight
trendy
try on
turtleneck
Velcro fastener
velvet
vest
V-neck
well dressed

wool
zipper

Unit 53

acne
AIDS
allergist
antibiotic
anxious
arthritis
black eye
blood pressure/test
break
bronchitis
bruise
bug
cancer
capsule
cardiologist
cast
chest pains
chiropractor
cold
congested
constipated
cough
depressed
dermatologist
diarrhea
dislocate
dizzy
earache
family doctor
fever
(fill a) prescription
flu
food poisoning
gastroenterologist
general practitioner (GP)
gynecologist
headache
heart attack
hemorrhage
hepatitis
hives
hyper
hypertension
hypochondriac
indigestion
infection

insomnia
internist
itch
lose (one's) appetite/voice
lump
nauseous
nurse
obstetrician
operation
ophthalmologist
osteopath
out of breath
pain
pediatrician
physical
pill
pneumonia
podiatrist
pregnant
psychiatrist
pulse
rash
rheumatism
rub
shivery
shot
sore throat
sprain
stomachache
stroke
stuffed up
sunburn
surgeon
tablet
temperature
tense
tired
ulcer
urologist
virus
weak
X-ray

Unit 54

airplane
airport security checkpoint
air-traffic controller
anchor
barge
book

brakes
bridge
bunk
bus terminal
cabin
captain
change (trains)
chauffeur
cockpit
commuter train
conductor
containership
crew
cruise ship
deck
departure
dining car
dock
driver
duty-free shop
emergency exit
engine/engineer
express
ferry
first officer
flight attendant
freight car
freight train
fuselage
galley
gangplank
garage
gas station
ground crew
handles
helicopter
hood
horn
journey
(jumbo) jet
land
landing
lighthouse
local train
lounge
mast
mechanic
miles per gallon (mpg)
motorist
nose
on time

overhead bin
passenger car
pickup
pilot
port
porter
porthole
purser
railroad crossing
recreational vehicle (RV)
rowboat
runway
service station
shipyard
signal
skipper
sleeping car
starboard
stranded
supersonic aircraft
tail
take off
taxi
ticket agent
tires
train station
transmission
travel
trip
truck
trunk
van
voyage
waiting room
wharf
wings
yacht

Unit 55

amusement park
bed & breakfast (B&B)
book
breathtaking
campground
check-in
checkout
cycle
double room
elder hostel
exhilarating
exotic
glamorous
go to the beach
hike
intoxicating
king-size bed
motel
nonsmoking room
ocean view
picturesque
queen-size bed
reservation
resort
river view
room service
shopping
sightseeing
single room
sublime
summer camp
sunbathe
swim
time-share
twin bed
unspoiled
wake-up call
youth hostel

Unit 56

addition
Celsius
centigrade
circle
circumference
cube
cubed
decimal
diagonal
diameter
divided by
division
equals
even number
Fahrenheit
feet
formula
fraction
inches
meter
minus
multiplication
octagon
odd number
opposite
oval
pentagon
percent
plus
point
prime number
pyramid
radius
rectangle
right angle
semicircle
sphere
spiral
square
square root
squared
subtraction
times
triangle

Unit 57

analyze
bioclimatology
biology
botany
cell phone
chemistry
combine
conclude
cryogenics
cybernetics
discover
dissect
ergonomics
experiment
field
genetic engineering
geopolitics
GPS navigation system
HD (high-definition) TV
hypothesis
identify
invent
laptop
manipulate

memory stick
molecular biology
MP3 player
nanotechnology
patent
physics
react
scanner
touch screen monitor
voice technology
webcam
zoology

Unit 58

address
back up
blog
bookmark
CD
chat room
computer graphics / hardware / software / virus
desktop computer
download
DVD
e-mail
FAQ (frequently asked question)
flash drive
gigabyte
google
hard drive
homepage
hotlink
hyperlink
IM (instant messaging)
Internet ("the Net")
laptop (computer)
link
log in
megabyte
memory
memory stick
modem
online
password
PC (personal computer)
RAM (random access memory)
search engine
social networking site
spreadsheet
tool
upload
username
virtual
Web page
Web site
webcam
Wi-Fi
wired connectivity
wireless
word processing
World Wide Web ("the Web")

Unit 59

advice
antenna
broadcast
cable box/TV
cartoon
censor
classified ad
comic book
commercial TV
crossword puzzle
detective show
digital video recorder (DVR)
documentary
drama
edit
editorial
feature article
flat screen TV set
game show
headline
horoscope
Internet TV
journal
magazine
(mass) media
movie
mystery
nature show
network TV
newspaper
pay-per-view
print
program
public TV
publish
radio
reality show
remote control
report
satellite dish/TV
section
situation comedy (sitcom)
soap opera
sports
Sunday edition
supplement
tabloid (newspaper)
talk show
variety show

Unit 60

appoint
branch
Cabinet
campaign
candidate
chambers
checks and balances
confirm
Congress
democracy
Democrat
dictatorship
elect
Executive Branch
federation
Highest Court
House of Commons
House of Lords
House of Representatives
independence
judge
Judicial Branch
judiciary
justice
Legislative Branch
limit
majority
majority party
member of Congress
member of parliament (MP)
monarchy

Index   223

nominate
parliament
parliamentary government
president
presidential government
prime minister
republic
Republican
run (for office)
senate
senator
Supreme Court
vice-president
vote

Unit 61

accomplice
accuse
acquit
airtight
arson/arsonist
burglar/burglary/burgle
charge
commit
defend
deliberation
deliver
evidence
ex-convict
felony
find (someone) guilty
fine
go to court
guilty
homicide
identity theft/thief
judge
jury
kidnap/kidnapper/
    kidnapping
lawyer
misdemeanor
murder/murderer
not guilty
parole officer
plead
proof
prosecutor
rob

robber/robbery
sentence
serve
set fire to
shoplift/shoplifter/shoplifting
smuggle/smuggler/smuggling
steal
swear off
testimony
time off
trial
try
vandalism
verdict
witness

Unit 62

airfare
ATM (automated teller
    machine)
auto loan
balance
bank loan
bank statement
bill
billing date
borrow
bounce
bus fare
(by) check
car loan
check (one's) balance
checking account
currency
debit card
due date
exchange rate
fare
fee
finance charge
home equity loan
(in) cash
income tax
inheritance tax
insufficient funds
interest
lend
make a deposit
make a withdrawal

monthly statement
mortgage
online banking
overdrawn
principal
property tax
salary
sales tax
savings account
student loan
train fare
transfer funds
tuition
(with a) credit card
withdraw money
write a check

Unit 63

believe (in)
Buddhist
conservative
conviction
convince
death penalty
doubt
eccentric
empiricist
fanatical
from (one's) point of view
idealistic
ideology
if you ask me
in favor of
in my mind
in my opinion
in my view
intellectual
left-wing
liberal
maintain
middle-of-the-road
moderate
moral
obsessive
odd
oppose
pacifist
peculiar
personal

philosophy
radical
religious
revolutionary
right-wing
suppose
suspect
traditional
unrealistic
vegetarian
view

Unit 64

anger
anxious
appreciate
apprehensive
cheerful
conflicting
confused
content(ed)
delighted
depressed
depression
disagreeable
disappointed
ecstatic
enthusiastic
excited
fed up
frustrated
furious
fury
grateful
in a rage
inspired
intense
livid
miserable
mixed up
nervous
overpowering
seething
sick and tired
thrilled
uncertain
upset
worried

Unit 65

affectionate (toward)
appall
appeal to
attracted (to)
can't bear
can't stand
care for
crazy about
darling
dear
desire
despise
detest
disgust
dislike
dread
enchanted by
enjoy
fall for
fall in love
fascinate
fond of
handsome
hate
honey
loathe
long for
look forward to
loving (toward)
passionate about
repel
revolt
sweetheart
tempted by
yearn for

Unit 66

angrily
anxiously
argue
beg
bitterly
boast
boldly
cheerfully
complain
confess
dejectedly
desperately
eagerly
enthusiastically
excitedly
furiously
gladly
gloomily
gratefully
groan
grumble
happily
hopefully
hopelessly
impatiently
insist
maintain
miserably
mumble
murmur
mutter
nervously
object
passionately
proudly
reluctantly
sadly
sarcastically
scream
shout
shriek
shyly
sincerely
speech impediment
stammer
stutter
threaten
urge
whine
whisper
yell

Unit 67

aromatic
bitter
deafening
déjà vu
extrasensory perception (ESP)
feels
finger

Index 225

foul
fragrant
gaze
glance
glimpse
grab
grasp
handle
hearing
hot
intuition
looks
loud
musty
noiseless
noisy
notice
observe
peer
perfumed
premonition
press
quiet
rub
salty
scented
sight
silent
sixth sense
smell/smelly
snatch
sounds
sour
spicy
stare
stinking
stroke
sweet
sweet-smelling
tap
taste/tasteful/tasteless
telepathy
touch
vile
witness

Unit 68

bit
bite
blink
blush
boredom
breath/breathe/breathing
burp
chew
cough
coughing
displeasure
dust
embarrassment
eyebrow
frown
grimace
grin
growl
hiccupping
lick
perspiration
perspire
rumble
shake
shiver
sigh
sneeze
snoring
suck
swallow
sweat
tremble
wink
yawn

Unit 69

a bit (of)
a drop (of)
a good/great deal (of)
a (little) bit
a lot (of)
a number (of)
absolutely
amount
average
awfully
completely
considerable
destroyed
dozens (of)
enormous
entirely
exhausted
extremely
fairly
gigantic
hot
huge
large
little
loads (of)
lots (of)
many
much
not much
number
plenty (of)
pretty
quite
rather
really
ruined
small
terribly
tiny
tired
tons (of)
totally
utterly
vast
very
weak
worried
wrong

Unit 70

about time
age
amnesty
at times
by the time
decade
digital age
drag on
elapse
era
for a time/while
for the time being
geological
historical

Ice Age
industrial
just in time
last
Middle Ages
occasionally
on time
one at a time
pass
penalty
period
punctually
run
spell
Stone Age
take
take your time
time
time and (time) again
vague

Unit 71

broad
broaden
broad-minded
deep
deepen
depth
extend
far
faraway
height
high
highly
length
lengthen
lengthy
local
long
long-distance
low/lower
narrow
nearby
shallow
short
shortcut
shorten
shortly
shrink
spread
stretch
tall
thin
wide
widening
width

Unit 72

alternative
automatic
certain
chance
choice
close down
compulsory
curiosity
exempt
force
have got to / have to
impossible
in need of
inevitable
lack
liable
mandatory
must
must not
need (to)
nonprofit
obligatory
obliged
obsolete
optional
petroleum
possible
probable
prohibition
recession
required
safe
shortage
unlikely

Unit 73

bank
beam
burst
chime
clang
construction site
crash
creak
dim
din
earplugs
fizzy
flash
flicker
glare
gloomy
glow
grit
hiss
irritating
lawnmower
noise
patter
pop
racket
ray
ring
roar
rumble
rustle
shine
somber
sound
sparkle
starting gun
thud
twinkle
unpleasant

Unit 74

assign
belongings
borrow
contribute
donate
estate
finance
generation
give away
giving
hand down/out/over
landlord/landlady
leave
lend

let go of
loan
mugger
occupy
owner
ownership
penniless
possession
present (someone) with
property
proprietor
provide (with)
rent
renters
sell
supply
tenants
theft
will

Unit 75

breakneck
crawl
creep
dawdle
derail
drift
drive
flow
flutter
fly
gale
heel
hurry
limp
march
move
pace
plod
rate
run
rush
sail
shuffle
snail's pace
speed
stir
storm
stroll

sway
swerve
tear
tiptoe
travel
velocity
walk (with a limp)

Unit 76

as heavy as lead
as light as a feather
bright
bulky
course
dazzling
dense
dim
downy
dull
fine
fluffy
fluid ounce (fl. oz.)
furry
gallon (gal.)
glare
gram
hollow
jagged
kilogram
liter
milliliter
ounce (oz.)
pint (pt.)
polished
pound (lb.)
prickly
quart (qt.)
rough
shady
shiny
silky
sleek
slippery
smooth
solid
sparse
sticky
surface
texture

thick
thin
to the touch
underfoot
vivid

Unit 77

accomplish
accomplished
accomplishment
achievable
achieve
achievement
aim
ambition
attain
attainable
attainment
come to (nothing)
cope
difficult
difficulty (in)
exceed
falter
fold
fulfill
fulfilling
fulfillment
go under
go wrong
goal
hard (time/work)
(have a) problem (with)
(have) trouble (with)
manage (to)
meet
misfire
miss (one's chance)
objective
reach
realize
succeed (in + -ing)
success
successful
successfully
surpass
target

Unit 78

a chip off the old block
a drop in the bucket
a fool's errand
a shot in the dark
barking up the wrong tree
be in a bind
be in seventh heaven
be out of sorts
be up to it
better days
child's play
down and out
enough on (one's) plate
feel down in the dumps
feel under the weather
flies in the face of
fly off the handle
give or take
give (someone) the cold shoulder
hit the sack
hold your horses
hold your tongue
idiom
just goes to show
keep mum
kid's stuff
leaves a lot to be desired
make a mountain out of a molehill
make ends meet
odds and ends
once in a blue moon
pain in the neck
pie in the sky
poke your nose in(to)
pull a fast one
rough and ready
sink or swim
sitting pretty
springing to mind
stick your nose in(to)
take the cake

Unit 79

announcement
as far as I'm concerned
as I was saying
as luck would have it
attract
bump into
by chance
come to think of it
console
decision
economy
emphasize
finalize
haven't seen (someone) for years
head for (trouble)
if all else fails
if worst comes to worst
if you ask me
immediately
interrupt
just in case
opinion
point
point of view
settle
speaking of
that reminds me
That's it
that's that
this and that
This is it
this, that, and the other
upset
what with one thing after another
when it comes to

Unit 80

as black as night
as blind as a bat
as busy as a bee
as cool as a cucumber
as dead as a doornail
as dry as a bone
as easy as falling off a log
as flat as a pancake
as fresh as a daisy
as good as gold
as hard as nails
as heavy as lead
as light as a feather
as quick as a wink
as quiet as a mouse
as red as a beet
as sick as a dog
as strong as an ox
as white as a sheet
as white as snow
brain like a sieve
clumsily
cruel
immobile
like a bull in a china shop
like a bump on a log
like a charm
like a hawk
like a horse
like a log
like a statue
like two peas in a pod
simile
spoiled
tough

Unit 81

all or nothing
antonym
atmosphere
back and forth
binomial
compromise
down and out
first and foremost
give and take
give or take
head to toe
here and there
high and dry
last but not least
law and order
leaps and bounds
more or less
neat and clean
odds and ends
off and on
on and off
out and about
part and parcel
peace and quiet
pick and choose

Index 229

prim and proper
ranting and raving
ready and able
rest and relaxation (R&R)
safe and sound
sick and tired
sink or swim
slowly but surely
sooner or later
synonym
take it or leave it
up and down

Unit 82

around the bend
as good as gold
as hard as nails
back stabber
betray
big mouth
bizarre
cold fish
eccentric
fast worker
get on (one's) nerves
good head for numbers / figures
have a change of heart
have a heart
have a heart of stone
have (one's) heart in the right place
have (one's) heart set on something
head of the class
head screwed on
heart of gold
intention
irritate
know-it-all
middle-of-the-road
moderate
nuisance
oddball
off the wall
over the top
pain in the neck
quick study
sensible

slacker
slow on the uptake
slowpoke
straight arrow
teacher's pet
unsympathetic

Unit 83

a dime a dozen
at death's door
be a bit down
be in a bad/foul mood
be in high spirits
be itching to
be on cloud nine
Capricorn
dead on (one's) feet
dead tired
eat a horse
exaggeration
feel a bit down
feel blue
frighten (someone) out of (his/her) wits
frighten (someone) to death
get carried away
haven't been (one's) self
head over heels
heart sank
jump out of (one's) skin
keep (one's) chin up
keep a cool head
Leo
long face
on the edge of (one's) seat
on top of the world
outing
patient
scare (someone) out of (his/her) wits
scare (someone) to death
scared stiff
Scorpio
seventh heaven
shaking in (one's) boots
startle
suspense
swell with pride

Taurus
temper
under the weather
up in arms
walk on air

Unit 84

affair
be in a bind
be in a fix
be in a (tight) spot
bull in a china shop
bury the hatchet
career
clarify
clumsy
dead end
dilemma
gesture
get a grasp of
get (one's) act together
get to the bottom of
go a long way
go back to square one
go hand in hand
happy medium
hold back
lay (one's) cards on the table
out of the woods
permanent
pins and needles
play (one's) cards close to one's chest
predicament
sit up and take notice
solution
stir things up
straighten things out
sweep (something) under the rug
take a back seat
take the bull by the horns
the light at the end of the tunnel
turning point

Unit 85

boast
bring home the bacon
butter (someone) up
chicken
cream of the crop
criticism
crow
cup of tea
epitome
first-rate
green thumb
ham it up
have (one's) cake and eat it, too
have a way with
head and shoulders above
icing on the cake
knock
light years ahead
miles ahead
modest
on the ball
out of this world
pick apart
praise
put (someone) down
put (something/someone) to shame
run down
scaredy cat
snake in the grass
surpass
take the cake
top-notch
tough nut to crack
trustworthy
worm (one's) way into

Unit 86

admit
(can't) get a word in edgewise
consult
deny
get the ball rolling
get to the point
give (someone) a talking to
ignorant

in a nutshell
inferior
long-winded
make heads or tails
notwithstanding
off the top of (one's) head
persuade
profile
proviso
reasonable
represent
scold
small talk
social
speak (one's) mind
speak up
stupid
talk behind (someone's) back
talk down
talk nonsense
talk shop
talk (someone) into
talking through (one's) hat
tough
warn
wrap up

Unit 87

acknowledge
admit
back
bite to eat
bothering
buy a lemon
couch potato
crash
drive a hard bargain
foot the bill
freshen up
hand it to (someone)
hang out
heel
incredible
make (quite a bit of) headway
negotiate
off (one's) chest
on (one's) mind
palm

pay through the nose
pay top dollar
preoccupied
progress
put (one's) feet up
relax
rip (someone) off
rip-off
rise and shine
sink (one's) teeth into
take a nap
thumb
tip of (one's) tongue
toe
tongue

Unit 88

A bird in the hand is worth two in the bush
Absence makes the heart grow fonder
advantage
advice
All that glitters is not gold
authority figure
cheap
criticize
definite
Don't count your chickens before they're hatched
Don't cross your bridges before you come to them
Don't put all your eggs in one basket
Familiarity breeds contempt
fault
interfere
invest
It's no use crying over spilled milk
moral
naive
Never judge a book by its cover
Never look a gift horse in the mouth
outward
paraphrase
partner

People who live in glass houses shouldn't throw stones
persuade
proverb
rumor
stingy
Too many cooks spoil the broth
visualize
warning
When the cat's away, the mice will play
Where there's smoke, there's fire
You can lead a horse to water, but you can't make it drink

Unit 89

abolish
compensate
compose
cosmetics
do a disservice
do a favor
do a good job
do aerobics / exercises / laps / sit-ups / sprints / weightlifting / yoga
do away with
do chores
do homework/paperwork
do nothing
do (one's) best
do something over
do the cooking / dishes / shopping
do (the) gardening / housework / laundry
do up
do without
make a bed
make a choice
make a cup of coffee / meal
make a decision
make a delivery
make a difference
make a fuss about

make a good or bad impression
make a living
make a mistake
make (a) noise
make a phone call
make a point of
make a profit
make a promise
make a suggestion
make allowances for
make an agreement
make an attempt
make an effort
make an excuse
make arrangements
make fun of
make money
make of
make off with
make out
make sense
make sure
make the best of
make the most of
make trouble
make up
make up for
make war
phrasal verb

Unit 90

bring about
bring back
bring down
bring on
bring out
bring out into the open
bring out the best in
bring out the worst in
bring (someone) around
bring (something) to light
bring to a head
bring to (one's) knees
bring up
capitalize
escort
expose
reintroduce
resemble

satisfaction
scandal
superiority
take advantage of
take after
take back
take care of
take everything in (one's) stride
take in
take it out on
take off
take on
take (one's) breath away
take out
take over
take part in
take place
take pride in
take up

Unit 91

annoy
critical
depressed
destroy
gathering
get along
get at
get away with
get back at
get behind
get by
get down to
get nowhere
get off
get off to a good/bad start
get out (of)
get out on the wrong side of the bed
get over
get rich quick
get rid of
get (someone) down
get the door
get the phone
get through
get to know
get up
get-together

investigation
irritate
manage
obtain
progress
recover
revenge
sneezing
throw away

Unit 92

criticize
extinguish
ignite
incite
instigate
mount
put away
put forward
put in (a good word)
put off
put (one's) foot down
put (one's) ideas across
put (one's) mind to it
put out
put (someone) down / off / on / out /up / up to
put two and two together
put up
put up with
putting on
reserve
set a good example
set aside
set fire to
set foot in
set in (one's) ways
set off
set on fire
set (one's) clock back/ahead
set (one's) heart/sights on
set out
set (someone) back
set the tone
set up
to put it another way
tolerate
turn off

Unit 93

as far as it goes
come across
come between
come into a fortune / money
come into bloom
come into contact
come into existence
come into fashion
come into operation
come into possession of
come into power
come into sight/view
come into use
come on
come out
come to
come to a conclusion
come to a halt/standstill
come to an agreement
come to an end
come to blows
come to grips with
come to mind
come to (one's) senses
come to terms with
come together
come up with
go back on
go bankrupt
go far
go for
go on
go through
go to great lengths
goes without saying
on the go

Unit 94

bother
break down
break into
break off
break (someone's) heart
break the record
forcibly
hallucinate
let down
let go of

let it slip
let (someone) be
let (someone) in on
let up
look down on
look forward to
look out
look up
rehearse
run
run in (one's) family
run into
run out
run through
see about
see eye to eye
see (someone) off
see the forest for the trees
see through
see to
seeing someone
seeing things
turn (to do something)
turn down
turn in
turn over a new leaf
turn up

Unit 95

aid
ax
back
bar
bid
blast
blaze
boost
boss
chief
clash
combat
curb
cut
deny
dive
drive
edge
FDA (Food and Drug Administration)

Index 233

flat
go-ahead
head
hike
key
link
loom
move
nod
ordeal
oust
pact
plea
pledge
plunge
poll
probe
quit
seek
soar
stall
talks
threat
vow
wed

Unit 96

aircraft
bills
bin
caution
container
counter
declare
destroy
disable
donation
environment
expense
extent
fine
fitting room
garment
hazardous
health
impose
lavatory
merge
monetary

penalty
physical
post
private property
prohibited
prosecute
receptacle
refund
refuse
reserved
rollerblades
skateboards
smoke detector
smoke-free
soliciting
spectator
tamper
teller
tow away
trash
trespassing
unlawful
vacancy
vehicle
violator

Unit 97

artificial
businessperson
camera operator
chair(person)
crew member
executive
firefighter
fisherman
flight attendant
gender-biased language
gender-neutral words
girl
human being(s)
humanity
labor
lady
male
man
man on the street
mankind
man-made
manpower

manufactured
Member of Congress
nurse
ordinary person
people
police officer
postal worker
repairman
sales representative
salesperson
spouse
staff
staff
synthetic
typical person
woman
work force
worker

Unit 98

abode
ad
along
apartment
beat
brainy
bucks
checks
children
clipped words
copy
cram
designated
disabled
folks
house
kid
lab
monosyllabic
nerd
Net
offspring
pal
paper
phone
place
regret
render
residence

seniors
slang
snooze
unattended
vacate
vet

Unit 99

Anglophone
arvo
Aussie
Australian English
barbie
beaut
bereaved
biggie
bizzo
Bollywood
bosom
Canadian English
chesterfield
common man
condoled
felicitate
first nations
footy
Francophone
G-day
Indian English
issueless
journo
loonie
milko
miscreant
Mountie
mozzies
oldies
Oz
riding (for)
truckie
ultra
undertrials
uni
walkabout
wearunders

Unit 100

aerial
antenna
apartment
apartment building
baby carriage
bank holiday
bank note
bathroom
bill
biscuit
block of flats
bonnet
boot
brief
candy
car park
carrier bag
cell phone
check
chips
closet
cookie
crosswalk
diaper
elevator
engine driver
engineer (on train)
eraser
faucet
first floor
flashlight
flat
freeway
french fries
garbage
gasoline
ground floor
highway
holiday
hood (of car)
kerosene
lift
line (of people)
lorry
mobile (phone)

motorway
nappy
national holiday
one-way
pants
pantyhose
paraffin
parking lot
pavement
petrol
pram
queue
return
round trip
rubber
rubbish
(Scotch) tape
second floor
sellotape
shopping bag
sidewalk
single
subway
sweets
tap
tights
to call (by telephone)
to ring
toilet
torch
trousers
truck
trunk (of car)
underground
underpants
undershirt
vacation
vest
waistcoat
wardrobe
WC
zebra crossing

Answer key

Many of your answers will depend on your own particular interests and needs. In some cases the Answer key can suggest answers only.

Unit 1

A
1. d
2. b
3. a
4. The most common twenty words in written English are (starting with the most frequent): *the, of, to, in, and, a, for, was, is, that, on, at, he, with, by, be, it an, at, his*. In spoken English they are: *the, and, I, to, of, a, you, that, in, it, is yes, was, this, but, on, well, he, have, for* (source: David Crystal, *The Cambridge Encyclopedia of Language*, 2nd edition, CUP, 1997, p. 86.)

B
1. *Possible answers:*
   a) a **chilly** day, **chilly** weather
   b) to **dissuade** someone from doing something
   c) **up to my neck** in work
   d) to be **independent** of someone or something / an **independent** country
   e) **get married** to someone, **get married** by a priest/minister/judge
2. a) **scissors** – used only in plural; if you want to count **scissors**, you have to say, e.g., **two pairs of scissors**.
   b) **weather** – uncountable noun
   c) **teach, taught, taught; teach** someone to do something; **teach** someone French.
   d) **advise** – uncountable noun; a piece of **advice**; verb = to **advise** (regular)
   e) lose, lost, lost; **lose** ≠ **loose**
   f) **pants** – used only in plural; if you want to count **pants** you have to say, e.g., *three pairs of pants*.
3. a) The **b** in **subtle** is silent.
   b) The final **e** in **catastrophe** is pronounced as a syllable, as it is in **apostrophe**. **Catastrophe** has four syllables.
   c) The stress is on the first syllable in **photograph**, and on the second syllable in **photography**. The "rule" is that the stress in long words in English frequently falls on the third syllable from the end of the word.
   d) The **w** in **answer** is silent, so the last syllable sounds like *sir*.
4. a) **guys** is informal, **persons** is formal and often used in legal texts, and **people** is a neutral term

D The picture is a good clue to help you understand **tortoise**. You may recognize the word **shell** in **shelled** (as in **eggshell**, for example). Similarly, your knowledge of **life** and **long** together with the context should enable you to figure out what **life span** and **longevity** mean. The whole context of the sentence should help you to figure out the meaning of **tended**. Some of the underlined words may be similar to words in your own language, which can be another useful way of working out the meaning of a word you have not seen before.

Unit 2

A
- *Possible answers:* **purr** (with **meow**), **scratch** and **lick**, **tail** or **claw** (with **paw**), and **tomcat** (with **kitten**)
- draw a line; write a line; point a gun; point a finger; utter nonsense; highly successful
- *Possible answers:* pricey, underpriced, price tag; to lend someone a hand, a handful, a handbag, underhanded. To find related expressions, you can use the

word's entry in a paper dictionary or you can type in the word in the search engine of an online dictionary.

B • *Possible answers:*

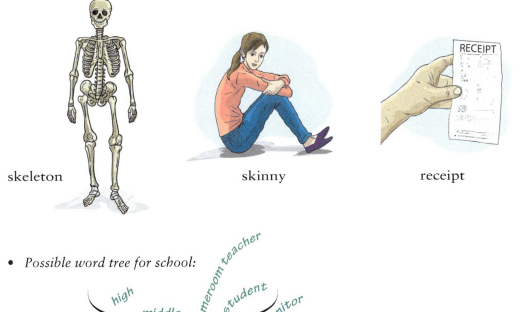

skeleton   skinny   receipt

• *Possible word tree for school:*

homeroom teacher, student, janitor, principal, attend, learn, study, get expelled from, skip (class), high, middle, elementary, calculus, physics, math — s c h o o l

• *Possible answers:*

original / brilliant / unusual / great / excellent	idea	shoot / edit / direct / star in / review	a movie	magnificent / breathtaking / superb / stunning / fabulous	view	kick / hit / bounce / catch / throw	a ball

• 1. drove   2. flown   3. Riding

Unit 3

3.1 The list is probably connected to a lesson or text about time. A possible organization might include bringing the **clock** words together in a word map or bubble network (**clock, wristwatch, hands, minute hand**); other words could then be added later (**hour hand, face/dial, digital**, etc.).

Tell the time and **What time is it?** could form a separate list of time phrases, to which others could be added, e.g., **Do you have the time? My watch is fast/slow.**

Answer key

Drowsy and **wide awake** could be treated as antonyms, and some notes about the usage of **beneath**, **under**, and **next to** would be useful. The list could also have information about parts of speech (*noun, preposition,* etc.) and pronunciation and word stress (*wristwatch* has the first syllable stressed).

3.2 **Theater** seems to be the obvious word. Note that **theater** has a physical meaning (the location of a play, movie or musical event) and a more abstract meaning (meaning putting on plays with actors)

3.3

synonyms	=		≠	*antonyms*
dominant, controlling	=	powerful	≠	*weak, ineffective*
prepared, willing	=	ready	≠	*unprepared, unwilling*
move, carry, convey	=	transport	≠	*remain, stand still*
devastate, wipe out	=	destroy	≠	*create, build*

3.4 Other testing systems include reentering any word you have trouble remembering, so that it appears more than once in the notebook. Another useful discipline is to set yourself a small, fixed number of words to memorize each week (e.g., 15–20) and to check them off in the book as you memorize them. You could also take any ten words from your book and put them on individual slips of paper or Post-It notes that you attach to furniture around your room or house (e.g., on the refrigerator door), so that you look at them frequently. It is a good idea to recycle (see or use again) key words, even if the activity that recycles the word is not difficult; just seeing the word again will help with your vocabulary learning.

Unit 4

4.1 *Possible answers:*
1. (countable nouns) style, association, conversation
2. (transitive verbs) have, include
3. (regular verbs) base, include, end
4. (adjectives) informal, colloquial, suitable, different
5. (prepositions) of, for, in, to
6. (uncountable nouns) pronunciation, slang
7. (intransitive verbs) be, refer, occur, begin
8. (irregular verbs) have, be, begin
9. (adverbs) extremely, mainly, frequently, very
10. (articles) the, a, an

4.2

Verb	*Infinitive*	*-ing form*	*Past participle*
define	to define	defining	defined
mean	to mean	meaning	meant
write	to write	writing	written

4.3
1. root – *form*; prefix – *in*; suffix – *al*
2. *formal*
3. unofficial, relaxed, casual (e.g., casual clothes)
4. *possible answers:* form, formality, formalize, formless, deform, reform, reformation, etc.

4.4 sy<u>lla</u>ble, coll<u>o</u>quial, pe<u>jo</u>rative, collo<u>ca</u>tion, <u>pe</u>riod, <u>co</u>mma, <u>se</u>micolon, a<u>pos</u>trophe (note that there are four syllables), <u>hy</u>phen, excla<u>ma</u>tion point, <u>ques</u>tion mark, pa<u>ren</u>theses, quo<u>ta</u>tion marks, <u>ca</u>pital <u>let</u>ter, <u>co</u>lon

4.5 1. chat – converse   4. beat – exhausted
        2. guy – man   5. hang out – relax
        3. put up with – tolerate

4.6 1. scheme   3. wordy   5. cunning
        2. skinny   4. stingy   6. smug

4.7 ( ) parentheses   ; semicolon   , comma
        ? question mark   – dash   " " quotation marks
        ' apostrophe   - hyphen   ! exclamation point

Unit 5

5.1 1. underwear   3. escape   5. piece of paper
        2. slide   4. get worse   6. mistake

5.2 1. education; (four syllables) **ca**, the third syllable, is stressed
        2. revision; (three syllables) **vi**, the second syllable, is stressed
        3. liberty; (three syllables) **lib**, the first syllable, is stressed
        4. length; only one syllable in the word
        5. passport; (two syllables) **pass**, the first syllable, is stressed
        6. brother; (two syllables) **bro**, the first syllable, is stressed

5.3 In the right-hand definition of **hairy**, synonyms are **frightening**, **dangerous**, and **exciting**.

There is no key for Unit 6.

Unit 7

7.1 High blood pressure, also called <u>hypertension</u>, is a common problem and needs <u>ongoing</u> <u>monitoring</u>. Doctors identify high blood pressure when the <u>sphygmomanometer</u> reading is 140/90 mmHg or more. This <u>malady</u> can lead to kidney <u>failure</u>, heart attacks, and other <u>debilitating</u> health conditions. Making positive changes in diet and lifestyle can significantly lower blood pressure in many cases. In certain cases, medication can be used to <u>remedy</u> this condition.

Check your understanding of the underlined words by using a dictionary. Then, use these notes about guessing meaning. The illustration can help you figure out some of the items.

hypertension: notice the commas and the phrase *also called*, which tells you it is giving a definition. This word means high blood pressure.
ongoing: look at the combination of words here – *on* and *go*. This means continuing.
monitoring: this is a verb acting as a noun. What kinds of actions would a common medical problem possibly require?
sphygmomanometer: you can guess that the machine around the arm is measuring the blood pressure.
malady: notice the *mal* part of the word. This generally means a negative thing, and because the word is a noun, you know it's a bad thing that leads to other very bad things; a sickness.
failure: if you know the verb *fail*, you can guess that this is the noun form.
debilitating: this adjective is used in a series of illnesses, so you can assume it is negative.
medication: this is a noun, the subject of the sentence. It is a form of the noun *medicine*.
After you figure out the next word, *remedy*, you will be able to determine that *medication* must be some type of medicine to help *remedy* the condition.
remedy: notice that this is a verb in the sentence – it describes what the medication will do (we assume it will probably cure or improve the condition).

7.2 *Possible answers:*
(These answers all give correct information in more detail than you would need to have provided in your own answers.)
2. *An echidna* must be a kind of animal or bird that people can eat. It is a type of anteater.
3. A *chisel* is something you use for shaping marble. It's a kind of tool used by sculptors.
4. A *tureen* must be a kind of very large bowl, a bit like a pot, used for soup.
5. To *clamber* means something like climbing with difficulty.
6. *Cranky* must be a bit like bad-tempered.

7.3 *Possible answers:*
2. Many countries require cards that show a person's identity for anyone who lives there.
3. I find Max to be a very kind person.
4. I've been terribly busy with work.
5. We walked down a street with trees along both sides of it towards the station.
6. The little boys were fascinated by the machine used for mixing cement.

7.4
1. anger that can't be controlled
2. feelings that are hostile to the current government
3. the person who used to be my boss (and no longer is)
4. drinks before dinner
5. a report that comes out either twice every month or every two months (both meanings of bimonthly exist)
6. letters that have not been delivered to the people they were addressed to

Unit 8

8.1
2. windshield wiper(s)
3. professional photographer
4. employee
5. dishwasher
6. artist
7. environmentalist

8.2
1. stapler
2. coffeemaker
3. MP3 player
4. hanger
5. monitor/computer

8.4
1. **a cleaner** – can be a thing or a person, e.g., a person who cleans in an office, or a substance/instrument for cleaning ("This cleaner will get the grease off your oven")
2. **a computer** – a thing [machine for computing]
3. **a dresser** – usually a thing [furniture to store clothing], but can sometimes mean a person who helps someone get dressed
4. **a dishwasher** – can be a person or a thing; a person who washes dishes, e.g., in a restaurant, or a machine that washes dishes
5. **a governor** – a person [the head of a state / regional government]
6. **an MP3 player** – a thing [machine for playing digital music]
7. **a marker** – a thing [something you write with]
8. **a singer** – a person who sings

8.5
2. doable
3. laziness
4. productive
5. outrageous

8.7
1. **timely** – it is an adjective. All the others are adverbs created by adding *-ly* to the adjective.
2. **compliment** – all the others are nouns from verb + **ment**, e.g., **appoint** + **ment**; there is no verb *compli*.
3. **handful** – all the others are adjectives; **handful** is a noun, meaning a pile of something about as big as you can hold in one hand, e.g., a handful of sand.
4. **worship** – all the others are nouns formed from noun + **ship**; there is no noun *wor*.

Unit 9

9.1
2. immature
3. inconvenient
4. irreversible
5. dissimilar
6. inefficient
7. impatient
8. unjust
9. disloyal
10. illogical

9.2
1. inedible
2. illiterate
3. unemployed
4. irreplaceable
5. illegal
6. antisocial

9.3
2. disagree
3. disprove
4. disliked
5. unload

9.4
1. a microwave
2. overqualified
3. a multinational company
4. a postgraduate
5. an ex-smoker
6. a submarine

9.5
2. are overworked and underpaid
3. oversleep
4. her ex-husband
5. reread them
6. misunderstood me
7. bilingual

Unit 10

10.1 The stress is on the underlined syllable in each of the words in the table.

Verb	Person noun	Abstract noun	Adjective
con<u>vert</u>	<u>con</u>vert	con<u>ver</u>sion	con<u>ver</u>ted
pro<u>duce</u>	pro<u>du</u>cer	pro<u>duc</u>tion, <u>pro</u>duce, <u>pro</u>duct, produc<u>tiv</u>ity	pro<u>duc</u>tive
con<u>duct</u>	con<u>duc</u>tor	<u>con</u>duct, con<u>duc</u>tion	con<u>duc</u>ted
im<u>press</u>	X	im<u>pres</u>sion	im<u>pres</u>sive
sup<u>port</u>	sup<u>por</u>ter	sup<u>port</u>	sup<u>por</u>tive
im<u>pose</u>	X	impo<u>si</u>tion	im<u>po</u>sing

10.2
1. It isn't easy to find synonyms for these words. The meanings are as follows: "She's shy and quiet and not very talkative. He finds it easy to talk and share his thoughts."
2. argues against
3. hold back
4. figure out based on the information available
5. made public
6. hold back, prevent

10.3
1. respect – look up to
2. postpone – put off
3. oppose – go against
4. inspect – look at
5. revert – turn back to
6. export – take/send out
7. divert – turn away

The two-word verbs (in the right-hand column) are more informal; you would expect to find them more in spoken English than in academic writing, for example.

10.4
1. deported
2. advertisements
3. introduce
4. oppressive
5. inspect
6. composed

> **follow-up**
>
> *Possible answers:*
> **spect** – circumspect behavior; a retrospective exhibition; a fresh perspective
> **vert** – an extroverted person; covert operations; a perverted sense of humor
> **port** – a hotel porter; reported speech; a portable television
> **duc, duct** – to reduce taxes; to induce labor; induction into the hall of fame
> **press** – blood pressure; compressed air; an original expression
> **pose, pone** – to pose for a photograph; to suppose something to be true; exposure to sunlight

Unit 11

11.1
1. amazement
2. attractiveness
3. complexity
4. discouragement
5. generosity
6. fear
7. friendliness
8. hope
9. kindness
10. hostility
11. prosperity
12. reason
13. resentment
14. sensitivity
15. warmth
16. wisdom

11.2
1. to achieve
2. to believe
3. to bore
4. to collect
5. to improve
6. to imagin
7. to invest
8. to own
9. to produce
10. to recognize
11. to replace
12. to think

11.3
1. bitterness
2. curiosity
3. brotherhood
4. chance
5. consciousness
6. stardom
7. reduction
8. neighborhood
9. sight
10. bitterness
11. rage (or anger)
12. originality

11.4
1. calm
2. aggressiveness
3. kingdom
4. illusion
5. partnership

> **follow-up**
>
> *Possible answers:*
> There are many more possibilities for the B suffixes but not many for the C suffixes.
> B **-ment** (un)employment, entertainment, involvement, requirement
>   **-ion** attraction, direction, diversion, rejection
>   **-ness** awkwardness, foolishness, loneliness, madness
>   **-ity** brutality, familiarity, productivity, superiority
> C **-ship** citizenship, sponsorship, championship
>   **-dom** officialdom
>   **-th** growth, wealth, stealth
>   **-hood** falsehood, nationhood, likelihood

Unit 12
When you are looking up compound adjectives in the dictionary, you may sometimes find the word listed under its second part rather than its first. Sometimes the word will not be listed at all if the meaning is absolutely clear from an understanding of the two parts.

If you are not sure whether a compound adjective is one word, two words, or hyphenated, check a dictionary. Be aware, however, that dictionaries sometimes differ, e.g., **absentminded** in one dictionary, but **absent-minded** in another.

Notice that the descriptions of Martin and Sonya on the left-hand page are lighthearted and exaggerated! They are not examples of good style – such long lists of adjectives would be inappropriate in a normal composition.

12.1
1. starry-eyed, wide-eyed
2. foolproof, fireproof
3. narrow-minded, open-minded
4. carefree, tax-free
5. hotheaded, lightheaded, hardheaded
6. broken-hearted, hard-hearted

12.2 *Possible answers:*

Positive:	self-assured	self-confident	self-possessed	self-sufficient
Neutral:	self-effacing	self-employed	self-evident	
Negative:	self-satisfied	self-serving	self-conscious	self-destructive

12.3
2. No, nearsighted.
3. No, handmade.
4. No, I prefer sugar-free food.
5. No, I like to fly first/business class.

12.4
1. up
2. on
3. back
4. of
5. out
6. down

12.5 *Possible answers:*

air-conditioned car/movie
bulletproof car/vest
duty-free perfume/liquor
first-class ticket/letter
handmade clothes/jewelry
interest-free credit/loan
last-minute decision/arrival
long-distance call/runner
longstanding arrangement/relationship
off-peak travel/hours
part-time work/job
so-called expert/specialist
sugar-free diet/cola
time-consuming work/preparation
top-secret information/file
world-famous actors/athletes

12.6 Here is one way of categorizing the words. There will be many other ways of categorizing them. What is important is not how you categorize them but the process of doing the exercise. The process should help you to learn the words.

Words connected with money: duty-free, interest-free
Words connected with comfort, safety, and convenience: air-conditioned, bulletproof, handmade, sugar-free
Words connected with time: last-minute, longstanding, off-peak, part-time, time-consuming

Unit 13

13.1 *Possible answers:*

Money	Health	Social issues
credit card bank account income tax Internet banking luxury goods business class	heart attack blood donor birth control family planning junk food blood pressure food poisoning hay fever	air-traffic control death penalty generation gap greenhouse effect labor force global warming brain drain public works race relations human rights birth control family planning grass roots mother tongue

13.2 *Possible answers:*
1. junk mail
2. computer program
3. bus driver
4. heartache
5. train station
6. word processing
7. sales tax
8. food processor
9. checking account

13.3
2. blood pressure
3. greenhouse effect *or* global warming
4. trademark
5. status symbol
6. death penalty
7. alarm system
8. junk food
9. Internet banking

13.4 *Possible sentences:*
1. "I get an enormous amount in the mail these days." (junk mail)
2. "I use a lot of these to run my computer." (computer program)
3. "This is a job that allows you to see a lot of the city." (bus driver)
4. "When you fall in love, you always risk feeling this." (heartache)
5. "This is where you should go if you like rail travel." (train station)
6. "It is so much more efficient than writing with paper and pen." (word processing)
7. "Things are already so expensive, and then we have to add this on." (sales tax)
8. "This is really convenient for chopping vegetables." (food processor)
9. "There's usually not much money left in it by the end of the month." (checking account)

Unit 14

14.1
1. leave the ground (of an aircraft)
2. burglaries
3. try to hide information
4. test performance
5. robbery
6. escape

14.2 *Possible answers*:
1. nervous breakdown
2. computer printout (*or* input, output)
3. final outcome (*or* output)
4. retail outlets
5. positive feedback (*or* outlook)
6. drastic cutbacks (*or* layoffs, downturn)

14.3
1. takeover
2. shakeup
3. crackdown
4. feedback, input
5. breakthrough
6. outlook

14.4
1. standoff
2. handouts
3. workout, push-ups
4. cleanup
5. holdup
6. turnout

14.5
1. **Outlook** means prospect or expectation; **lookout** is a person watching out for an enemy or danger.
2. **Outbreak** means a sudden appearance (e.g., of war, disease); **breakout** means escape (e.g., from prison)
3. **Setup** means a an arrangement or plan; **upset** means disturbance.
4. **Outlay** means amount of money spent on something; **layout** means the way something is arranged (e.g., the **layout** of a page or a room)

Unit 15

15.3 *Possible answers:*

Food	Politics	The arts	Sports
carafe cuisine delicatessen frankfurter hamburger kumquat marmalade molasses sauté smorgasbord spaghetti tea tofu vanilla yogurt	coup democracy embargo guerrilla junta ombudsman tsar	academy avant-garde ballerina drama easel guitar origami piano soprano waltz	judo karate kayak kung fu lasso ski slalom snorkel yacht

15.4 *Possible answers:*
Clothes: anorak shawl caftan pajamas boutique taffeta bazaar
Things in a house: futon mattress alcove carafe patio balcony
Animals: mosquito poodle dachshund mammoth lemming jackal cobra
Geographical features: fjord tundra steppe landscape

15.5
2. longstanding vendetta
3. strawberry yogurt
4. clinical psychology
5. gourmet cuisine
6. noisy kindergarten
7. total embargo
8. pleasure cruise
9. ruling elite
10. ecological catastrophe

15.6
2. garage – French
3. guru – Indian
4. tomato – Spanish
5. intelligentsia – Russian
6. coffee – Turkish
7. haiku – Japanese
8. anonymous – Greek

Unit 16

16.1
1. <u>M</u>ister Henry Chen
<u>P</u>ost <u>O</u>ffice <u>B</u>ox 2020
<u>S</u>aint Louis, <u>M</u>issouri
<u>U</u>nited <u>S</u>tates <u>o</u>f <u>A</u>merica

2. <u>Doctor</u> Maria Rivera
   430 Yonge <u>Street</u>
   <u>Apartment</u> 5 (Apt.)
   Toronto, <u>Ontario</u> (Ont.)
   <u>Canada</u> (Can.)

3. Lowe Plastics, <u>Incorporated</u> (Inc.)
   7 Bridge <u>Road</u>
   Freeminster
   <u>United</u> <u>Kingdom</u> (U.K.)

Note: In U.S. addresses, there is a two-letter abbreviation for every state, such as **MO** for **Missouri**, but some people write out the full word in addresses. Similarly, the Canadian province of **Ontario** might either be abbreviated or written as a full word.

16.2
1. Bachelor of Arts
2. Federal Bureau of Investigation
3. Professor
4. mind your own business
5. Test of English as a Foreign Language
6. to be announced
7. extension (telephone number)
8. frequently asked questions
9. condominium
10. self-contained underwater breathing apparatus

Note: In (3), **Prof.** can be a title, short for *Professor*, in which case it is pronounced as the full form. As a clipping (see section E), **prof** is used informally and pronounced as a one-syllable word.

16.3
```
From     : Mister Braneless
Sent     : Monday, March 24, 2010
Subject  : laboratory equipment
To       : All staff
copy to  : Ms. Hothead, Supply Department

All new laboratory equipment should be registered with the
Supply Department, Room 354 (extension 2683). New items
must be registered before five o'clock in the afternoon
on the last day of the month of purchase, that is, within
the current budgeting month. For your information (a
reminder): All numbers must be recorded.
```

16.4
2. ASAP
3. typo
4. Mrs.
5. PIN
6. OPEC
7. laser
8. R&D

Unit 17

17.1
1. someone who wants to be like someone else, especially someone famous (from *want to be* spoken quickly)
2. the process of using fewer natural resources and becoming more environmentally aware
3. clothes for overweight or large people
4. television programs that document non-actors in contrived situations
5. ordinary mail sent through the postal service
6. a television commercial that lasts 15 to 30 minutes

17.2
1. downsizing/outsourcing
2. telecommuting
3. spam
4. technophobe
5. spin doctors
6. cybercafé
7. family leave
8. blended family

17.3
1. tourists who travel to places with unspoiled natural attractions, such as wildlife, wetlands (a blended word: **eco** for ecology or environment + **tourist** = **ecotourist**)
2. a building that has chemicals that make the people inside sick
3. etiquette, or manners, on the Internet (a blended word: **net** + **etiquette** = **netiquette**)
4. software that is given away, or costs nothing (a blended word: **free** + **software** = **freeware**)
5. fear of computers (**cyber** for "computer" and **phobia** for "fear" = **cyberphobia**)

Unit 18

18.1
1. last
2. meter
3. friend
4. late
5. rein
6. head

18.2
1. dome
2. plead
3. wand
4. boot
5. doubt
6. though

18.3
1. Your <u>k</u>nowledge of <u>p</u>sychology shou<u>l</u>d help soften the blow.
2. It was an <u>h</u>onest mistake when the <u>p</u>sychiatrist <u>w</u>rote down the <u>w</u>rong name.
3. It shou<u>l</u>d take you a ha<u>l</u>f an <u>h</u>our to follow the <u>w</u>hole recipe for sa<u>l</u>mon.
4. I dou<u>b</u>t that we cou<u>l</u>d <u>w</u>rap all these presents before Chris<u>t</u>mas.

18.4
1. sus<u>pec</u>ted, <u>sus</u>pect
2. ob<u>ject</u>, <u>obj</u>ect
3. con<u>flic</u>ting, <u>con</u>flict
4. in<u>sult</u>, <u>in</u>sult
5. in<u>creas</u>ed, <u>in</u>crease
6. per<u>mit</u>, <u>per</u>mit
7. pro<u>gress</u>, <u>pro</u>gress
8. <u>con</u>duct, con<u>duc</u>ting

18.5
1. cooperate
2. compound
3. vegetable
4. conflict
5. subtle
6. honorable
7. pneumonia
8. reinforce

18.6
1. <u>pho</u>tograph, pho<u>tog</u>raphy, pho<u>tog</u>rapher, photo<u>gra</u>phic
2. <u>pol</u>itics, po<u>lit</u>ical, poli<u>ti</u>cian
3. e<u>con</u>omy, eco<u>nom</u>ical, eco<u>nom</u>ics
4. psy<u>chol</u>ogy, psy<u>chol</u>ogist, psycho<u>log</u>ical
5. psy<u>chi</u>atry, psychi<u>at</u>ric, psy<u>chi</u>atrist
6. mathe<u>mat</u>ics, mathema<u>ti</u>cian, mathe<u>mat</u>ical

Unit 19

19.2
1. growl
2. grumpy
3. mashed
4. clinked
5. crash
6. groaned *or* grumbled
7. gash
8. drizzling *or* sprinkling

19.3
1. spit (spat, spat)
2. grumpy
3. spit [a long, thin metal spike on which meat is put for roasting]

19.4
1. an angry animal growls
2. a dish falling on the floor smashes
3. a bored child wriggles
4. someone with asthma wheezes
5. a church bell clangs

19.5
1. gargle – to move a liquid around in your mouth and throat without swallowing
2. mumble – to speak softly and indistinctly
3. creak – to make a sound like an unoiled hinge
4. whack – to hit something very hard

19.6
1. children **giggling**
2. a referee **whistling**
3. someone **clicking** with a mouse
4. someone **sprinkling** salt on his/her food
5. food **sizzling** on the grill

> ### follow-up
>
> *Possible answers:*
>
> *cl:* **clap** or **clatter**; both represent fairly sharp sounds. **To clap** is to applaud with your hands. **To clatter** is to make a long, continuous resounding noise, like hard metallic things falling on a hard surface.
>
> *gr:* **gripe** and **grudge**; both have unpleasant meanings. **To gripe** is to complain, often accompanied by grumbling. **To hold a grudge** is to be unwilling to forgive someone for something bad they have done.
>
> *sp:* **spatter** or **spill**; both have an association with liquid or powder. **To spatter** means to splash or scatter in drips. **To spill** means to cause or allow a liquid to pour out of a container, so it goes beyond the edge, usually causing waste.
>
> *wh:* **whirl** and **whisk**; both have associations with the movement of air. **To whirl** means to move quickly around and around. **To whisk** means move or sweep quickly through the air.

Unit 20

20.1
2. It's no use (juice)! I can't use (snooze) this gadget.
3. The violinist in the bow (go) tie took a bow (now).
4. He's the lead (deed) singer in the heavy metal group "Lead (head) Bullets."
5. Does he still suffer from his war wound (mooned)?
6. I wound (round) the rope around the tree.
7. I didn't mean to tear (wear) up the contract, but I was so angry.
8. Now that the party is starting to wind (find) down, let's go home.

20.2
2. waste
3. sole
4. pane
5. allowed
6. through, phase
7. peel
8. write, right
9. week

20.3
1. "You're too young to smoke."
   This is a play on words on the two meanings of **smoke** – to smoke a cigarette and a fire or chimney smokes [gives out smoke].
2. He wanted to draw the curtains.
   This is a play on words on two meanings of **draw**. One means make a picture and the other means pull (curtains) open or closed.
3. A nervous wreck.
   A **wreck** is a boat or ship that, for example, hits a rock and sinks to the bottom of the sea. A **nervous wreck**, however, is an expression commonly used to describe someone who is extremely nervous.
4. Because it's full of dates.
   This is a play on words on the two meanings of **dates**. One meaning refers to time (e.g., 1492, 2001) and the other to a sweet fruit that comes from a kind of palm tree.

5. A newspaper.
   When we first hear the question, we assume the word red is a color, like black and white. But the word is really the verb **read** (same pronunciation as **red**) – the past participle of the verb **to read**. Of course, a newspaper is black and white and people read it all over. **All over** is another play on words: It could mean everywhere or all over the newspaper. (*Note*: Jokes and riddles like this one are usually spoken, not written, because the play on words is based on the sounds.)

20.4 1. (a) tea (b) tee 3. (a) mail (b) male
2. (a) pear (b) pair 4. (a) meat (b) meet

Unit 21

21.1 1. Before / Prior to
2. Till then / Until then / Before that / Before then
3. By the time / When
4. While/When
5. Previously / Earlier / Before that
6. As soon as
7. When/Once/After
8. The moment / The minute / Just as

21.3 *Possible answers:*
2. . . . study overseas.
3. . . . I usually feel bloated.
4. . . . look at the clock to see what time it is.
5. . . . lived in the same house.
6. . . . reading a book.
7. . . . have studied vocabulary every day.
8. . . . will double-check that I have all my reservations made.
9. . . . upset.
10. . . . used it to call a few friends.

Unit 22

22.1 1. **as long as / providing (that) / provided (that)** are all possible answers; **on condition that** is possible too, but it sounds a little stronger.
2. **In case of**; you can also say **In the event of**, which is sometimes seen in notices and regulations.
3. **If**
4. Since this is legal/official language, **on condition that** would be appropriate, or **provided that**; **as long as** is also possible but sounds a little too informal.
5. **Supposing / Suppose / What if**

22.2 *Possible answers:*
1. You cannot enter unless you have a visa. *or* You may enter provided (that) you have a visa.
2. You can't go in unless you're over 21. *or* You may enter provided (that) you are over 21.
3. Visitors may enter the mosque on condition that they remove their shoes. *or* You may go in as long as you take off your shoes. *or* You may not enter unless you remove your shoes.

22.3 1. No matter where she goes, she always takes that dog of hers.
2. I don't want to speak to anyone, whoever it is.
3. Whatever I do, I always seem to do the wrong thing.
4. However I do it, that recipe never seems to work.
5. No matter which color I choose, I always end up liking another color better.

22.4 *Possible answers:*
1. For the authors of this book, who are teachers, the prerequisites are a university degree and teaching qualifications.
2. Many people might move if they were offered a good job in another area. Others might not move under any circumstances.
3. In the United States, the normal admission requirements are a high school diploma, good grades, and acceptable scores on the Scholastic Aptitude Tests (SATs).
4. Some people might say, "I would lend a friend some money on the condition that they promise to pay me back by a specific date."

Unit 23

23.1 *Possible answers:*
1. The new tax law **brought about / led to / gave rise** to changes in the tax system.
2. An electrical fire was **caused by / due to** faulty wiring.
3. A violent storm **caused** widespread flooding. *or* **Owing to / Because of** a violent storm, there was widespread flooding.
4. Food shortages **sparked (off) / provoked / ignited** riots in several cities.
5. Declining profits **caused / led to** layoffs and salary cuts.
6. More Internet advertising has **led to / generated** increased sales.

23.2
2. The reason I didn't call you was (because/that) I'd lost your phone number. *or* My reason for not calling you was . . . (acceptable, but sounds more formal)
3. I will not sign the contract, on the grounds that it is illegal.
4. Lawmakers passed a new bill with the aim of balancing the budget. *or* The aim of the new bill passed by lawmakers was to balance the budget.
5. I wonder what her motives were in sending everyone flowers.
6. The high salary prompted her to apply for the job.

23.3 *Possible answers:*
1. The road was blocked due to a terrible snowstorm.
2. Owing to the cancellation of the performance, everyone got a refund.
3. The service was terribly slow. Consequently, the customers got angry.
4. There was a transit strike. As a result, we had to walk home.

23.4
1. for
2. of
3. from
4. with, of
5. given, to

Unit 24

24.1 *Possible answers:*
1. I agree (*or* more formal: I acknowledge) that you weren't entirely to blame, but you have to take *some* responsibility.
2. He conceded that we had tried our best, but he still wasn't content.
3. The company acknowledges (*or* concedes) that you experienced some delay, but it does not accept liability. (**Acknowledge** is fairly formal and therefore appropriate in formal, legal situations like this one.)
4. OK, I admit I was wrong and you were right; he is a nice guy.

24.2 *Possible answers:*
1. on the contrary
2. on the other hand
3. huge discrepancy
4. After all
5. despite all that (*or* in spite of it all)
6. world of difference
7. It's all very well
8. Admittedly

24.3

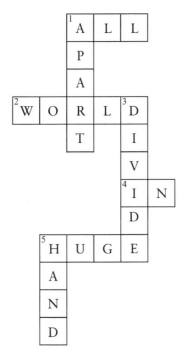

Unit 25

25.1 *Possible answers:*
1. Pursuant to / Further to
2. In addition to / As well as / Apart from / Besides
3. etc. / and so on / and so forth
4. in addition to / as well as / apart from / besides
5. Furthermore/Moreover

Comments: In (2) and (4), the choice is wide, but the writer would probably choose different phrases to avoid repeating herself.

25.2
1. Physical labor can exhaust the body very quickly. Similarly, excessive study can rapidly reduce mental powers.
2. My cousin turned up, along with some classmates of his.
3. As well as owning a big chemical factory, he runs an enormous oil business.
   or He owns a big chemical factory as well as running an enormous oil business.
4. She was my teacher and a good friend to boot.
5. In addition to being the scientific adviser, I also act as consultant to the director.

25.3
1. I work part time as well as **being** a student, so I have a busy life.
2. Besides **having** a good job, my ambition is to meet someone nice to share my life with.
3. Apart from **having** many other responsibilities, I am now in charge of staff training.
4. In addition **to** a degree, she also has an advanced certificate. *or* In addition to **having** a degree, . . .
5. My father won't agree. **Likewise**, my mother's sure to find something to object to.
6. He said he'd first have to consider the organization, then the system, then the finance, and **so forth / and so on**.

Unit 26

26.1
1. fact
2. issue
3. belief
4. problem
5. evaluation
6. view

26.2
1. issue (best here because it is something everyone is debating and disagreeing on; **question** or **controversy** are also OK)
2. problem/matter/situation (**crisis** or **dilemma** if it is really serious)

3. question (**mystery** would also be possible)
4. topic
5. approach / response / solution / answer

26.3
1. Situation in Sudan worsening daily
2. New approach to cancer treatment
3. No resolution for unemployment numbers
4. Scientist rejects claims over fast food
5. Proposal to raise cable rates draws fire
6. Solution to age-old mystery in Kenya

Unit 27

27.1 "<u>Well</u>, <u>where should I start</u>? It was last summer and we were just sitting in the garden, <u>sort of</u> doing nothing much. <u>Anyway</u>, I looked up and … <u>see</u>, we have this <u>kind of</u> long wall at the end of the garden, and it's … <u>like</u> … a highway for cats, <u>for instance</u>, that big fat black one you saw, <u>well</u>, that one considers it has a right of way over our vegetable patch, <u>so</u> … <u>where was I</u>? <u>Yes</u>, I was looking at that wall, <u>you know</u>, day-dreaming as usual, and all of a sudden there was this new cat I'd never seen before, <u>or rather</u>, it wasn't an ordinary cat at all … I <u>mean</u>, you'll never believe what it was …"

Comments:
Well is often used to shift the conversation to a different type or topic (here from the ordinary conversation to a story).

Where / How should I start / begin? ("begin" is much more common in written language than in spoken). This is a very common marker at the beginning of a story or monologue while the speaker is composing his/her thoughts.
Anyway is probably the most common marker in spoken story-telling to divide up the story into its different stages (introduction / main plot / resolution, etc.)
See is often used in informal talk instead of **you see**, when someone is clarifying or explaining something.
Like, sort of and **kind of** are often used when the speaker hesitates, or to make something less precise, a little more vague.
Well here is used to focus on an important point.
So is very commonly used to mark the beginning of the next event in a story.
Where was I? is used when we want to come back to the main subject we were talking about after an interruption or diversion into another point or topic.
Yes is often used when we resume what we were talking about; it does not have to be an answer to a question from someone. **No** is also used in exactly the same way and could have been used here instead of **yes**.
You know is used here to mean "you can guess what I was like."
Or rather is used when you change to a different word or a better / more accurate way of saying what you want to say.
I mean is used when you want to explain something or expand or illustrate what you are saying.

This extract is typical of the number of markers found in everyday informal talk. The speaker is not a "lazy" or "bad" speaker; everyone uses markers, even if they are not conscious of it or do not want to admit it! Informal conversation *without* markers sounds rather odd and strained, and a little too formal.

27.2
1. Yes, there is a lot of work to do. **Anyway**, I must rush now, I'll call you tomorrow.
2. A: It is so hot in Mexico City just now!
   B: **Of course**, it is summer.
3. **After all**, money is not the most important thing in life. I really do believe that.
4. I never got a chance to tell him. **Still**, I'm seeing him next week. I'll tell him then.
5. There're two reasons I think he's wrong. **A**, he has the facts wrong; and **b**, his conclusion doesn't make sense.

27.3 *Possible answers:*
1. A: Are you a football fan?
   B: **Well,** I like it; I wouldn't say I was a fan.
2. A: I'll take care of these.
   B: **OK,** that's everything.
   A: **Fine/Great,** so see you next week.
   B: **Good.** That was a very useful meeting.
3. A: It was last Monday. I was coming home from work. I saw this ragged old man approaching me. **Anyway,** I stopped him . . .
   B: Jim Dibble!
   A: **Hang on!** Let me tell you what happened first.
4. A: Which number is yours?
   B: *(pause)* **Let me see** . . . it's this one here, yes, this one.
5. A: He's looking exhausted.
   B: Yes, he is.
   A: **Of course,** he has an awful lot of responsibility, so it's hardly surprising.
6. A: What do you mean, "cold?"
   B: **Well,** She's not friendly, very distant, **so to speak.** Last week I gave her a big smile and she . . . **like,** scowled at me.
   A: **Well,** What do you expect? **Look,** I've seen the way you smile at people, it **sort of** makes them feel uncomfortable.

> **follow-up**
>
> If it is difficult or impossible for you to get hold of tape-recordings of natural conversation, there are tapes and transcripts of everyday English conversation in R. Carter and M. McCarthy, *Exploring Spoken English* (Cambridge University Press, 1997), where you will find a wide range of spoken discourse markers in actual use, with commentaries.

Unit 28

28.1
1. First of all / Firstly / First
2. in other words
3. For example / For instance
4. Next
5. Lastly
6. In summary *or* in sum (more formal). (**In conclusion** would not be suitable here, since it just means "this is the end of the text," whereas this sentence provides a summing up of the arguments in the text.)

28.2
1. this will not be discussed
2. to correct or modify something
3. moving to a more specific point
4. to finish off
5. this document is about another one
6. read something earlier in the text

28.3
1. actually
2. the following (introducing a list)
3. further (as in *further details/information*)
4. in other words / that is to say (meaning to restate information in a new way)
5. in summary, to sum up, in sum

28.4 *Sample letter:*

> Dear Editor,
>
> **Regarding** the article in your newspaper about the closure of Bridgeport Hospital, I would like to express my strong opposition to the proposal for **the following** reasons. **First,** the nearest other hospital is 50 miles away. **Second,** 200 people work at the hospital and they will lose their jobs and the whole region will suffer; **that is to say,** the hospital makes an important contribution to the local economy. **Finally,** it is the only hospital in the region with a special cancer unit. But **leaving aside** the economic and medical questions, the hospital is obviously being closed for political reasons, and this is quite wrong. **To sum up,** the closure of our hospital would be a disaster both for the people and for the economy of this region.
>
> Sincerely yours,
> Ms. Anne Greene

Unit 29

C *Possible answers:*
cheese, spaghetti, bread, cake, lettuce, yogurt, fish, milk, juice, etc.

29.1
1. no article
2. no article
3. a study
4. no article
5. no article
6. no article

29.2

Uncountable	Countable
cotton	shirt
work	job
information	fact
baggage	suitcase
advice	idea
travel	trip
soap	toothbrush
fuel	engine

29.3 *Possible answers:*
soap, toothpaste, shampoo, makeup, underwear, clothing, writing paper, film, medicine

29.4
1. We had such terrible **weather** last night! The storm knocked out the **electricity** for hours.
2. I love antique **furniture**, but I would need **advice** from a specialist before I bought any. My **knowledge** in that area is very poor.
3. His **research** is definitely making great **progress** these days. He has done a lot of original **work** recently.
4. If your **luggage** is too heavy, it will cost a lot of **money** to bring it.

29.5 Possible answers:
Can I have **a** broom?
Can I have **some** detergent?

Can I have **some** shampoo?
Can I have **some** flour?
Can I have **a** knife?
Can I have **some** soap?

29.6 *Possible answers:*
An **actor** needs a lot of determination, talent, creativity, discipline, empathy, and some training.
An **athlete** needs great determination, stamina, discipline, and a lot of commitment.
A **doctor** needs a lot of patience, compassion, and goodwill. A little bit of charm also helps, and a lot of commitment and training is needed.
A **firefighter** needs courage, training, determination, and discipline.
A **teacher** needs great patience, empathy, a lot of energy, a little bit of creativity, intelligence, and some training.
A **writer** needs a lot of creativity, talent, and intelligence.

Unit 30

30.1
1. tongs
2. sunglasses
3. scissors
4. tweezers
5. binoculars
6. pliers

30.2 overalls, socks, underpants, pants/slacks/jeans, tights, shorts

30.3
1. pajamas
2. proceeds
3. whereabouts
4. authorities, goods
5. blues

30.4
1. pants
2. aerobics
3. tongs
4. clothes

30.5
After teaching **gymnastics** for years, I decided that I wanted to be a rock star and I moved to Los Angeles. I got a room, but it was on the **outskirts** of the city. The owner didn't live on the **premises**, so I could make as much noise as I liked. The **acoustics** in the bathroom **were** fantastic, so I practiced playing rock music and rhythm & **blues** there. I went to the **headquarters** of the musicians' union, where a guy in pink **shorts** and large **sunglasses** told me he liked my music but hated my taste in **clothes**.

Unit 31

31.1 *Possible answers:*
2. Most people have **a cloth** somewhere in the kitchen to wipe the work surfaces and in case they spill something. People who like to make clothes might have **cloth** at home, usually in a room where a sewing machine is kept.
3. For those who like to use **peppers** in cooking (e.g., bell peppers, chili peppers, jalapeño peppers), they would be found in the kitchen. Most people have **pepper** (together with salt) in their kitchen or dining room.
4. You would have some **paper** around so you can write on it or use it to print something. Many people enjoy getting a **paper** so they can read about daily news.
5. Some people have **a fish** (or **several fish**) swimming around in a tank or fishbowl in their living room. Of course, for cooking, **fish** would usually be found in the kitchen.
6. Most people keep **glasses** (for drinking) in the kitchen, dining room, or other rooms. Most homes also have **glass** somewhere, usually in the windows.

31.2 *Possible answers:*
1. Can I have a chocolate?
2. Can I have some pepper?
3. Can I borrow some coffee?
4. Can I have some turkey?
5. Can I have some wine?

Answer key

31.3 *Possible answers:*
2. I drove over some glass. *or* There was glass on the road.
3. How about some pepper?
4. There was a hair in it.
5. Oh, it's a thread. I'll just cut it off.

31.4
1. **Painting** (uncountable) can be an occupation or a hobby. **A painting** or **paintings** are individual works of art, each created by someone.
2. **A noise / noises** would mean one or more particular sounds. **So much noise** (uncountable) can mean many sounds (usually unpleasant) that might go on over a period of time.
3. **Light** (uncountable) usually means light to see by, e.g., electric light. In its countable form, as in the request "Can I have **a light?**" it usually refers to a match or lighter to light a cigarette or pipe.

Unit 32

32.1
1. swarm
2. school
3. gang
4. set
5. team/group

32.2
1. pigs
2. a book
3. a hospital
4. cats

32.3
2. a herd of elephants
3. a row of chairs (in a line)
4. a swarm of bees
5. a pile of clothes
6. a pair of socks

32.4
1. There's a stack of tables in the next room.
2. There's a crowd of people waiting outside.
3. The staff is well paid.
4. He gave me a set of six sherry glasses.
5. She gave me a bunch of beautiful roses. (*or* a beautiful bunch of roses)
6. We brought a bundle of firewood to burn in the bonfire.

32.5
a whole **host** of questions
a **barrage** of complaints
a **string** of wild allegations
a **series** of short answers

Unit 33

33.1
2. a rumble of thunder
3. a cloud of smoke
4. an article of clothing
5. a flash of lightning
6. a blade of grass
7. a drop of rain
8. a means of transportation

33.2
2. My mother gave me **a piece of / bit of** advice that I have always remembered.
3. Suddenly a **gust of** wind blew him off his feet.
4. Would you like another **piece/slice of** toast?
5. Let's go to the park – I need a **breath of** fresh air.
6. I can give you an important **bit of / piece of** information about that.
7. I need to get some **pieces of** furniture for my apartment.

33.3

33.5 Possible sentences:
1. In wartime, many villages went through a state of siege several times.
2. The company has been going through a state of flux ever since the top executive resigned.
3. Everything seems to be in a state of confusion at the moment, but I'll sure it'll all be smoothed out before the wedding.
4. We moved over a month ago, but we are still in a state of chaos.
5. It's important for job applicants to be in a good state of mind before an interview.

Unit 34

34.1 2 <u>cartons/bottles</u> of milk
4 <u>cans/bottles/six-packs</u> of soda
a <u>can</u> of tuna fish
a <u>package/box</u> of chocolate chip cookies
a large <u>box</u> of matches
a <u>jar</u> of honey
2 <u>bottles/cans</u> of mineral water
a <u>sack/bag</u> of rice

34.2
1. pot
2. barrel, bottles, crate
3. bottles, cans, barrels, six-packs, crates
4. *any five of these:* bottle/carton (of milk or juice), jug (of milk or juice), mug (of coffee), box (of cereal), jar (of jam), glass (of milk or juice), bowl (of sugar), basket (of fruit)
5. (shopping) bag and basket
6. carton, bottle, can, glass, jug

34.3
1. a jar of peanut butter
2. a box of laundry detergent
3. a carton of orange juice
4. a tube of skin cream
5. a can of tomato sauce
6. a bag/sack of apples
7. a box of tissues
8. a bottle of cooking oil
9. a carton of eggs
10. a bottle of dishwashing liquid

34.4 *Possible answers:*
2. tool, match
3. gallon, milk
4. beer, soda
5. packing, wooden
6. fruit, fish
7. wine, hour
8. flower, tea

Answer key 257

Unit 35

35.1
1. Argentinean, Venezuelan, Costa Rican, Panamanian, Mexican, Peruvian, (note the v), Ecuadoran/-ean/-ian, Bolivian, Uruguayan, Paraguayan, Colombian, Salvadoran/-ean/-ian, Nicaraguan, etc.
2. Ukrainian, Yugoslavian, Croatian, Serbian, Slovenian, Bulgarian, Bosnian, Romanian, Albanian, Mongolian, Moldavian, Czechoslovakian, Russian, Georgian, etc.
3. *Other groupings:* – i adjectives seem to be Muslim and/or Middle Eastern countries; four of the -ese adjectives are Asian.

35.2
2. Italy → Italian
3. Canada → Canadian
4. Vietnam → Vietnamese
5. Jordan → Jordanian
6. China → Chinese

35.3
1. A **Spaniard** named as new UN leader
2. **Britons** have highest tax rate in EU
3. **Canadian** elections today
4. Police arrest **Dane** on smuggling charge
5. **Iraqi** delegation meets **Pakistani** president
6. Four gold medals for the **Portuguese** team!

35.4
1. Languages most widely spoken, in order, are Chinese, English, Spanish, Hindi, Arabic. (source: *The Cambridge Encyclopedia of Language*, Cambridge University Press)
2. China, India, the United States, Indonesia, Brazil (as of the publication of this book!)
3. If we take Scandinavia as strictly the geographical peninsula, then Sweden and Norway are the only countries completely in Scandinavia. If we consider it more as a language family, then Denmark and Iceland can be added, and if as a cultural family, then Finland can be added too.
4. A difficult question! However, most linguists seem to agree on around 5,000 mutually incomprehensible tongues. There are, of course, many more dialects.
5. Inuit is an Eskimo language, and its speakers may be found in northern Canada.
6. Malays, Chinese (or various ethnic subtypes), and Indians (many are Tamils and Sikhs).

Unit 36

36.1
1. slush
2. sleet
3. frost
4. blizzards
5. snowdrifts
6. thaws
7. melts

36.2 *Note:* Some of these combinations form one solid word and some remain as two words.
1. thunderstorm
2. torrential rain
3. downpour
4. heat wave
5. hailstones
6. snowdrift
7. hurricane warning
8. overcast sky

36.3 *Possible answers:*
2. It was scorching/boiling/sweltering last month. *or* There was an awful heat wave last month.
3. It's stifling/muggy/humid today.
4. We had terrible floods.
5. There was a blizzard that night.
6. There was a very bad drought.
7. There was a strong breeze / gust of wind. OR It was very blustery.
8. After the hurricane/gale/tornado, the damage was unbelievable.

36.4   2. *good*: warm, mild, or even cool (if it has been a very hot day) and preferably dry; *bad*: cold, windy, or wet weather
3. *good*: clear, sunny, dry, breezy weather; *bad*: gales, high winds, hurricanes, storms, wet weather, mist/fog
4. *good*: clear, dry, but not too hot; *bad*: cold, wet, and windy weather or humid, muggy weather, smog or haze
5. *good*: dry, no wind, warm nights; *bad*: wet, windy, snowy weather

Unit 37

37.1   *Possible answers:*
2. . . . the fair/white, bald guy (*or* straight-haired / curly-haired man).
3. . . . scruffy and messy (*or* sloppy) looking.
4. . . . the slim, dark-haired one.
5. . . . a teenager / in her twenties / twenty-something. (Another useful expression is "She's only a youngster," for a person who is a teenager or who is still very young.)

37.2   *Possible answer:*
1. The author who wrote this exercise is tall, with brown hair that is going gray; he's white, in his forties, and thinks he's good looking! What about you?

37.3   *Possible answers:*
Will Prowse: curly blond (*or* fair) hair; fair complexion; thin face
Louisa Yin: long, straight, dark hair
Sandra King: brunette, dark wavy hair; stocky or heavy build, round face
Jake "Dagger" Flagstone: bald, with beard and mustache; muscular build

Unit 38

38.1   1. bright – stupid   4. cruel – kindhearted
2. extroverted – introverted   5. generous – tight-fisted
3. rude – polite   6. unsociable – gregarious

38.2   2. sociable   6. extravagant
3. pessimistic   7. argumentative
4. assertive   8. sensitive
5. inquiring

38.3   *Possible answers:*
2. If you speak without worrying about how the other person will feel, you are blunt.
3. If you think carefully before doing something risky, you are sensible.
4. If you believe everything you read in a newspaper, you are naive.
5. If you are calm even in stressful situations, you are even-tempered.
6. If you like to do things differently from other people, you are unconventional.

38.4   *Possible answers:*
2. Nancy's usually blunt.   6. I find Annie self-assured.
3. Jim's really stubborn.   7. Molly is somewhat inquiring.
4. Paul can be assertive.   8. Jack is kind of weird.
5. Dick is awfully ambitious.

Unit 39

39.1   1. This is Jack. He's my roommate. *or* He and I are roommates.
2. We were classmates at Lincoln High School, weren't we? *or* You were a classmate of mine . . .
3. She and I were teammates (on the softball team).

39.2 *Possible answers:*
John Crosby and Bill Nash are colleagues.
Bill Nash and Josh Yates are acquaintances.
Lan Nguyen is Bill Nash's ex-wife.
Bill Nash is Lan Nguyen's ex-husband.
Lan Nguyen and Nora Costa were Olympic teammates.
Ana Marquez and Nora Costa were classmates.
Ana Marquez is Fred Park's wife.
Fred Park is Ana Marquez's husband.
Fred Park and Josh Yates's are colleagues.
Fred Park and Lan Nguyen were once acquaintances.
Laura Fine is Josh Yates's significant other.
Laura Fine and John Crosby worked at the same school.

39.3 *Possible answers:*
1. A teenage pop music fan might not see eye to eye with his/her parents, might worship or idolize a pop star, might dislike but might (secretly!) respect a strict teacher, and surely gets along with his/her best friend.
2. An administrative assistant might like another administrative assistant or might not get along well with her/him; might despise or hate the boss, or perhaps look up to him/her; and might be attracted to a very attractive co-worker.
3. A 45-year-old bachelor might dislike teenagers or look down on them, or might like them; he might be repelled by an ex-girlfriend, or the ex might still turn him on.

39.4
1. Dave and Phil don't see eye to eye. *or* … don't get along.
2. I had a falling out with my boyfriend last night.
3. We had an argument but now we've made up.
4. His girlfriend gets along well with his mother.
5. Dana had a big fight with her fiancé and broke up with him.

Unit 40

40.1
1. attic
2. landing
3. hall or hallway or foyer
4. master bedroom
5. garage
6. driveway
7. laundry room
8. den or study

40.2
1. basement
2. attic
3. patio/porch
4. front hall (*or* foyer)
5. ironing board
6. (electrical) outlet
7. condominium (*or* condo)
8. studio apartment (*or* studio)

40.3
2. a bathroom cabinet
3. the garage
4. a living room or den, next to a TV set
5. a den, a kitchen, a living room, or a master bedroom
6. the kitchen or laundry room
7. anywhere inside or outside a house
8. the kitchen

Unit 41

41.1 *Possible answers:*
2. My car broke down / wouldn't start. *or* My car battery was dead / had run out.
3. Our washing machine broke down / stopped working.
4. You sprained or twisted your ankle.
5. I cut my finger.
6. The batteries in my radio/camera have run out / are dead.
7. I seem to have misplaced my glasses / contact lenses / etc.

41.2
1. break down – this means "fail mechanically"; **break** and **smash** both mean break physically.
2. stain – means "leave a mark"; **fall down** and **bump** both refer to ways you can injure yourself.
3. come off – refers to pieces falling off an object; **spill** and **leak** both refer to liquids.
4. flood – refers to an excess of water; **cut** and **bruise** are both types of injury.

41.3 *Possible answers:*
1. Call the bank / credit agency and get them to cancel it immediately.
2. Call a plumber to fix the leak.
3. Sew it back on.
4. Get it repaired or buy a new one if it is beyond repair.
5. Put ice on it immediately.
6. Reset it. *or* Get a new battery.

41.4
1. vase – crack
2. sofa cushion – rip
3. faucet – drip
4. car – dent
5. elbow – bang
6. old coat – wear out

41.5 *Possible answers:*
2. . . . locked myself out.
3. . . . fell down and cut my knee.
4. . . . the batteries are dead / run down
5. . . . dented the car behind me. (*or* smashed/banged into another car)

Unit 42

42.1
2. Drought; if the plants and trees are **withered**, they are probably dying because they have no water, and since the earth is **cracked** [hard, with a pattern of deep lines over it], it suggests it is very dry.
3. Earthquake; a **tremor** is a trembling movement of the earth. Note how disasters of various kinds can **strike**, e.g., The hurricane **struck** the coastline at noon.
4. A violent storm or wind, such as a hurricane/typhoon/tornado; if you **board up** your house you cover the windows and doors with wooden boards to protect them.
5. War, battle, or an attack of some kind, or extreme unrest; **shells** and **mortars** are projectiles that cause explosions when they strike.

42.2

Verb	Noun: thing or idea	Noun: person/people	Adjective
destroy	destruction	-------	destructive
erupt	eruption	-------	-------
explode	explosion	-------	explosive
injure	injury	the injured	injured
starve	starvation	the starving	starving
survive	survival	survivors	-------

42.3
1. has happened / getting worse (**spreads** means get bigger)
2. getting worse / heading for a major disaster (a **time bomb** ticks like a clock and eventually explodes)
3. disaster was avoided (the bomb was **defused** – made safe)
4. disaster was avoided (**all survive** means no one died)
5. is happening (**smashing** – pushing through something in a destructive way)
6. disaster has happened / is happening (if you **heed** a warning, you take note, and do something; here the warning was ignored)

42.4 1. victims 3. casualties
2. refugees 4. survivors

42.5 1. malaria 2. cholera or typhoid 3. rabies

Unit 43

43.1
1. nursery school / preschool
2. elementary school / primary school / kindergarten
3. elementary/primary
4. junior high / middle
5. private/parochial
6. scores
7. major
8. bachelor's
9. graduate
10. lecturer/professor

43.4
1. I have to study all night; I'm **taking** a test tomorrow.
2. Congratulations! I hear you **aced** your exams!
3. After finishing high school, she went directly to **college**.
4. **Public** schools in the U.S. are free.

43.5 *Possible questions:*
1. Did you get a scholarship or a grant to study?
2. Until what age do students have to attend school in the U.S.?
3. You look really tired. What've you been doing?
4. Did you pass / do well on / ace your exam?
5. Did your kids go to preschool / nursery school?

Unit 44

44.1
1. CEO, executive
2. union representative
3. unskilled worker, entry-level employee
4. white-collar worker
5. supervisor, boss
6. accountant

44.2
2. health care – psychiatrist, surgeon
3. engineering – biotechnical engineer, mechanical engineer
4. arts/entertainment – dancer, singer, costume designer
5. journalism – radio/TV announcer
6. computer/technology – software developer

44.3 *Possible answers:*
2. This person was **laid off**.
3. This person **works the night shift**.
4. She's **been promoted**. / She **got a promotion**.
5. This person **was fired**.
6. He quit his job. (*or* he **resigned**)
7. You are a **workaholic**.

44.4
1. get/have/find   4. applied
2. living   5. offered
3. work   6. moonlight

Unit 45

45.1 *Possible answers:*
1. bowling
2. windsurfing
3. auto racing

4. pool/billiards, but could, of course, apply to a number of other sports too, particularly target sports (golf, archery, bowling, etc.)
5. horseback riding, cycling, motocross

45.2
2. paddle, ball, net
3. stick/cue, chalk, balls
4. bat, glove, baseball
5. basketball, net/hoop
6. bowling ball, pins, lane
7. saddle, horse, bridle
8. racquet, squash ball
9. soccer ball, goal/net
10. racquet, tennis balls
11. goggles, bathing suit
12. surfboard

45.3
1. A long jumper
2. a jockey
3. a racecar driver
4. a discus/javelin thrower
5. a gymnast
6. a hockey player
7. a long-distance runner
8. a pole-vaulter

45.4
1. broken/set
2. lost or been beaten
3. win
4. holds
5. take up

45.5 *Possible answers:*
2. golf (golf course) or horse racing (racecourse)
3. usually boxing or wrestling
4. baseball, football, soccer, field hockey, and many others
5. ice skating, ice hockey, roller skating
6. bowling
7. downhill skiing
8. running, jogging, racing (racetrack)

Unit 46

46.1 *Possible answers:*
2. sculpture (The verb **stand** is often associated with statues; it could also be architecture, if Peace is interpreted as the name of a building or huge monument.)
3. a performance of a play at a theater (Plays are divided into **acts** – major divisions – and **scenes** – smaller divisions.)
4. dance (**Movement** and **rhythm** are the clues.)
5. poetry (**Rhyme** – having the same sounds at the ends of lines – is sometimes thought of as a necessary quality of poetry.)
6. painting (**Oil**-based and **water**-based paints are the main types of paint used by artists.)
7. architecture (We talk of the **design** of a building.)
8. plays (Drama texts in written form.)
9. probably a novel, but it could be any book divided into **chapters**, e.g., an academic textbook.
10. the movies (When a movie is shown at a theater, we sometimes say it's on the **big screen**.)

46.2
2. What's the name of the **publisher** of that book you recommended? Was it Cambridge University Press? (An **editorial** is an article in a newspaper or magazine giving the opinions of the editor on matters of interest/concern.)
3. "Do I dare to eat a peach?" is my favorite **line** of poetry in English. (A **stanza** is a group of lines that make up the divisions of a poem or song.)
4. He's a very famous **sculptor**; he did that statue in the park, you know, the one with the soldiers. (**Sculpture** is the name of the art form; **sculptor** is the person who does it.)
5. Most of the (**short**) **stories** in this collection are only five or six pages long. They're great for reading on short trips. (A **novel** is a long work, usually more than 100 pages. Here **short story** or just **story** is clearly what the speaker is referring to.)

6. The cast wore beautiful **costumes** in the new production of the play. (**Costumes** are clothes worn by the actors; the **sets** are the scenery, furniture, etc., representing the location of the play.)

46.3 *Possible questions:*
2. Was the play (or movie) a success?
3. Would you like a ticket for the concert tonight?
4. What's the architecture like in your hometown?
5. Was it a good production/performance?
6. What's playing at the Arts Theater this week?
7. Do you like ballet?

46.4 *Possible answers:*
1. *Citizen Kane*
2. *Seven Samurai*
3. *The Rules of the Game*
4. *The Godfather*
5. *Dr. Strangelove*

Unit 47

47.1
1. A track is one individual song or piece of music that is part of an album. An album usually contains ten or more tracks.
2. These are all ways for musicians to share recordings of their work. An MP3 file is data stored electronically that can be transferred easily with little quality loss. A CD is a compact disk (made of shiny plastic with a metal surface).
3. A hit is a successful single (usually – although albums can be referred to as hits as well if they sell particularly well) and a single is one song issued/released individually.
4. Orchestral music is written for a full orchestra and so can only be played in a large hall, and chamber music is classical music written for a small group of people so that it can be played in a small room.
5. Country music is a particular style of U.S. music based on the folk music of the southern and western U.S.; folk music is traditional music from any part of the world.

47.2 The pictures are intended to suggest the following types of music but if they suggest different types of music to you then that is no problem – there cannot really be said to be right and wrong answers here.
1. classical music
2. country music
3. pop music
4. jazz (or blues) music

47.3 *positive:* soothing, relaxing, rousing, sweet, soft, innovative (note that some people will use this word with positive connotations while for others it has negative connotations)
negative: loud, deafening, discordant, tuneless

47.4
1. practice
2. hum
3. chords
4. read
5. arranged
6. ear
7. whistling

47.5 *Possible answers:*
1. Yes, it was "Nothing from Nothing" by Billy Preston.
2. Answers will vary.
3. I particularly enjoy folk music, guitar music, and rock music.
4. I love flamenco music.
5. I'm not that keen on contemporary classical music as I find it rather discordant.
6. I sometimes like to have background music on – something reasonably rousing, some Irish folk songs or some songs from musicals, for example.

Unit 48

48.1 *Possible answers:*
Found in salads: cucumbers, spinach, carrots, green/red peppers, lettuce, cabbage, radishes, celery
Onion-family vegetables: leeks, onions, shallots
Grow underground: carrots, potatoes, turnips, beets
Usually long-shaped: cucumbers, zucchini, corn, eggplant
There are, of course, other possible groups too, e.g., green or yellow vegetables, leafy vegetables, vegetables that are better raw/cooked, vegetables you like/hate.

48.2
1. hot, spicy
2. salty
3. sour
4. sugary
5. bitter, strong
6. bland, tasteless

48.3
1. These fries are greasy/oily.
2. This steak is overcooked/overdone.
3. This stew is too salty.
4. This is tasteless / very bland.
5. This roast beef is awfully fatty.

48.5
1. calf – veal; deer – venison; cow – beef; pig – pork, ham, bacon
2. Answers will vary.

Unit 49

49.1
1. volcano
2. mountain range
3. waterfall
4. cliff
5. geyser
6. glacier, mountains
7. peak or summit of a mountain
8. gorge

49.2 Brazil is **the** fifth largest country in **the** world. In **the** north, **the** densely forested basin of **the** Amazon River covers half **the** country. In **the** east, **the** country is washed by **the** Atlantic. **The** highest mountain range in South America, **the** Andes, does not lie in Brazil. Brazil's most famous city is Rio de Janeiro, **the** former capital. The capital of Brazil is now Brasilia.

49.3 *Possible answers:*
1. Scotland
2. country
3. the north of Britain
4. agriculture
5. the Clyde
6. the Western Highlands
7. Ben Nevis
8. Overfishing
9. water pollution

49.4
2. turbulent river/sea
3. steep gorge/hill/rise
4. dangerous cliff/ridge/gorge
5. shallow brook/bay/creek
6. tall mountain / mountain range / cliff
7. rocky coast/mountain
8. long coastline/river

49.5 Possible answers:
1. The chemicals released by spray cans can destroy the ozone layer.
2. Organic farming means fewer chemicals are put into farmland and, eventually, our bodies.
3. Recycling means that fewer natural resources need to be used to produce goods.
4. Answers will vary.

Unit 50

50.1
1. in New Mexico, a state in the Southwestern U.S.
2. There are many attractions, particularly those connected with the arts: museums, theaters, studios, and galleries, in addition to restaurants, nightclubs, churches, public buildings, and historic businesses. Most display the distinctive Santa Fe-style of architecture.
3. adobe
4. the Plaza
5. the Rio Grande and the Rocky Mountains
6. The climate is pleasant; there are four seasons.

50.3 *Possible answers:*
1. natural history museum
   science museum
   modern art museum
2. sports center
   shopping center
   city center (downtown)
3. higher education
   private education
   public education
4. basketball court
   squash court
   federal court
5. nightclub
   country club
   social club
6. employment agency
   travel agency
   real estate agency

Unit 51

51.1
1. a mammal
2. pollen
3. *possible answers:* groundhog, tortoise, and bear
4. the cheetah
5. the dove
6. breathing
7. Answers will vary depending upon year of answer.
8. Answers will vary.

51.2
graceful willow
noble eagle
prickly porcupine
rough bark
sweet-smelling rose petals
sturdy oak
wriggly worm

51.3
1. roots
2. claws; trunk/bark
3. hoof
4. bud
5. branches/twigs
6. Snails

51.4 The words underlined below are worth learning. You can use them when talking about other animals too.

Camel - A <u>mammal</u> of the family Camelidae (two <u>species</u>): the Bactrian, from cold deserts in Central Asia and <u>domesticated</u> elsewhere, and the dromedary, which has one hump, not two; <u>eats</u> any vegetation; <u>drinks</u> salt water if necessary; closes slit-like <u>nostrils</u> to exclude sand; humps are stores of energy-rich <u>fats</u>. The two species may <u>interbreed</u>: the offspring has one hump; the <u>males</u> are usually <u>sterile</u>, while the <u>females</u> are <u>fertile</u>.

51.5 The description of an elephant from the same encyclopedia is given below as an example. While it is unlikely that you would need or want to write anything quite so technical, look at it carefully and pick out any vocabulary that could be useful for you to learn.

Elephant - A large mammal of the family Elephantidae; almost naked gray skin; massive forehead; small eyes; upper incisor teeth form tusks; snout elongated as a muscular, grasping trunk; ears large and movable (used to radiate heat).
There are two living species. The <u>African elephant</u> is the largest living land animal, with three subspecies. The <u>Asian elephant</u> has four subspecies. The African is larger with larger ears, a triangular tip on the top and bottom of the trunk tip (not just on the top), and obvious tusks in the female.

If you chose to write about another animal or plant, compare your description if possible with one in an English-language encyclopedia.

Unit 52

52.1
1. heel, soles
2. laces (*or* shoelaces)
3. slippers
4. belt
5. hem, buttons

52.2
1. fits
2. tried on
3. take off, put on
4. matches
5. take off

52.3 *Possible answers:*
2. silk, cotton
3. denim
4. cotton, wool
5. suede, wool, leather, cotton
6. cotton, silk, wool, corduroy
7. silk, cotton
8. leather, wool, cotton, suede, corduroy

52.4 *Possible answers:*
The man is wearing brown corduroy pants, a leather jacket that is open, a plaid vest, and a plain blue shirt. He is wearing a baseball cap and sneakers with laces. The woman is wearing a plain skirt, a leather belt with a buckle, a polka-dotted sweater, a paisley print scarf around her neck, and leather high-heeled shoes. She is carrying a leather bag and leather gloves.

Unit 53

53.1 *Possible answers:*
1. indigestion, a stomachache
2. bronchitis, lung cancer or other allergic reactions
3. bruises, broken bones, (eventually) arthritis
4. a broken leg
5. sunburn
6. rash, hives, food poisoning
7. being out of breath
8. an itch, a lump
9. indigestion, nausea, diarrhea, food poisoning
10. hypochondria

53.2
1. hepatitis – fever, weakened condition, yellow color of skin
2. pneumonia – dry cough, high fever, chest pain, rapid breathing
3. rheumatism – swollen, painful joints or muscles, extreme stiffness
4. an ulcer – burning pain in abdomen, pain or nausea after eating
5. the flu – headache, aching muscles, fever, cough, sneezing

53.3
2. for giving injections (*or* shots)
3. for holding down the tongue while examining the throat
4. for taking someone's temperature
5. to check the patient's weight

53.4
1. Rub this cream on and stay out of the sun.
2. You'll have to have your leg put in a cast.
3. You'll need some shots before your trip.
4. You'll have to take an antibiotic, drink plenty of liquids, and get as much rest as possible.
5. We'll contact the surgeon to schedule you for an operation.
6. Take one pill/capsule/tablet three times a day after meals.

53.5
2. a cardiologist
3. a psychiatrist
4. an allergist
5. an obstetrician *or* gynecologist
6. an osteopath *or* chiropractor
7. a podiatrist
8. an ophthalmologist

Unit 54

54.1

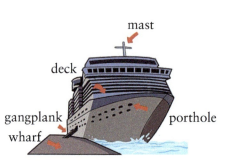

54.2 fender, rearview mirror = automotive, parts of vehicle
balloon, glider = types of air transportation
deck chair = water, associated facilities
sail, oar, rudder = water, parts of vehicle (boat or ship) (**rudder** can also be part of a plane)
gas pump, freeway, toll booth = automotive, associated facilities
bus driver = automotive, people working with it
baggage claim, metal detector, check-in counter = air, associated facilities
canoe = water, kinds of vehicle

54.3
1. flight/plane/trip
2. trunk
3. hood
4. garage
5. mechanic
6. out
7. airport security
8. departure lounge
9. delayed (*or* canceled)
10. train
11. dining

Unit 55

55.1 *Possible answers:*

Vacation place	Advantage	Disadvantage
resort	lots of activities	expensive
motel	convenient	not many facilities
bed & breakfast	less impersonal than hotels	less freedom
campground	cheap	uncomfortable, bugs
summer camp	kids: lots to do parents: kids out of the house!	kids: homesick parents: expensive
youth hostel	cheap	no privacy
time-share	can be very comfortable	same place every year

55.3 *Possible answers:*
1. Can I book a double room with a double / queen-size / king-size bed (*or* with two beds / twin beds), please?
2. Can I book a single room with a double / queen-size / king-size bed, please?
3. Do you have a nonsmoking room? *or* Can I book a nonsmoking room, please?
4. Could I have a wake-up call at 6 a.m., please?
5. What time is checkout?
6. Can I have room service, please?

55.4 *Possible answers:*
2. breathtaking : Traveling up the coast of Alaska was breathtaking .
3. exhilarating: Paragliding over the beach was the most exhilarating time I've ever had!
4. exotic: For a boy from Georgia, the ancient temples of Cambodia seemed so exotic.
5. intoxicating: Swimming with dolphins was absolutely intoxicating – what an incredible experience!
6. glamorous: This hotel and casino are so glamorous – I hope I see some movie stars!
7. unspoiled: Those long stretches of unspoiled coastline in southern Baja California are a delight.
8. sublime: Visiting the Buddhist temples of South Korea was a sublime experience for me.

55.5 The Smiths stayed at a <u>campground</u> last summer. Every day Mrs. Smith <u>sunbathed</u>, and Mr. Smith <u>went sightseeing</u>. The children <u>cycled</u>, and they <u>traveled</u> around the island. One day the family <u>went on / took</u> an excursion to a local castle. The castle had a gift shop, so they could <u>go shopping</u>.

Unit 56

56.1
1. One, three, five, seven
2. Two, four, six, eight
3. Four squared is (*or* equals) sixteen.
4. Seven to the third power (or seven cubed) is (*or* equals) three hundred and forty-three.
5. E equals mc squared; it is Einstein's relativity formula in which E = energy, m = mass, and c = the speed of light.
6. two pi r; this is the formula for the circumference of a circle in which r = the radius of the circle. π (pi) is the mathematical symbol for 3.14159 . . .

56.2
1. Seventy-nine percent of American women diet each year, yet ninety-five percent of those diets fail.
2. Zero degrees centigrade/Celsius equals thirty-two degrees Fahrenheit.
3. About fifteen percent of children under age ten are left-handed.
4. Two-thirds plus one-quarter (*or* one-fourth) times four squared equals fourteen and two-thirds.
5. Two million, seven hundred (and) sixty-nine thousand, four hundred (and) twenty-five people live in my city.
6. The inflation rate was three point five percent last year and point four percent (*or* zero point four percent) last month.

56.3
triangle: *triangular*   sphere: *spherical*   square: *square*
rectangle: *rectangular*   circle: *circular*   oval: *oval*
cube: *cubic*   octagon: *octagonal*   spiral: *spiral*

56.4
1. forty-six point six percent
2. nine hundred (and) seventy-nine meters
3. one thousand eight hundred (and) ninety-two cups or eighteen hundred (and) ninety-two cups
4. thirty-three years; nineteen sixty-one
5. (zero) point four square kilometers

56.5
  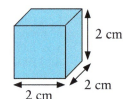

Unit 57

57.1
computer programmer
genetic engineer
molecular biologist
physicist
zoologist

57.2

1. cell phone – a phone that is small and mobile
2. MP3 player – a small machine that plays high quality sound from a digital file
3. scanner – a machine that makes electronic copies of documents and photographs
4. HD (high definition) TV – a television that has sharp images and high quality sound
5. laptop – a computer that is portable
6. memory stick – a small device that holds a large amount of information to transfer between computers
7. webcam – a small camera that records moving pictures and sound onto the Internet
8. touch screen monitor – a screen that responds when you touch it

57.3
2. combination
3. conclusion
4. discovery
5. dissection
6. experiment/experimentation
7. invention
8. patent

Unit 58

58.1
1. webcam
2. spreadsheet
3. desktop computer
4. flash drive
5. laptop

58.2
1. search engine; googled
2. virus
3. webcam
4. laptops / laptop computers
5. Wi-Fi
6. downloading
7. e-mail
8. back up

58.3
2. scanned
3. clicked
4. crashed
5. attachment
6. down

58.4
1. check your e-mail
2. log in to a social networking site
3. click on a hyperlink
4. surf the Internet
5. back up your hard drive

Unit 59

59.1
1. detective show / movie
2. documentary / nature show
3. sports
4. game show
5. news and weather
6. talk show

59.3
1. A news anchor reads the news on television.
2. A narrator tells a story while actors perform the story.
3. A game show host hosts a show with contestants.
4. A camera operator runs the camera for a film or TV show.
5. A foreign correspondent sends news or commentary from abroad.
6. A copy editor edits writing (or copy) for the media or the press.
7. A columnist writes a regular feature for a newspaper or magazine.
8. A critic writes or broadcasts reviews of books, movies, music, etc.

59.4
1. remote control
2. digital video recorder (DVR)
3. cut/edited
4. tabloid newspapers / tabloids
5. AM
6. magazine
7. section
8. satellite

Unit 60

60.1
1. independence
2. appointed/nominated
3. running
4. elected
5. federation

60.2
1. branches
2. judiciary
3. Republicans
4. houses
5. election
6. campaign
7. majority
8. judges

60.3

Abstract noun	Person noun	Verb	Adjective
dictatorship	dictator	dictate	dictatorial
election	elector	elect	elective
politics	politician	politicize	political
presidency	president	preside	presidential
representation	representative	represent	representative

60.4 *Possible answers:*
1. U.K., Sweden, Belgium
2. *presidential system:* Mexico, France; *parliamentary system:* Canada, Australia
3. Iceland
4–6. Answers will vary.

Unit 61

61.1
1. robbed; stole
2. was stolen; robbed

61.2
1. commit a crime
2. accuse someone of a crime
3. charge someone with a crime
4. serve a sentence of 15 months
5. try a case
6. find someone guilty
7. time off for good behavior
8. the case went to court
9. the jury found him guilty
10. deliver a verdict

61.3
1. convicted / found guilty
2. (had) defended
3. felony
4. sentenced
5. serve
6. acquitted

61.4 *Possible answers:*
People connected with the law: prosecutor, detective, member of a jury, parole officer, witness
Crimes: smuggling, burglary, shoplifting, arson, homicide, kidnapping
Punishments: prison, fine, death penalty, lethal injection, probation

Unit 62

62.1
1. interest: money chargeable on a loan or paid to savers
2. mortgage: a loan to purchase a home or property
3. an overdrawn account: a bank account with a negative balance
4. savings account: an account that is used mainly for keeping money
5. checking account: an account that checks are drawn on for day-to-day use
6. tuition: money paid for education
7. sales tax: tax paid at the time of a purchase
8. insufficient funds: the reason a check bounces
9. student loan: money you borrow to pay tuition and fees at a university
10. online banking: using the Internet to access your accounts

62.2
1. inheritance tax
2. loans/lends
3. fare
4. balance, finance charge
5. overdrawn, bounce
6. online banking, transfer

62.3 **Mortgage rates higher:** Most people who have a mortgage without fixed rates and anyone who wants to get a mortgage would not be happy.
Inheritance tax eliminated: People whose families have a lot of money would love this, but most people without a lot of family money would either not care or dislike it because it would mean other taxes might go up.
No wage increase this year: Most people who earn salaries would not be happy.
Sales tax lowered: Most consumers would be happy to see this.
U.S. dollar falls: It depends. People living in the U.S. who don't buy a lot of imported goods wouldn't care one way or the other. Visitors to the U.S. would be happy because it means they spend less of their own currency and get more value for the money they exchange into dollars. Some people in countries whose currency is tied to the dollar would be unhappy because it would devalue their currency. Consumers who buy U.S. products in other countries would be happy if lower prices resulted.
Interest rates down: People who want to borrow money or take out a loan, or those who regularly pay finance charges on credit cards, would be happy. However, those who live on fixed incomes from bank interest would not be happy.

Unit 63

63.1
1. I've always <u>doubted</u> that she really loves him.
2. Claudia <u>maintains</u> that the teacher has been unfair to her.
3. I was <u>convinced</u> (that) I had been in that room before.
4. He <u>feels/felt</u> (that) we should have tried again.
5. I <u>suppose</u> (that) the government will raise taxes again soon.

63.2

1.	What do you think	of	the new teacher?
2.	I've always been opposed	to	wasteful government spending.
3.	Are you in favor	of	higher taxes?
4.	I have strong views	on/about	educational policy
5.	Do you believe	in	life after death?
6.	Let's look at it	from	your parents' point of view.

63.3 *Possible answers:*
2. idealistic/unrealistic/fanatical
3. middle-of-the-road / moderate
4. fanatical/obsessive
5. conservative/traditional
6. radical/revolutionary

63.4 *Possible sentences:*
1. I believe in God / the existence of God.
2. I'm conservative about finances but liberal when it comes to social policy.
3. I doubt that the weather will improve anytime soon.
4. If you ask me, the best way to learn English is to practice it every chance you get.
5. It has always seemed odd to me that you park on a driveway and drive on a parkway!
6. I'm in favor of long prison sentences but opposed to capital punishment.

Unit 64

64.1

Adjective	Abstract noun	Adjective	Abstract noun
furious	fury	frustrated	frustration
anxious	anxiety	cheerful	cheerfulness
grateful	gratitude	enthusiastic	enthusiasm
ecstatic	ecstasy	apprehensive	apprehension
inspired	inspiration	excited	excitement

64.2
1. confused
2. depressed
3. frustrated
4. disappointed
5. worried
6. fed up
7. upset
8. thrilled

64.3
2. exciting (excited)
3. inspired (inspiring)
4. depressing (depressed)
5. confused (confusing)
6. frustrating (frustrated)

64.4 *Possible answers:*
2. I felt apprehensive before my first trip abroad.
3. I was very happy when I got my first paycheck.
4. My father was in a terrible rage when he discovered a big dent in his parked car.
5. My friend was miserable for days when she broke up with her boyfriend.
6. I was seething when I realized that I could not get a refund for the computer software.

7. People are sick and tired of all the politicians' lies.
8. Most of my classmates are nervous right before an exam.
9. I am content with my life as a student.
10. My parents were delighted when they saw my grades this semester!

Unit 65

65.1

Verb	Noun	Adjective	Adverb
–	affection	affectionate	affectionately
appeal	appeal	appealing	appealingly
attract	attraction	attractive	attractively
disgust	disgust	disgusting/disgusted	disgustingly
hate	hatred	hateful/hated	hatefully
–	passion	passionate	passionately
repel	repulsion/repellent	repulsive	repulsively
tempt	temptation	tempting	temptingly

65.2
2. I can't stand jazz.
3. His art appeals to me.
4. Beer revolts me. / I find beer revolting.
5. She yearns for her true love.
6. I'm not looking forward to the exam.
7. I fell for him from the start.

65.3
1. b 4. a
2. a 5. b
3. b

65.4
1. women 4. steal
2. birds 5. the future (or everything!)
3. spiders

Unit 66

66.1 *Possible answers:*
2. complained/whined 5. urged
3. begged 6. grumbled/complained
4. complained/grumbled

66.2
2. The boy whined that he never got to be first in line. *or* The boy whined about never getting to be first in line.
3. He begged me to help him. (*or* He begged for help.)
4. She complained/grumbled that the hotel was filthy. (*or* She complained/grumbled about the hotel being filthy.)
5. He urged Jim to try harder.
6. He grumbled/complained that the plan would never work.

66.3
2. objection 6. insistent
3. beggar 7. argumentative
4. confession 8. whiny
5. threatening

66.4
1. whisper, mutter, mumble, murmur
2. yell, shriek, scream, shout
3. groan, grumble, whine

66.5

Adverb	Adjective	Noun
bitterly	bitter	bitterness
cheerfully	cheerful	cheerfulness
enthusiastically	enthusiastic	enthusiastically
furiously	furious	fury
gratefully	grateful	gratitude
miserably	miserable	misery
reluctantly	reluctant	reluctance
sarcastically	sarcastic	sarcasm

66.6 *Possible answers*:
1. "We can easily break into the bank," she said <u>boldly</u>.
2. "I love that new movie!" she said <u>enthusiastically</u>.
3. "Look at this new high-definition TV!" he said <u>excitedly</u>
4. "Thank you so much," he said <u>gratefully</u>.
5. "I wish you'd hurry up," he said <u>impatiently</u>.
6. "I love you so much," she said <u>passionately</u>.
7. "I'll go if you really want me to," he said <u>reluctantly</u>.
8. "You look really busy," he said sarcastically.
9. "I don't know anyone here," she said <u>shyly</u>.
10. "Of course, I believe you," he said <u>sincerely</u>.

Unit 67

67.1 *Possible answers:*
2. That smells wonderful.
3. This tastes delicious.
4. That sounds terrific. *or* That is deafening!
5. He/She smells disgusting.

67.2
1. witness
2. glimpse/glance
3. stare/gaze
4. observe/notice

67.3
1. noticed
2. tapped
3. grasped
4. press
5. stroked
6. gazed

Note: In (6) we would probably say **gaze**, rather than **stare**, at a view. You might gaze at something you admire or find interesting without knowing it.

67.4
1. salty
2. sweet
3. hot/spicy
4. sour
5. spicy/hot
6. bitter

67.5 *Possible answers:*
1. aromatic
2. smelly/stinking
3. scented/perfumed
4. fragrant
5. vile/stinking
6. musty

67.6 1. telepathy   3. déjà vu
2. intuition   4. premonition

Unit 68
68.1 2. to blush   5. to wink
3. to shiver   6. to sigh
4. to blink

68.2 2. Someone is snoring.   5. Someone's stomach is rumbling.
3. Someone is yawning.   6. Someone has burped.
4. Someone is hiccupping.   7. Someone is sweating *or* perspiring.

68.3 1. sneeze   4. grin
2. frown   5. wink
3. yawn   6. snore

68.4 1. sneeze/cough   3. lick
2. grimace   4. chew

Unit 69
69.1 *Possible answers:*
2. That's a gigantic amount of money to waste!
3. That's a considerable number of people.
4. So it'll be about average again this year.

69.2 *Possible answers:*
small: minuscule, minute, insignificant, minimal, tiny
large: overwhelming, excessive, sizable, substantial, tremendous

69.3 1. tiny / minimal / minute / minuscule (Note the pronunciation of the adjective **minute**. The stress is on the second syllable, and the vowels are pronounced differently from those in the noun **minute**.)
2. overwhelming/tremendous
3. excessive/tremendous
4. sizable/substantial
5. excessive

69.4 *Possible answers:*
1. a lot of
2. plenty of / lots of
3. much
4. a good deal of / a great deal of / a lot of
5. Many / A lot of / A number of

69.5 *Possible answers:*
2. I might feel/be utterly exhausted / extremely tired.
3. I might feel/be rather/quite/pretty confused
4. I might feel/be utterly amazed / completely astounded / awfully surprised
5. I might feel/be a little bit / rather sad

Unit 70
70.1 1. period   4. time/while
2. age/era   5. spell
3. era

70.2 1. No, it wasn't. In fact, it's always late.
2. Just in time to catch the last train!
3. It's about time!
4. No, by the time I left work, it was too late.
5. At times.

70.3 *Possible answers:*
2. You're just in time for tea/coffee!
3. By the time you get this card, I'll probably already be there.
4. I'd rather talk to you one at a time, if you don't mind.
5. Could you use the old printer for the time being? The new one's being repaired.
6. It can get extremely cold at times in . . .
7. I'll do my best to get to the meeting on time.
8. It's about time (she got a job)!

70.4 *Possible answers:*
1. . . . **takes** about two hours.
2. . . . **run/last** for about an hour on high resolution.
3. . . . **lasted** three winters.
4. . . . **dragged on** for ages.
5. . . . have **elapsed/passed** since then, but people still remember that day.
6. . . . **pass** quickly.
7. . . . **take** your time.
8. . . . **lasted/ran/dragged on** for more than three hours.

Unit 71

71.1
1. . . . shortened?
2. . . . very tall.
3. . . . a shortcut.
4. . . . widened it / . . . 've widened it.
5. . . . deep.

71.2
1. the width of the room
2. to lengthen
3. a broad/wide range of goods
4. a long-distance call
5. shallow water
6. faraway/distant places

71.3
1. it's much bigger now.
2. it's a lengthy procedure.
3. to give us more room.
4. there's a wide range available.
5. you should broaden it.
6. for miles along the river.

71.4
1. at, of
2. in
3. from (*or possibly* at)
4. from, to

71.5
1. is spreading
2. stretches/extends
3. extend
4. shrinking

Unit 72

72.1
2. . . . must / need to / have to / 'll have to / 're required to put down a deposit.
3. . . . is compulsory/obligatory/mandatory for young people.
4. . . . must / have to / 've got to take it to the cleaners.
5. . . . forced him to hand it over.
6. . . . compulsory/required/mandatory in high school.

72.2 *Possible answers:*
2. Most people usually suffer from a lack of time or of money.
3. Attending classes every day and completing homework is compulsory for students in many countries.
4. Most people feel they are in need of more time and money, and millions of people in the world are in need of food and shelter.
5. Death is certainly inevitable for all of us.
6. If you are an adult, you probably no longer have to be home at a specific time every night.
7. Police officers and firefighters are exempt from traffic laws when they are dealing with emergencies.
8. Maybe as a child you were forced to eat some foods you didn't like.

72.3 *Possible answers:*
2. absolutely **impossible**
3. highly/quite **probable**
4. highly/extremely **unlikely**
5. absolutely **inevitable**
6. absolutely/quite **certain**

Note: Some English speakers may have different opinions about the above collocations. These answers are provided as guidelines only.

72.4 *Possible answers:*
1. It is quite possible that petroleum will become obsolete within the next 50 years.
2. Rain in the Amazon forest within eight days is highly probable.
3. A human being living to 150 some day is highly unlikely.
4. My becoming a professional musician is . . . ?

Unit 73

73.1
1. **Racket** would be an ideal word here.
2. **Sound** or **sounds** since it is obviously pleasant. The uncountable meaning (**sound**) describes continuous sound; the countable meaning (**sounds**) means *different* sounds.
3. **Noises/sounds** if you mean different sounds, but **noise/sound** is also possible here if you interpret "some" to mean not a plural number, but *one* sound of "a certain, unidentifiable type," e.g., *Some animal must have gotten into the garden last night; look at these footprints.* (It's not clear what kind of animal.)
4. **Din** would fit best here; **racket** and **noise** are also possible.
5. **Noise/sound** (uncountable without **a**); **noise** is probably a better choice because the sentence implies something unpleasant.

73.2 *Possible answers:*
1. hiss
2. crash *or* clang
3. rustle
4. thud
5. bang
6. rumble
7. roar
8. creak

73.3
1. I saw a beam of light coming through the window. It was a police officer holding a flashlight.
2. The jewels sparkled in the sunlight. I'd never seen such a beautiful bracelet.
3. The candle began to flicker in the breeze. Then it died, leaving us in complete darkness.
4. The first rays of the sun shone into the room. It was clearly time to wake up and start the day.
5. The glare of the truck's headlights momentarily blinded me. I pulled over to the side of the road.

73.4
1. a
2. c
3. b
4. a

Unit 74

74.1
1. donated/left
2. left
3. lent
4. presented

74.2
1. handed down
2. hand out
3. let go of
4. gave away
5. hand over

74.3 *Possible answers:*
1. your wallet/bag/money
2. furniture/jewelry
3. handouts/tests
4. an antique / a set of books

74.4 *Possible questions:*
1. Do you rent this house?
2. Could I borrow your camera? / Would you lend me your camera?
3. Does the school provide/supply textbooks?
4. Would you like to contribute/donate something to cancer research?
5. What does it cost to rent a car?

74.5
1. properties
2. loans
3. landlords
4. tenants
5. owner/proprietor
6. estate
7. borrowed
8. properties/property
9. possessions
10. belongings/possessions

Note: In (8), the answer could be **properties**, meaning many different buildings or parcels of land, or **property**, meaning all the holdings taken together.

Unit 75

75.1 *Possible answers:*
2. a river
3. a car, motorcycle, or other vehicle
4. a train
5. a tree; a flagpole, telephone pole, or other kind of pole
6. a bird

75.2 *Possible answers:*
2. a stream; blood flows through the body (i.e., through the veins); ideas and words can flow
3. an insect, a baby
4. a bird's or butterfly's wings, an article of clothing on a clothesline in the wind, a person's eyelashes, a curtain in the wind
5. Anything moving slowly on water may be drifting if it's not being guided, e.g., a boat or a piece of wood; snow on the ground may drift; a person can drift through life (moving without any sense of purpose or direction); your thoughts can drift to something or someone (it happens unintentionally).
6. A street can run east and west or north and south. It can also run through a city. A movie/meeting/lecture runs for a certain length of time. People can run through a script or speech in preparation for a performance, speech, or even a meeting.

75.3 *Possible answers:*
2. if you wanted to be late for something, e.g., something unpleasant
3. if you weren't in a hurry or you weren't very interested or enthusiastic about something you were doing, e.g., if you plod along at your studies without making much progress
4. if a bee flew onto your nose
5. if you are very angry with someone
6. if you injured your leg or foot and had difficulty walking on it
7. if you came home very late or got up very early and didn't want to wake anyone
8. if you were nervous or anxious about something or awaiting some important news
9. if you had some free time and wanted to relax, for example, on a pleasant weekend you might stroll (around) in the park (*also* **go for a stroll**)
10. if you were late for an appointment

75.4
1. rate
2. pace
3. velocity
4. speed
5. pace
6. rate
7. speed

Unit 76

76.1 *Possible answers:*
2. polished/smooth
3. slippery
4. prickly
5. rough/coarse
6. fluffy/furry
7. jagged
8. coarse
9. downy/fluffy
10. smooth/shiny

76.2 *Possible answers:*
1. the metal surface of an appliance
2. a heavy-duty carpet, a doormat, a basement floor
3. a highly varnished tabletop, a mirror, the surface of a table
4. a cat or dog, a fur coat
5. stockings, someone's fine hair, silk clothing

76.3 *Possible answers:*
1. This is about average for a baby.
2. Yes, a half liter a day would be about 3.5 liters a week, just under a gallon.
3. The person writing this weighs about 172 lbs., or 72.5 kg.
4. 16 ounces is a pound, or about 454 grams. It's *more* than enough for two (normal) sandwiches.

76.4 *Possible answers:*
1. a big cat, such as a panther or leopard
2. a fish, an eel
3. a bear, a panda
4. a porcupine

76.5 shiny/vivid
shady/dull
coarse/rough
dense/sparse
dazzle/glare

Unit 77

77.1
1. attain / reach / achieve / meet / fulfill / realize
2. fulfill/realize/achieve
3. realize/achieve
4. manage
5. succeed, went
6. misfired / came to nothing / failed
7. surpassed/exceeded
8. cope

77.2

Verb	Noun	Adjective	Adverb
-------	ambition	ambitious	ambitiously
-------	difficulty	difficult	-------
expect	expectation	expected, expecting	expectedly
fail	failure	failed, failing	-------
realize	realization	realizable	-------
target	target	targeted	-------
trouble	trouble	troubling, troublesome, troubled	-------

Comments:
difficult: has no adverb in English; we say "We did it **with difficulty**."
targeted: "Our sales campaign is designed for a **targeted** [specifically chosen] group."
failed: "They have made three **failed** attempts to save the company."

failing: **failing** health
unfailingly: "failingly" doesn't exist, but **unfailingly** does, e.g., "She is **unfailingly** honest;
you can trust her completely."
troubling: "We have seen some very **troubling** [worrisome] developments recently."
troublesome: "They are a **troublesome** [cause trouble] group of students."
troubled: "I've been feeling rather **troubled** [worried with problems] lately about my daughter."
expecting: A woman who is pregnant is **expecting** (a baby). For this meaning, **expecting** is sometimes used without an object (informally).

77.3 1. I'm amazed that you can cope **with** all the work they give you.
2. She succeeded **in rising** to the highest rank in the company.
3. Do you ever have trouble **using** this photocopier? I always find it difficult.
4. I've **managed** to get all my work done this week, so I'm taking a long weekend! (**accomplish** usually has a direct object, e.g., *I've accomplished a lot this week.*)
5. I have **a** hard time driving to work with all the traffic.
6. We've **accomplished/achieved** a great deal during this past year.

77.4 *Possible answers:*
2. It would probably soon **fold** or **go under**.
3. I'd have it checked.
4. Perhaps I'd talk to the teacher or get a tutor.
5. Perhaps I'd try again, or abandon it and cut any losses.
6. I'd congratulate myself and then set new (and higher) goals!

Unit 78

78.1 2. bucket   5. block
3. plate   6. shot
4. handle

78.2 *Possible answers:*
Be + prepositional phrase:
be in a bind [be in a difficult situation or predicament], **be up to it** [be capable of something], **be out of sorts** [be unwell]

With 's:
child's play [very easy] and **a fool's errand** [a wasted/pointless effort to get something] (See Unit 81 for more of these.)

With hold:
hold your tongue [be silent], **hold your horses** [wait before acting/speaking]. **Hold your tongue** could also go with **keep mum** [be silent] because they are very close in meaning. The difference is that **hold your tongue** is often used in aggressive commands, e.g., *Hold your tongue, you!* [Shut up!]

Binomials (phrases joined by and, but, or):
rough and ready [basic / lacking in comfort], **odds and ends** [small items difficult to group along with others], **give or take** [as in *It'll cost $700, give or take $50*, meaning between $650 and $750 approximately]. **Sink or swim** [you have to succeed or fail, but there is no middle area] (see Unit 81)

78.3 2. springs   5. 're sitting
3. flies   6. leaves
4. just goes

78.4 1. go to bed
2. a stronger, more informal version of **child's play** [simple, too easy]
3. clearly this means more than just "unemployed," since he didn't have a home; it means totally without money or property, living and sleeping on the streets

4. not talking, or behaving in an unfriendly way
5. infrequently / not often

Unit 79

79.1
1. to think of it
2. ask me
3. Speaking
4. reminds me
5. I was saying

79.2
1. this and that *or* this, that, and the other
2. that's it
3. this is it!
4. that's that

79.3
1. come to think of it . . .
   if worst comes to worst . . .
   when it comes to . . .
2. as luck would have it . . .
3. if all else fails . . .
4. if worst comes to worst . . .
5. as far as I'm concerned . . .
6. what with one thing after another . . .

79.4

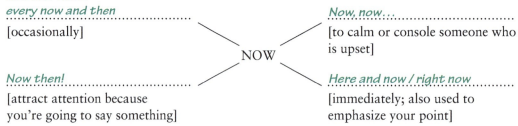

1. Do you want me to do it here and now / right now, or can it wait?
2. Now then, everybody, listen carefully. I have news for you.
3. I bump into her in town (every) now and then, but not that often.
4. Now, now, everything will be better soon.

Unit 80

80.1
1. bone
2. ox
3. mouse
4. dog
5. bat

80.2
2. as busy as a bee
3. as flat as a pancake
4. as fresh as a daisy
5. as red as a beet

80.3
1. a) slept
   b) falling
2. a) snow
   b) a sheet

80.4

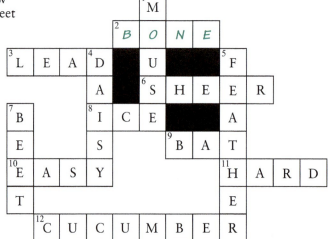

80.5
1. He/She has eyes like a hawk.
2. It worked like a charm.
3. She/He eats like a horse.
4. He/She has a brain like a sieve.
5. He/She stands there like a statue.

Unit 81

81.1
2. part and parcel
3. neat and clean
4. first and foremost
5. sick and tired
6. ranting and raving
7. pick and choose
8. down and out
9. peace and quiet
10. leaps and bounds
11. now and then
12. here and there

81.2 *Possible answers:*
1. The new mayor promised that law and order would be a priority.
2. The house looks neat and clean now for our visitors.
3. I'm sick and tired of traffic jams. I'm going to start using the train.
4. My command of English vocabulary has improved by leaps and bounds since I've been using this book.
5. There are lots of courses in this university, so you can pick and choose.
6. I've seen her now and then, taking her dog for a walk.

81.3
1. high and dry
2. safe and sound
3. ready and able
4. prim and proper
5. give and take

81.4
1. or
2. or
3. to
4. or
5. but
6. but

Unit 82

82.1
1. ... of gold.
2. ... as nails.
3. ... as gold.
4. ... study.
5. ... slowpoke.

82.2
1. a know-it-all
2. the teacher's pet
3. a straight arrow
4. at the head of the class
5. a slacker or lazy-bones (*note*: singular in form)

82.3
1. ... a heart of stone.
2. ... have a heart!
3. ... his heart in the right place.
4. ... a change of heart.
5. ... have my heart set on it.

Another example of a key-word family might be **eye**:
He only has **eyes for** Mary. [He never looks at other women.]
She has **an eye for** antiques. [She is good at spotting them.]
He has **eyes in the back of his head**. / He has **eyes like a hawk**. [said of someone who never misses anything, especially when other people are doing something wrong]
Look up **eye** in a dictionary and see how many more idioms there are using the word.

82.4 get on your nerves (always with possessive: my, our, John's, etc.)
be a pain in the neck (always used with **the**)
stab you in the back (always used with **the**)

82.5
1. an oddball
2. middle-of-the-road
3. over the top

Unit 83

83.1 *positive:*
to be in seventh heaven
to be/feel head over heels
negative:
to feel/be a bit down
to feel blue

83.2 *Possible answers:*
2. I would feel blue, or even be in a foul mood.
3. I would be on cloud nine / walking on air / in high spirits.
4. I would feel blue *and* be in a foul mood or down in the dumps.
5. I would feel a bit down / blue / not myself.
6. I would be on cloud nine / in seventh heaven / walking on air / head over heels.

83.3
1. . . . to death / out of my wits.
2. . . . the weather.
3. . . . cloud nine.
4. . . . out of my skin.
5. . . . eat a horse.

83.4 *Scorpio:*
itching to [have a great desire or longing to do something]
(to be) on the edge of your seat [to be impatient, excited, in suspense, waiting for something to happen]

Leo:
to be up in arms [to be very angry and protesting loudly]
to be a dime a dozen [not special, cheap]

1. This new MP3 player is really just **a dime a dozen**.
2. I've been **on the edge of my seat** all day. What happened? Tell me!
3. We enjoyed our vacation, but by the end of it, we were **itching to** go home.
4. Everyone was **up in arms** when they canceled the outing.

83.5
1. shaking in your boots
2. swell with pride
3. under the weather
4. be carried away

Possible answers:
1. That mugging had me **shaking in my boots**.
2. Seeing him in the graduation procession made his parents **swell with pride**.
3. Why don't you go home? You really look **under the weather**.
4. I know I shouldn't have listened to her lies, but I got **carried away** by her charming personality.

Unit 84

84.1
1. take a back seat
2. stir things up
3. the light at the end of the tunnel
4. the bottom of things
5. spot
6. up and take notice
7. grasp of
8. my cards on the table

84.2 You might find some of the following idioms and expressions, along with others, depending on your dictionary:

2. come to a **dead** end
a **dead** duck [an idea, plan, or person that's doomed to fail; beyond hope]
a **dead** ringer [someone who looks just like someone else]
I wouldn't be caught **dead** . . . [something you would never do, wear, etc.]
dead to the world [sleeping very deeply]
3. play your **cards** close to the chest
in the **cards** [destined / very likely to happen]
play your **cards** right [deal with situations skillfully]

              play your trump **card** [use your best advantage]
              hold all the **cards** [have all the power, control]
    4. **straighten** things out
        straighten someone out [explain something so someone changes]
        The **straight** and narrow path [a conservative lifestyle]
    5. **stir** things up
        cause a **stir** [cause great excitement or anger among everyone]
        stir-crazy [extremely restless because of feelings of being trapped]
        stir-fry [vegetables, meat, etc., fried quickly on high heat in a lightly oiled pan]

84.3   2. a compromise
        3. in great suspense
        4. are found together in the same place and connected to one another
        5. safe / out of danger

84.4   *Possible questions:*
        1. Are you still arguing all the time with Walter?
        2. Has your new job been a success?
        3. Should I call him? Or maybe send a thank-you note?

Unit 85

85.1   *Possible answers:*
        1. The hotel we were staying in was **out of this world**.
        2. Joe is **head and shoulders above** the other kids when it comes to arithmetic.
        3. This restaurant **puts** all the other restaurants in town **to shame**. *or* This restaurant is **head and shoulders** above all the other restaurants in town.
        4. You're **miles / light years ahead** of me in understanding all this technology; I'm impressed.
        5. The **cream of the crop** from our university went on to business school. *or* The topnotch graduates . . .

85.2   1. scaredy cat   3. to be on the ball
        2. to have a green thumb 4. to butter someone up

85.3   1. (3) to be on the ball / first rate / top notch
        2. (4) to butter someone up
        3. (1) scaredy cat
        4. (2) to have a green thumb

85.4   *Possible answers:*
        2. Al is **a snake in the grass**.
        3. Steve has **a way with** babies; just look at how they react when they see him.
        4. He often **runs down / knocks** his school.
        5. She **picks apart** everything I say.
        6. She wants a promotion, a company car, and a raise, yet she can't even get to work on time. **She takes the cake! / She wants to have her cake and eat it too!**
        7. Your dinner parties **put** mine **to shame**.
        8. She is always **crowing** about her high grades.

85.5   1. There is a verb **to ham it up**, which can be used to criticize an actor's performance if it is overdone and grossly exaggerated; we can call such an actor or actress **a ham**.
        2. If you don't like something or somebody, you can say *It / He / She just* **isn't my cup of tea**, which means you do not feel attracted to it or to the person.
        3. If you say something is **icing on the cake**, you are praising it as something extra good on top of something that is already good. *Flying first class was wonderful, and being met at the other end by a limousine was icing on the cake.*
        4. If you call a person a **nutcase, as nutty as a fruitcake**, or **nuts**, you mean they are mad/crazy or perhaps eccentric. Also, **a tough nut to crack** is a difficult problem or a person who is difficult to understand or convince.

5. If you say someone **brings home the bacon,** it means he/she earns a living and supports his/her family, which is usually seen as praise.

Unit 86

86.1 *Possible answers:*
2. . . . a word in edgewise.
3. . . . heads or tails of what Meg is saying.
4. . . . behind George's back / are talking about George behind his back.

86.2
1. wrap up
2. in a nutshell
3. the ball rolling
4. the point

86.3
1. speaks
2. talk
3. talking
4. through

Unit 87

87.1
1. Yoko is **driving a hard bargain.**
2. Henry should **get it off his chest** by telling Mark how he feels.
3. Julie knows the name of the song but just can't remember. It's on **the tip of her tongue.**

87.2
1. Can I tell you about a problem I have? I just have to **get it off my chest.** It's been **on my mind** for a while now.
2. They charged us $200 for a tiny room without a TV. It was a **rip-off!** *or* They really **ripped us off!**
3. We'll have just enough time to get **a bite to eat** before the show.
4. **I've got to hand it to her,** Maria handled the situation admirably. *or* **I've got to hand it to Maria;** she handled . . .
5. I think I'll just go upstairs and **take a nap,** if nobody minds.
6. We had to **pay through the nose** for the apartment, but we had no choice. *or* We had to **pay top dollar** for the apartment . . .

87.4
1. foot the bill
2. put your feet up
3. couch potato

> ### follow-up
>
> **to be under someone's thumb:** *Since they got married, she's really kept him under her thumb.*
> **to hold one's tongue:** *I'm going to hold my tongue. The last time I said anything it only caused trouble, so this time, I'll say nothing.*
> **the cat's got your tongue:** *Now that you have my attention, it seems like the cat's got your tongue.*
> **to be head over heels in love (with someone):** *Mike's head over heels in love. He talks about Jeanne all day long and blushes every time her name's mentioned.*
> **to toe the line:** *The boss gave him a very hard time yesterday about his lazy attitude and all his absences. He warned him he might lose his job. He's going to have to toe the line from now on.*
> **to tiptoe / to walk on tiptoe:** *We'll have to tiptoe past the children's bedroom. I don't want to wake them up.*
> **eating out of the palm of your hand:** *She has her boyfriend eating out of the palm of her hand.*
> **to get someone's back up:** *Sally won't get any sympathy from her co-workers; in fact, quite the contrary, she seems to get everyone's back up with her selfish attitude.*
> **to back out (of):** *We agreed to become business partners, but she backed out (of it) at the last minute.*
> **to do something behind someone's back:** *He's always talking about his friends behind their backs. That's why they don't stay friends.*

Unit 88

88.1
1. Never look a gift horse in the mouth
2. Don't put all your eggs in one basket.
3. It's no use crying over spilled milk.

88.2
1. . . . shouldn't throw stones.
2. . . . the mice will play.
3. . . . there's fire.
4. . . . but you can't make it drink.

88.3
1. Never look a gift horse in the mouth. [Both proverbs advise you to take advantage of good fortune when you have it in front of you.]
2. Don't cross your bridges before you come to them. [Both proverbs warn you not to anticipate future events.]
3. Never judge a book by its cover. [Both proverbs warn against trusting the external or superficial features of something.]
4. Familiarity breeds contempt. [*Absence makes the heart grow fonder* says that if you cannot be with someone or something, you will love the person / the thing more. *Familiarity breeds contempt* says that being with someone / something too much makes you come to hate the person / the thing.]

Unit 89

89.1
2. constitutes (**make up** with this meaning is usually used in the passive)
3. fasten
4. inventing
5. succeeding *or* progressing
6. arranged
7. write

89.2
2. without
3. of
4. out
5. up

89.3
1. . . . make of that statement.
2. . . . make the most of . . .
3. Do them up or . . .
4. . . . make out that they . . .

89.4 *Possible answers:*
Work: do the housework / the laundry / some gardening / the dishes / the shopping / the cooking / homework / paperwork / business with; **make** a living / money / a bed / a profit / a cup of coffee or tea / a meal / photocopies / delivery.
Trying, succeeding, and failing: do your best / a good job / harm / without / nothing; **make** money / an attempt / an effort / a mistake / the most of / the best of / a success of / a good or bad impression / trouble / a point of / allowances for / choice.
Things you say: make a promise / arrangements / an agreement / a phone call / a suggestion / a decision / an excuse / fun of / believe / a fuss about / noise / a point of.
Physical things: do aerobics / chores / exercises / gardening / laps / sit-ups / sprints / weightlifting / yoga. **make** war / love / noise / effort / a gesture / a face.

89.5
1. your best
2. profit
3. mistake
4. a good impression
5. housework/chores
6. favor
7. damage

Unit 90

90.1
1. back
2. about
3. over
4. on
5. out
6. up

90.2

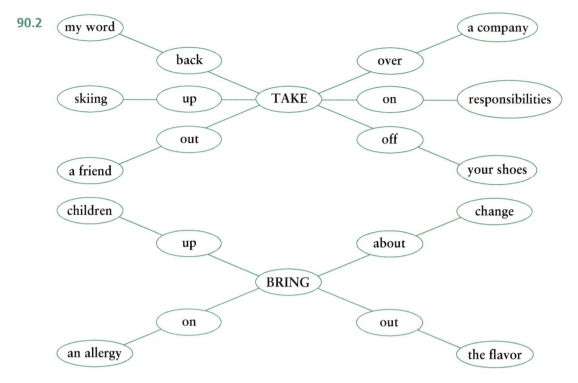

90.3 *Possible answers:*
2. She **takes after** her father.
3. I've **taken up** tennis recently.
4. It really seems to have **taken off** now.
5. I'll **bring him around** somehow.
6. Probably because it **took off** two hours late.
7. To **bring about** change.

90.4
1. The story of the movie *takes place* in Casablanca during the war.
2. Today's newspaper *brings to light* some fascinating information about the president.
3. How does he always manage to *take things in his stride*?
4. The view from the top of the hill took my breath away.
5. He *took advantage of* her weakness at the time and she sold the car to him.
6. The main function of a nurse is to *take care of* the sick.
7. Whenever you're upset, you always *take it out* on the children.

90.5
1. to take it in your stride
2. to take part in
3. to take care of
4. to bring to a head
5. to take pride in
6. to take my breath away

Unit 91

91.1 *Possible answers:*
I don't **receive** interesting offers through e-mail very often these days. However, an unusual one came this morning. It was titled "Are little things **depressing you**?" It went on, "If so, **purchase/buy** some of our special pills today. Taking just one in the morning will help you **succeed/manage** at work, at home, or at school. It will stop the feeling that you're **making no progress** in life and will ensure that you **become** rich and successful with little effort on your part. Go to our Web site and pay just $25 online today, and you will **receive** your tablets and your key to success within 10 days."

91.2 1. through   4. along
2. over   5. know
3. by

91.3 1. You are very late in completing a critical project. How did I get so far behind?
2. Someone is about to throw something away. Don't get rid of that yet!
3. Your roommate is still asleep and has an important meeting in 30 minutes. Get up! You're going to be late!
4. Someone has done something very cruel to you. Just you wait! I'll get back at you one of these days!
5. Some people have stolen your money. They'll never get away with this.

91.4 *Possible answers:*
1. . . . my favorite coffee mug.
2. . . . I spilled water on the manager's desk.
3. . . . work in nice weather like this.
4. . . . going to the meeting.
5. Living in such a noisy place . . .

91.5 *Possible sentences:*
She was the first to **get off** [disembark from] the plane.
I don't understand what you are **getting at**. [suggest, try to say]
They are due to **get back** [return] at 6:00.
You **get ahead** [succeed, be promoted] in that company only if you are related to the boss.
I'd like to **get in touch with** [communicate with] my old friends from school.
Get off my back [Stop nagging/criticizing me!], will you?
Get lost! [Go away, stop bothering me!; (very informal)]
Get a life! [often spoken in jest to tell someone to stop being boring or silly; (informal)]

Unit 92

92.1 1. They have recently <u>established</u> a committee on neighborhood crime.
2. We try to <u>reserve</u> some money for our summer vacation every week.
3. The new ad campaign <u>cost us</u> over two million dollars.
4. If we hadn't <u>departed</u> so late, we would have arrived on time.
5. The government's unpopular new taxes <u>caused</u> a wave of protests.
6. When we cross the International Date Line, should we <u>change</u> our clocks to an earlier time?

92.2 *Possible answers:*
2. an idea / a proposal
3. an appointment / customers
4. ideas/opinions
5. a guest / a sign
6. a fake smile / clothes
7. papers/tools
8. someone's behavior / a bad situation

92.3 *Possible answers:*
2. Yes, it <u>set me back</u> quite a bit.
3. I haven't had time to <u>put things away</u> yet.
4. Yes, of course, I can <u>put you up</u>.
5. You're <u>putting me on</u>!
6. He <u>set the tone</u> for the entire meeting.

92.4 *Possible answers:*
1. He is very <u>set in his ways</u>.
2. Why do you always <u>put him down</u>? Don't you realize how sensitive he is?
3. She has <u>set her sights/heart on</u> becoming president of the company.
4. Please <u>put your mind</u> to the problem at hand.
5. She threw lighter fluid on the trash and <u>set fire to it / set it on fire</u>.
6. This is the first time I've ever <u>set foot</u> in the southern hemisphere.

7. You really should put your foot down with the children or there'll be trouble later.
8. If Ms. Martin doesn't set a good example, the children certainly won't behave.
9. To put it another way, I won't do it at any price.

Unit 93

93.1
1. ... to a decision.
2. ... to mind ...
3. ... into bloom/blossom.
4. ... to a standstill.
5. ... to an end.
6. ... into operation/existence/use ...
7. ... to blows.
8. ... into view/sight.

93.2
2. checked
3. being published
4. choose
5. used
6. become conscious

93.3
1. It goes without saying,
2. went to great lengths/effort
3. on the go
4. go far
5. as far as it goes

93.4
1. Her firm went bankrupt.
2. It's a fight, I think.
3. Seven-thirty, normally.
4. Over $1,000!
5. Right after the news.
6. Everything is finally coming together.

93.5 *Possible answers:*
1. ... an interesting article on vocabulary
2. ... a bitter divorce.
3. ... smoking is bad for your health.
4. ... the death of a loved one.
5. ... a disagreement about money.

Unit 94

94.1
1. through
2. to/about
3. down
4. up
5. down
6. forward

94.2
1. Why can't she see through him?
2. I ran into Jack at the library yesterday.
3. I cooked dinner yesterday. It's your turn (to do it) today.
4. I thought I was seeing things when I saw a monkey in the garden.
5. I wish you'd let me be.
6. When she left him, it/she broke his heart.

94.3 *Possible answers:*
1. ... the roads will be closed.
2. ... of the rope and fell.
3. ... studying English every day!
4. ... she refused to speak to him.
5. ... she would be leaving her job soon.
6. ... coffee.

94.4 *Possible answers:*
1. I very much regret turning down an opportunity to work in Canada.
2. A train I was on once broke down, making me very late for an important interview.
3. When I was younger, I didn't see eye to eye with my parents very often. It was probably because different generations often see things differently.
4. Stubbornness and good looks both run in my family.
5. Every New Year I resolve to turn over a new leaf – I decide to reply to all my e-mail messages promptly and to be generally much more organized.

6. I have to see to the car, which has been making strange noises.
7. My own home has never been broken into, but a friend's house was once when I was staying with him.
8. I usually turn in by 11 p.m. on weekdays, later on weekends.

94.5 *Possible answers:*
look
Now that his hair is turning gray, he's beginning to **look his age**.
I can always tell when my sister is lying because she won't **look me in the eye**.
see
His parents have promised to **see** him **through** college.
It's hard to find your way around this building – I'll **see** you **out**.
run
I **ran over** a nail when I was driving and got a flat tire.
She **ran up** an enormous bill at the department store.
turn
Please **turn down** your radio – I can't concentrate.
I **turned in** my homework a day late.
let
Let sleeping dogs **lie**.
This skirt is too tight – I'll have to let it out.
break
I'm **broke** – can you lend me 10 dollars until payday?
Breaking in new shoes can be painful.

Unit 95

95.1 2. complaint at a school
3. research about diet and health
4. marriage of a famous person
5. investigation about government is stopped
6. study involving work and sleep

95.2 *Possible answers:*
2. Steps are being taken with the aim of providing more work for people.
3. Approval has been given to place restrictions on the use of water.
4. A man resigned from his job after undergoing some kind of unpleasant experience there.
5. A public opinion survey has investigated how people spend their money.
6. The electric company is trying to increase the rates people pay for electricity.

95.3 2. investigate   5. tries to stop
3. verbally attacks   6. increases/encourages
4. asks for

95.4 Make sure that you note down not only the headline but also a brief indication of what the story was about so that the headline makes sense when you review your work later.

Unit 96

96.1 2. at a zoo
3. on a road or highway
4. outside a fitting room in a store
5. on a wall
6. on a city street or other public place where there are trash cans / bins
7. on a cigarette package
8. in a bank or store
9. many public areas, such as airports, restaurants, malls, etc.
10. in a parking lot or garage
11. outdoors, possibly in a residential or business area, or in a park
12. on an airplane

96.2
1. to bring a legal case against
2. a container, can, or bin
3. someone who goes on private property without permission
4. money paid as a punishment
5. to ask for something (usually money) or try to do business
6. to forbid something
7. someone who disobeys the rules/law
8. to damage, misuse, or alter something improperly
9. a means of transportation, such as a car
10. no smoking allowed

96.3
1. You would see this sign at Customs (e.g., at an airport). It lets people know that this is the way to go if they do not have any goods to pay duty on.
2. You would see this at a sports stadium or playing field. It warns people who are watching the game that they must not throw anything onto the field or they will be forced to leave.
3. You would see this sign in a store. It lets customers know that they can only return goods they have bought there for a refund within the first 14 days. (common for electronics and software)
4. This would be an outdoor sign on a city street. It warns people that they would be breaking the law by throwing trash (papers, food, etc.) into the street.
5. You would see this sign on a road or highway. It lets drivers know that two lanes will become one very soon, and if they are driving in the right lane, they should try to move into the left lane.
6. You would see this sign in a store. It warns people that if they steal things from the store while pretending to shop, they will be arrested and taken to court.
7. You would see this on a road or highway, just before a construction area. It warns that the area is more dangerous and the speed limit will be lower and the fines for driving over the speed limit will be twice the usual amount.
8. This might be a neon (electric) sign outside a hotel or motel. It tells people that there are no rooms available right now.

96.4
1. Eating and drinking prohibited. No food or drinks in the store.
2. Post no bills.
3. No soliciting. / Soliciting prohibited.

96.5
1. This means that if you break an item (even accidentally), you must pay for it. You would probably see this sign in a store.
2. This is a street sign that means "absolutely no parking." It would be seen on a sidewalk near a curb, where people might want to park their cars. (This sign is often identified with New York City.)
3. This is based on the motto on US currency – "In God We Trust." It means that everyone has to pay at the time they buy something. You might see this sign in stores.

Unit 97
97.1 *Possible answers:*

> **Now Eagle Airlines offers even more to the business traveler who needs comfort!**
>
> Let us fly you to your destination in first-class comfort, served by the best-trained flight attendants in the world. Successful businesspeople know that they must arrive fresh and ready for work no matter how long the journey. With Eagle Diplomat-Class you can do just that.
>
> And, what's more, your spouse can travel with you on all international flights for half the regular fare! Your secretary can book you on any of our flights 24 hours a day. All you or he/she have/has to do is book online at eagleair.com or pick up the phone and call 800-555-1234.

97.2
mankind – human beings
unmanned – unstaffed
forefathers – ancestors
foreman – supervisor
cleaning lady – housekeeper

97.3 *Possible answers:*
1. We'll have to elect a new chair/chairperson next month.
2. Several firefighters and police officers were hurt in the riots.
3. The airline reports that its flight attendants are on strike.
4. I wonder what time the postal worker comes every day.
5. Is this fabric natural or synthetic?
6. Her brother's a nurse, and she's a doctor.
7. TV news reporters and camera operators rushed to the scene of the accident.
8. If you don't like the new tax system, write to your member of congress.
9. A sales representative/person for the company will stop by and leave samples.
10. This radio program likes to conduct interviews of average/ordinary people.
11. Be careful! There are workers working on the side of the road.
12. We'll be meeting a group of businesspeople from overseas.

97.4
1. barber - M
2. secretary - F
3. farmer - M
4. dressmaker - F
5. hairdresser - F
6. teacher - F (professor is often marked as M)
7. detective - M
8. dancer - F
9. burglar - M
10. butcher - M

Note: Even though these words seem to bring to mind one gender or the other, it is best not to assume that someone in any of these occupations belongs to either gender, unless you know for certain. Also, this social markedness varies within English-speaking cultures and can shift over time.

Unit 98

98.1
2. a pal – a friend
3. snooze – a light sleep or nap / to sleep or to take a nap
4. a cop – a police officer
5. brainy – smart/intelligent/intellectual
6. a nerd – someone who is boring and awkward, sometimes intelligent

98.2 *Possible answers:*
1. JIM: Ann, can you lend me 50 <u>bucks</u>?
   ANN: What for?
   JIM: To pay the rent on my <u>apartment</u> (or <u>place</u>).
2. MOM: Where's today's <u>paper</u>?
   DAD: Mary might have it. She was looking at the <u>ads</u>.
   MOM: Well, where is she?
   DAD: In her room, talking on the <u>phone</u>.

98.3
1. In this situation, *residence* is too formal. A classmate would probably say: "Should we go to your *place* or mine?"
2. *Offspring* would be too formal for this situation; *children* (neutral) or *kids* (informal) would be the normal words. *Offspring* would be suitable for legal contexts, religious language, serious history books, and scholarly books/articles.
3. People who work together or share an institutional context (such as universities and colleges) often develop a high degree of acceptable informality, so clipped words and other short forms (like *lab*) are widely used by everyone and are not considered disrespectful.
4. The use of *kids* here sounds out of place compared with the formal tone of the rest of the letter, so it is too informal; *children* would be the preferred word. Over the phone, however, the same person might say, "Let me tell you about our new clothes for kids" in order to create a friendly relationship with the customer.

98.4 1. to regret   4. permitted
         2. unattended   5. folks
         3. beat   6. cram

98.5 *Possible answers:*
1. It's a way of saying "You must pay your bill today" or "Don't leave without paying." You might see this sign in a doctor's or dentist's office.
2. It means that you must get out of a seat if there are older people or disabled people who would like to sit there. You usually see this sign on buses and trains.

Unit 99

99.1
1. We were driving down the Trans-Canada Highway when we saw a <u>Mountie</u> in the rearview mirror.
2. Let's meet at the Eaton <u>Centre</u>.
3. The <u>reeve</u> of this city is a <u>Francophone</u>.
4. All I've got is a <u>loonie</u>.
5. I don't like the <u>colour</u> of paint that you've chosen for the front door.

99.2
1. journalist; university
2. business
3. afternoon
4. adults/parents
5. football
6. a long walk away from it all

99.3
1. people awaiting trial
2. underwear
3. have no children
4. the general public
5. someone with extreme views
6. the Mumbai (Bombay) film industry

99.4
1. Australian English: *We got really bitten by mosquitoes at yesterday's barbecue.*
2. Canadian English: *That's a nice sofa.*
3. Indian English: *The police caught the bandit/thief.*
4. Australian English: *My brother is a truck driver.*
5. Indian English: *We took my father to the hospital last night because he had a pain in his chest.*
6. Canadian English: *At my university, I am studying the culture of the indigenous peoples of Canada.*

Unit 100

100.1
1. American English is *labor*; British English is *labour*.
2. British English is *centre*; American English is *center*.
3. American English is *realize*; British English is *realise*; however, the ending *-ize* instead of *-ise* is becoming more common in British English these days.
4. American English is *theater*; in British English it is spelled *theatre* (and a *movie theater* would be called a *cinema* in British English).
5. British English is *neighbour*; American English is *neighbor*.
6. British English is *industrialise*; American English is *industrialize*.

100.2 *The pictures represent:*

	American English	British English
2.	line	queue
3.	elevator	lift
4.	baby carriage	pram
5.	candy	sweets
6.	undershirt	vest
7.	gas/gasoline	petrol
8.	truck	lorry
9.	diaper	nappy
10.	flashlight	torch

100.3
1. Let's take the underground.
2. Please pass the biscuits.
3. It's in the wardrobe.
4. Would you like chips with that?
5. I'll ring you tonight.
6. It's in the boot.
7. Let's check under the bonnet.
8. Single or return?
9. He left the tap on.
10. Excuse me, where's the toilet/WC?

100.4
1. The British man, because people do not usually talk about needing to change their underclothes (*pants* in British English), although he might well express the desire to change outer clothes (*pants* in American English and *trousers* in British English).
2. (a) two flights in the U.K. and (b) one flight in the U.S.
3. A British English speaker would ask for a bill in a café.
4. (a) over his shirt in the U.S. and (b) under his shirt in the U.K. (*Note*: These are two different articles of clothing.)

100.5 *Possible answers:*

American English	*British English*
eggplant	aubergine
zucchini	courgette
French fries	chips
potato chips	potato crisps
roast (of meat)	joint
can opener	tin opener
trash can	rubbish bin
dishcloth	tea towel
counterclockwise	anticlockwise
unlisted (telephone number)	ex-directory
slowpoke	slowcoach
talk show	chat show
swimsuit	swimming costume
run (in a stocking)	ladder
suspenders	(clothing) braces
to like	to fancy
intermission	interval
orchestra seats (in a theater)	stalls
news clipping	news cutting
realtor / real estate agent	estate agent
checking account	current account
windshield (of car)	windscreen
license plate (of car)	numberplate
fast lane (highway)	outside lane
wrench	spanner
football	American football
soccer	football/soccer